Pennies From An Angel

Innocent Lives Behind A Crime

Lisa,

To a very special young Lady who is full of life. Keep Dreaming - your life is full of possibilities. I feel blessed that you have come into my life. - What a gift you are - Always Believe,

Love ya -
Janie

Pennies From An Angel

Innocent Lives Behind A Crime

Tamara Pelosi with Susan Semerade

Mill City Press, Inc.
212 3rd Avenue North, Suite 570
Minneapolis, MN 55401
612.455.2294
www.millcitypublishing.com

ISBN - 1-934937-40-1
ISBN - 978-1-934937-40-2
LCCN - 2008939670

Cover Design by Bonni Campbell www.campbelldesignstudios.com
Typeset by Peggy LeTrent

Printed in the United States of America

For My Children,

Rachelle, Danny and Tony

Author's Note

Out of respect or out of necessity, I have changed
some of the names of the people who appear in
these pages.

To the best of my ability, I have told my story as *I*
remember it - from my perspective.

PART I

The Early Years

1981 - 1999

Prologue

*"Even if you have been banished to the most distant
land under the heavens, from there the Lord your
God will gather you and bring you back."*
—Deuteronomy 30: 4

When the bludgeoned naked body of New York millionaire Theodore Ammon was found in his East Hampton
country estate and my husband Dan Pelosi became the primary
suspect, my life and the lives of my children were never the
same again. The horrendous events began on October 21, 2001,
my youngest son's eleventh birthday. I didn't think I would ever
be able to hold my head up in public again.

On that fateful day in the middle of October, I was still
legally married to Dan and as emotionally attached to him as
I had been for twenty years - even though he had already left
me for Generosa Ammon, Ted Ammon's soon to be very rich
ex-wife. I thought this was another of Danny's flings, that he'd
soon tire of her and come home to me like he had done in the
past. But Generosa was different than the other women; she was
wealthy and powerful. She introduced my low-income blue-collar husband into a world the working poor can only read about
– the world of the ultra rich. She dressed Danny in Armani suits
and custom made tuxedoes, she even took him to the opera.
I foolishly thought the phase would pass. I never thought of

telling the S.O.B. to stay the hell out. I am one of those loyal women, who like a dog after being kicked in the ribs crawls to his master and licks his hand. But the phase didn't pass. Dan chose to abandon his family and leap feet first into what he must have believed was a pot of gold. Surely he thought he died and went to heaven. I just died inside.

In comparison to what my life was like while married to Dan - affairs, abuse, financial debt, insanity, let alone the horror of living behind a nationally publicized crime - I'd say my life is fairly calm, or as much as any single parent's life can be. With kids there's always something or another to deal with, and as upsetting as these incidents might be, they're not life altering. I can handle them.

Today I can sit on my back porch, snuggled in my fleece robe and enjoy the autumn sun setting over the massive oak without the fear of reporters or detectives at my door. I can open a newspaper and not dread seeing Danny's face on the cover. I am able to listen to the news on the radio and not get knots in my stomach at the sound of Danny's name. Time is healing. I have come a long way.

Unfortunately it took a catastrophic and nationally publicized event for me to find the courage to lift the veil of illusion that I hid behind all those years and discover deep within me a reservoir of courage and strength I didn't know existed.

ONE

Yo, What's Up?

*We cannot tell what may happen to
us in the strange medley of life. But we can decide
what happens in us —how we can take it, what we do
with it – and that is what really counts in the end.*
—Joseph Fort Newton

Once upon a long time ago there was this short boy named Danny Pelosi that looked as if someone put a bowl on his head to cut his hair, but the bowl must have been too big because his bangs hung down into his eyes. Danny was the class clown and often disrupted the room with his wisecrack and poking fun of the teachers behind their backs. His favorite trick was to sneak up behind the girls and snap their bra straps. Dan was a smart kid and got great marks on his tests even though he rarely, if ever, did his homework. I had known him since junior high school. We were in the same grade, and usually had the same classes. He would sit behind me and throw spitballs at my back and write me love notes telling me one day he was going to marry me. I thought he was a jerk. I already had a boyfriend who was older and taller and somewhat mature, certainly in comparison to Danny. But by the fall of our senior year, this short kid with the Buster Brown haircut and the alfalfa cowlick that stood straight up, sprouted like a weed. He had grown several inches over the summer and developed noticeable biceps.

Danny transformed from a goofy gangly boy into a tough guy, like John Travolta's character Danny Zuko in *Grease*, minus the sideburns and pompadour. In other words, a hoodlum. That of course made me Olivia Newton John's good girl Sandy Olsson, and I was.

I fell in love with this bad boy that spoke in the Brooklyn/ Bronx – "Yo, what's up" dialogue, with his Marlboro wedged between his teeth. I wasn't the only one stirred by the new cool Dan. Right from the start Danny had a way with the girls. Most days he could be spotted strutting around in his black leather jacket blowing smoke rings into the air showing off to a bunch of silly giggling girls who ogled all over him as if he were the 'Fonz' himself. He could have chosen any one of them, but it was me he hounded.

Everyone who knew Danny warned me from the beginning to stay away from him. I was told he was bad news and he was bound to break my heart. But it was too late. I was madly in love, or as much in love as a teenager would know. Dan was everything my former boyfriend wasn't - funny, daring, adventuresome, exciting, bold, gregarious, fun-loving. But it was those large brown Cocker Spaniel eyes that did me in, the ones that melt you into voluntary submission.

Whether consciously or subconsciously, Danny was a master at manipulation, so cunning, so smooth, so easily he wrangled and maneuvered me until he got exactly what he wanted. I didn't care what people said, or how much they tried to warn me. I was seventeen. I lived in the day, not in the future. He told me to trust him and I did. He said he would never hurt me. I believed him.

I was in my first year at the local community college, when I found out I was pregnant. Dan didn't hesitate for a second. "We'll get married," he said. "What's the big deal? We were gonna get married anyway."

"Are you sure?" I couldn't contain my excitement. This was my dream. To be married, have a baby, a white picket fence.

"Yea, I'm sure. It'll be cool."

Well it wasn't cool, but I didn't know that then.

I went to the clinic that week. A middle-aged nurse, who wasn't as much plump, as padded, sat next to me. In a motherly voice she confirmed I was indeed pregnant. In almost a whisper she told me it wasn't too late to have an abortion. An abortion was not an option in my mind. I was getting married. I was in love.

Dan and I parked down by the water later that evening. The night was brisk and mingled with a trace of salty air. I snuggled in his arms under a full moon that reflected off the bay. We were enchantingly in love.

We decided it would be best to break the news to our parents right away. Neither of us had any doubts about our future, but we weren't sure how our parents were going to handle this bit of news.

We went to my home first. My mother was at her desk researching a psychology paper that was due the next day; the two of us were going to the same college. I tapped on her door and stepped in the room. Danny waited in the hallway.

"Danny and I have something to tell you." I said timidly.

The pen fell from my mother's hands, her face paled, she let out a deep sigh.

"When?" Was her only question.

Mothers have that gift of knowing without the need for words. In fact my mother revealed to me that a few weeks earlier she had a dream I was pregnant. In her dream she was more upset with the fact that she was going to be a grandmother at thirty-six while her friends were still having babies.

Danny tiptoed in behind me. "Don't worry, *Mom*," he said in a nervous laugh, "I'm not running away or nothing. I'm gonna marry her." He swallowed a big gulp. "I love Tami."

With remorse in her voice Mom repeated the same words the nurse said earlier that day. "You can have an abortion...."

"Mom, I love Danny," I cut in not letting her go any further. "He loves me, we want to get married."

"Oh dear God." My mother wrapped her arms around me and choked back tears. "This is not what I wanted for you. Don't you want to finish college, travel, see the world?"

I was sorry to hurt my mother. She wasn't keen on Danny from the start, she remembered him as the kid that always caused a ruckus on the Little League field. I knew she didn't want me to go out with him. In time he sort of grew on her as he did everyone else. Like most parents, she wanted more for her child. Mom didn't want me to follow in her footsteps, a pregnant teenager married too young, but there was no swaying me. My mind was made up.

My father took the news well in his own dysfunctional way. He had been asleep on the couch with the TV blaring when Danny gave him the news. In a half sleep he read Danny the riot act then went back to his horizontal position and was snoring before we left the room.

I felt embarrassed to face Dan's parents. I liked them and didn't want them to think less of me. Naturally they weren't happy about the situation; Dan and I were only eighteen years old. Unlike my father, Dan's dad sat us down, but directed his lecture to his son. He said he was proud that Danny did not run from his responsibility, but he warned Dan that he could kiss his friends good bye. He reminded Danny that he would soon have a wife and a baby and that *we* would need to come first.

"It will be a long rocky road," his dad said in a stern fatherly voice, "but if you love, honor and respect each other you may have a chance."

Maybe we would have had a chance had we loved, honored and respected not just each other, but ourselves as well. Statistically though, we were doomed from the start, two juveniles with about as much maturity as a preadolescent. I didn't even know how to do a load of laundry.

We planned a wedding.

TWO

A Wedding, A Honeymoon, A Baby

"Life is no brief candle to me. It is a sort of splendid torch which I have got hold of for the moment, and I want to make it burn as brightly as possible before handing it on to further generations."
—Greg Bernard Shaw

The insanity began on the first day of spring, March 21, 1982, my wedding day. It rained like a monsoon. One grandmother said that meant good luck and the other just shook her head and clucked her tongue with a foreboding shadow across her face. The latter was definitely onto something.

We had a simple old-fashioned Italian-American family wedding at the local yacht club a few towns over. Early on the morning of the wedding, my aunt and uncle were at my house organizing a decorating committee. In less than three hours the room that overlooked the water was decorated with white crepe streamers that were hung crisscross from the ceiling; the tables were dressed in wedding finery; favors and place cards were set at each seat, and floral arrangements in shades of lavenders and yellows, sat on the center of every table.

We rushed home to get ourselves ready. Our small house was packed with relatives; females giggling, screaming and squirming into gowns and males yelling at us to get out of the bathroom.

My mother wore a simple silk cream-colored knee length

dress; her glossy short tawny brown hair, was slightly combed back over her ears revealing delicate pearl button earrings. She was trim and youthful enough to be the bride herself. We were often mistaken for sisters. We were only eighteen years apart.

It was a treat to see my father out of his scruffy construction work clothes and dapper in a new pinstriped gray double-breasted suit. He was tall, a little over six feet, with rugged features and weather worn skin. With a touch of silver in his hair, my grandmother told him he resembled a young Clark Gable. He was proud of me, and proud to walk me down the aisle.

Family and friends had gathered at the church, patiently waiting in the pews for me, the bride, to walk down the aisle. I was in the vestibule with the wedding party. Everyone was there, *but* Danny. The guys teased me and said that Danny got cold feet. I laughed along with them but inwardly I was afraid, maybe he did get cold feet.

Eventually Danny strolled into the church with his brother who rounded him up at the pub having a beer with the bartender.

"Hey, did you guys think I wasn't gonna make it?" He cracked jokes about having one last beer as a single guy. His tie was crooked and his hair and tuxedo were wet from the rain. I didn't care. He kept his promise. We were going to be married.

I felt like a princess in my long lace gown. I was able to fit into my size five dress without any telltale signs of a belly. I wore a white wide brimmed hat with a trailing white satin ribbon and carried a small bouquet of yellow roses which accentuated my recently permed blonde hair.

My father hooked his arm in mine, gave my hand a tender squeeze, dabbed at a tear in his eye, and down the aisle we went.

Danny was waiting for me at the altar in his gray tuxedo. Someone had straightened his tie. He was sporting a ridiculous grin on his face. His best man gave him a jab in his arm and Danny poked him back. The bridal party chuckled. But the stonefaced pastor didn't find it very amusing. He cleared his throat with an audible, "ahem."

The ceremony was officially underway.

"Do you Daniel John Pelosi, take this *woman* ..."

"Yea I guess so." It sounded more like a question than an answer. We snickered to ourselves careful not to be reprimanded.

"Do you Tamara Ann Shore take this *man*..."

"Yes I do." I answered shyly.

"I now pronounce you husband and wife."

Husband? Wife? Us? We looked at each other and broke up. Even we knew we looked more like teenagers dressed for the prom.

The rain let up long enough for us to get from the church to the yacht club without getting drenched. My grandfather proudly chauffeured us in his almost new 1980 Lincoln Town car. We were last in a procession of cars beeping horns and flashing headlights.

It was a wonderful wedding. I could not have been happier. We feasted on homemade foods several of my relatives offered to cook. Big Momma made her famous sausage and peppers, Uncle Frank whipped up a mean eggplant parmigiana, and my grandparents cooked pounds of lasagna. There was enough food to feed an army of guests with hearty appetites. The liquor flowed, the music played, we danced to the *Tarantella*, crooned along with the old timers and mashed wedding cake in each other's face to the roar of our friends. This was, by no stretch of the imagination, a high-priced gala event of the season. It was families gathered in affection and support, who toasted us a long life of love and health and to live happily ever after. I was too young, too gullible and too downright dumb to know that happily ever after only exists in fairy tales.

We set out for our honeymoon, two foolish happy kids in a souped up 1968 red Camaro headed for the Poconos. We drove most of the way with the bottom of my wedding gown sticking out the car door. I hadn't a clue I was supposed to change into

7

something more appropriate. In fact I had never even packed for myself before and wound up forgetting half my things. When we stopped for gas I needed to use the ladies room. I stepped out of the car and landed in a huge puddle. The entire bottom of my gown got soaked. We drove the rest of the way to our honeymoon resort with me in my muddy, filthy wedding gown and Danny in his stained and wrinkled tuxedo. But I was in heaven. And it continued to rain.

We arrived at the resort and sashayed to the lobby in our rumpled wedding attire, holding hands and giggling like the two kids we were and registered as Mr. and Mrs. Daniel Pelosi.

We were a married couple on our honeymoon, yet too young to toast our marriage with a glass of champagne. We looked so young in fact that many of the guests at the resort mistakenly thought we were part of a school trip that was there the same time we were. We didn't care what anyone thought. We were happy. We were in love. We had life in the palms of our hands.

We returned from five fun filled days at the Poconos as Mr. and Mrs. Pelosi. Once at home, it was obvious we were not quite prepared to take on the responsibilities of adulthood, let alone marriage.

In all honesty, life continued more or less as it had before. The only difference was Danny moved into my bedroom. My mother did her best to turn my girlish bedroom with its dozens of stuffed animals and frilly curtains into something a little more fitting for a married couple, with one exception: we needed to squeeze together on my single twin bed.

In the mornings Dan would go off to work with my father and I went back to school. My mother did everything from grocery shopping to cooking and cleaning and doing the laundry. It wasn't a bad arrangement as far as I was concerned.

I took that summer off from school and hung around the pool with my pregnant belly and my single girlfriends. I was the only one in the crowd who was married. I don't think I had made the connection that in a few months I would actually be giving birth to another living being. I had never even changed a baby's diaper or held a newborn. I was totally ignorant about the stages of pregnancy, the development of the fetus and the entire birthing process. I guess I didn't pay attention in those parenting classes we had in high school. Danny's experience with babies was limited to the one niece and nephew he had that he occasionally saw when his mother was babysitting.

To show how completely immature we were, Danny's idea of a gift to me was a little white mouse. Not diapers for the coming baby, not bottles, not even a rattle. A living breathing rodent with a long tail and beady red eyes! He thought this was a grand gift and, pathetically, so did I. Maybe this small creature had something to do with the nesting syndrome women experience just before the baby is born. I'm not sure how a mouse is related to nesting, but the day poor Henry died a tragic death in the jaws of my mother's fat drooling Lab, I went into labor.

I have to give credit where credit is due and admit that Danny did his best the night when I went into labor. In fact Danny was at my side when all three of our children were born. What happened in between those pregnancies is a whole other story. But I'll just stick with one thing at a time.

When Danny got home from work and I told him I thought I was in labor, he insisted he take me to the hospital. Of course I wasn't ready for the hospital at that point. The doctor sent me home and told me to do some walking. Danny and I walked up and down the road and around the block until it got too chilly and too dark. Danny's friend Jackie happened by. The three of us sat on my bed, they played Ping-Pong video and I counted the contractions the way my mother explained it to me. Jackie got bored and went home. Danny took over the job of keeping track of the contractions. It was well into the middle of the night before I made it back to the hospital. Danny held my hand the whole time and did his best to be supportive. My labor didn't appear to be progressing very fast. I had mild contractions that lasted for several hours. Danny took the nurse's suggestion and took a break in the lounge. Within minutes he was asleep on the tattered leather couch. I dozed off too. I woke up to warm water gushing over my legs. Not having a clue what was going on, I yelled for the nurse. Within minutes I was hurried to the delivery room. With a grunt and a groan and a little push, what felt like a slippery fish came sliding out. Eureka! I had a baby!

My daughter Rachelle entered the world on a warm September day in 1982. A precious little bundle. Her face was as round as a brand new penny, with a dot of a nose and soft golden peach fuzz for hair. Her skin so translucent I could see the veins on her forehead and the rhythmic pulse on her temples. I knew immediately she would have her daddy's big brown eyes. She was a flawless little being.

Danny was dumbstruck. The nurse handed him his daughter. He hesitated, "You sure I'm not gonna break her or anything?" He sat on the bed next to me. "She's so little, Tam. I ain't never held nothing this little." He kissed her tenderly on her forehead. The doctors and the nurses said we looked too young to be having a baby. They were right; we looked young because we were young. So young that during my stay at the hospital while the other women who had delivered their babies were watching soap operas and talk shows, I had on cartoons.

- THREE -

Preview of Insanity

*If we do not change our direction, we are likely
to end up where we are headed.*
—Ancient Chinese Proverb

In the four days that I was in the hospital, my father and other relatives built an adorable little apartment in the basement of my parents' home. My mother told me how they worked around the clock and developed an efficient working system. While the men put up walls, installed the plumbing and electric, the women cleaned up after them and made the meals. With my father's talent and eye for design he constructed our little place in a way that it didn't have that basement look about it. He dug out around the side of the house and installed glass sliding doors, which opened up to a small private deck creating a sunny and airy space. Rachelle's room was the one room that was completely finished with carpeting, dressing table, diaper pail, and even pictures on the walls. My mother painted the walls a pale mint green and decorated the room with the gifts from my baby shower. The white crib was fully set with Winnie the Pooh sheets, bolsters and comforter and a Winnie the Pooh mobile over the crib. My aunt had made a frilly skirt for the bassinet out of white cotton lace and tulle. I was astonished at all they accomplished in such a short time.

The only room not completed was the kitchen, which

was fine with me. Making a pot of coffee and grilled cheese sandwiches was the extent of my cooking abilities. My mother continued to run the household, do all the grocery shopping and cook our meals. All Danny and I needed to do was climb a few steps and sit down to a nourishing dinner.

Neither Danny nor I behaved as adults. Whenever we got into a squabble, which was often, I'd run upstairs to my mother's and complain to her just as I had done when I was a twelve-year-old snitching on my younger brother, Roger. For a while my mother played the role of mediator and would sit the both of us down and give each of us ample time to say our piece. Eventually she tired of our childish bickering and in no uncertain terms told me it was about time I acted like a married woman.

When I finally stopped whining to my mother, Danny and I actually began to settle into our new roles. Dan shopped around at the second hand stores for used furniture and proudly came home with a carload of other people's junk. Before long the kitchen was finished and we bought a stove and I began to play wife. I attempted to do some cooking. More accurately I was burning meals, boiling water until it evaporated and melting the food in plastic containers to an unidentifiable blob that stuck to the bottom of the microwave. Beyond the squabbles and the nonsense bickering we were getting on as well as any two people adjusting to the transition of marriage and a baby.

We did our best with what little knowledge and experience we had. We loved each other. We loved our daughter. To prove his love, Danny had Rachelle's and my name tattooed on his left arm. His first tattoo. A beautiful dove with two banners that bore our names. A symbol of our love and unity.

I was on top of the world. I had Danny, our baby and a place of our own, even though I spent more time upstairs in my mother's home than I did in mine. Except for the change in living arrangements, all else remained pretty much the same. Dan hung out with the guys and I went out with the girls; afterwards we would meet up at some common destination.

It seemed perfectly normal to me that my mother was more or less raising Rachelle. She went from cooking our meals to caring for our baby. I was like the big sister. I relied on my mother for everything, from how to change a diaper, what to feed her and whatever else I didn't know, and there was a lot that I didn't know. Obviously this suited my mother as well. At least for a while.

The night Rachelle came down with pneumonia and was running a temperature was the turning point for both my mother and me. I had gone out with my friends heedless to the fact that my nine-month-old daughter was sick.

I was in the middle of having a really swell time when I got a call from my mother. It was before cell phone days, which meant she needed to track me down. In no uncertain terms she told me to get home. It took my baby girl's illness for me to accept the responsibility of motherhood. It was as if I was plucked out of my little girl world and deposited into the world of adulthood. Unfortunately it wasn't the same for Danny; he preferred the world of Peter Pan.

It wasn't long after that night that our innocent marital squabbles turned into feuds. Feuds escalated to brawls. Brawls manifested into battles. Battles brought on raging wars.

When Danny got home from work, he'd brush right by me, jump in the shower, mumble something about he had to meet some guy about something and take off. I was left sitting at the kitchen table alone. On Saturday morning he'd leave to buy a pack of cigarettes and stumble in after midnight reeking of alcohol. On Sundays he'd be passed out in bed. Monday the routine started all over again. By Friday he didn't even bother to come home from work. He left earlier and earlier in the evenings and stayed out longer and later.

I was preoccupied with his whereabouts and tortured myself unmercifully. I rode around looking for him in the local bars. It didn't matter if I was on my way to school or if I would be late for a class; I *had* to find him. I never did. By the time I got to my class I was a wound up ball of nerves, barely able to

13

concentrate.

When Dan was home I'd scream like an old fishmonger. I demanded to know where he was and what he was doing. When he'd leave I'd beg him to stay home. He'd ignore me and walk out the door. I'd pace the floors, chew my fingernails and stare at the minutes slowly ticking away on the clock. I would call Danny's friends; they each claimed to have no idea where Danny was. I'd check with the hospitals for accidents. I even called the police precincts. When I'd come to the realization that he wasn't injured, dead or in jail, I'd drag my innocent baby with me in search of her father.

Having a baby didn't stop Danny from partying and it didn't stop me from jumping in my car and scouting the neighborhood. In the cold of winter and usually in the middle of the night I'd bundle this precious child and go on the hunt for my missing husband. I was obsessed with finding him. When I did, I'd storm into the bar, make a hideous scene and a fool of myself. In the end, all it did was keep him out longer.

My father told me not to worry so much. "Dan has to sow his oats, give him time, better he get it out of his system while you're both young."

I gave him a long time. I gave him the majority of my life.

There was always some event or episode with Danny, from barroom fights to scrabbles with police. We fought almost every night. It had become a regular routine.

I had lost a tremendous amount of weight from the constant stress; living under pressure had become the norm, not the exception.

My only form of escape was to spend some time with my cousins up island. I'd take the train and lug a baby, a stroller, a diaper bag and all the paraphernalia that goes with the territory. I foolishly and immaturely thought I was spiting Danny by spending a weekend at my cousin's house. I took great satisfaction in the fact that I was with single women and that Danny had no idea where I was. Of course it never occurred to me that I had no idea where he was either. I did a pretty good job of convincing myself that I didn't care what Danny was up to and actually believed I was having fun.

It was around 1985 when Danny spent his first time in a rehab for some sort of scrap with the law. He was offered thirty days in jail or thirty days in a rehab. Danny wasn't a fool, he opted for the rehab. He had thirty days of rest, three meals a day and probably slept like a baby. I plodded along working on my Associates Degree, cared for a baby and believed he would come home cured. Dan wasn't cured. He proceeded to pick up where he left off.

The insanity continued for years, nothing changed. Dan drank. Dan partied. I held steadfast to my foolhardy illusion that one day we would be that happy little family I fantasized about.

If I thought what I had been living was insanity, it was merely a mild preview of what lay ahead. Of course while living in the madness it simply became a part of my everyday life. I never recognized the progression of dysfunction. There was no definitive line down the middle letting me know what was normal and what was not normal or what was acceptable and what was not acceptable. It just was.

There was nothing unusual about Dan's staying out until the wee hours of the morning. He usually created a situation that would give him the excuse he needed to bolt out the door. On one particular evening it was the car insurance. I told him the insurance was going to expire unless he made the payment before the final expiration date, which happened to be the next day. Dan threw a twenty-dollar bill at me and stormed out the door. I'm not sure what he expected me to do with twenty dollars since the bill was over one hundred.

It had gotten to the point that I preferred when Danny wasn't home; then I could concentrate on my schoolwork. When he was around he belittled me and told me it was a waste of my time. He said I wasn't going to amount to anything anyway.

I went to bed around midnight, but couldn't fall asleep. I

tossed and turned, jumping with a start at every sound. The sun was already coming up when I heard Danny's noisy muffler and the crunch of the gravel on the driveway. On the one hand I was relieved he was finally home, safe and sound, not dead somewhere. On the other hand I wished he were dead so I could have peace in my life. I dreaded the confrontation we would inevitably have. I was tired of his lies and his promises.

Danny stumbled in the door, banged into the coffee table, and cursed his way to the couch and passed out. The stench of alcohol consumed the small apartment. I prayed to God to keep my mouth shut. Every fiber of my being knew I should not go into the living room. The best thing for me to do was nothing, stay in bed and hope for some sleep. I fought back the rage welling up inside me, but to no avail. I charged out of the bedroom like a crazy woman. Danny was sprawled out on the couch, his mouth wide open like a dead fish, saliva drooling down his chin. The repulsive sight sent me over the edge. In a wild rage I punched him in his shoulder and slapped him hard across his drunken face.

"You make me sick!" I screeched at him.

He grabbed me by my wrists and yanked me down.

"You're nuts, you're fucking nuts!" He yelled back at me and pinned me to the floor.

I spit in his face and kicked him in the groin, not caring what he would do to me. "Get out of this house, get out, get out, get out!" I shrieked hysterically.

"You want me out, bitch, huh? You want me out? I'm outta here!"

He grabbed his shoes and jacket, fled out the door and squealed out of the driveway, burning rubber all the way down the road.

My body trembled from blind fury. I had completely lost control of my emotions.

I had turned into a lunatic. Me, the person who was too shy to raise my hand in school, the one who stood in the background while the other girls flirted with the boys and asked *them* out on dates. How the hell had all this happened? And what was I doing to my precious daughter?

Rachelle was crouched in the corner of her little bed, weeping silently. She wrapped her skinny self around my body like a baby monkey and tucked her small head under my chin. This discerning two and a half-year old with two-inch pigtails that stuck straight out the side of her head, patted *me* on the back.

"Don't cry Mommy," she quivered.

My mother knocked at my door a few minutes after Danny screeched down the road. She did her best to stay out of my affairs, but that was nearly impossible with me living downstairs. My father completely avoided the situation in my marriage by conveniently burying his head under the sand.

On countless occasions my mother attempted to talk with me about the insanity of my life. I usually listened with half an ear. Her own life with my father was far from normal. They didn't have horrible fights like Dan and I, but my father was a compulsive gambler. Growing up we were either dining at expensive restaurants or eating potatoes and eggs for dinner. No one in my family was divorced. The women in particular put up with abuse in every form, from alcoholism to violent outbursts of rage. My mother hoped that I would be the one to take a stand and break the cycle of women who remain married, for better or worse, to men undeserving of our love.

By the time Danny got home that night I had scrubbed the apartment from top to bottom, made one of his favorite meals and had my hair done. I believed if I kept a cleaner house, cooked a better meal and looked prettier, Danny would change. He didn't. I tried another strategy; I bought a new sexy see-through purple nightgown. That caught his attention. He told me I looked beautiful.

"All the guys are married to dogs," he said. "Not me, my wife's a knock-out."

Danny decided we needed another child, a boy. He assured me things would be different if we had a boy. He would teach him how to throw a ball, hook a fish, take him to the ballgames, all the things he said he couldn't do with a girl.

The sexy nightie might not have kept Danny home, but it did get me pregnant. By this time I was down to ninety pounds from one hundred fifteen, rather scrawny on a five foot four inch frame. I avoided looking at myself in the full-length mirror. I was all bones, my ribs stuck out, my hips protruded, my chest caved in under my collarbone. I was a walking skeleton. But if I had a boy Danny would settle down. I prayed in earnest for a boy.

Danny was confident we were going to have a son. He took a one-eighty turn and dove into the *good* Danny character. We settled into a comfortable routine and actually had pleasant conversations over dinner. He willingly turned his paycheck over to me which allowed us to catch up on some bills and have a little left over for a night at the movie. Some nights we cuddled in front of the TV with Shelly (our knick-name for Rachelle) nestled between us, stuffing our bellies with hot fudge sundaes. For the first time in three years Danny cared for his daughter while I was at school. More shockingly he bought me a new electric typewriter as a token of his support for my academic efforts. There was a glimmer of light on the horizon.

Our lives were on a smooth and even keel no little bumps in the highway of life. Even my pregnancy was easy. With a clear mind I was able to maintain a 3.9 average. School was a pleasure, not a torture. I stopped waiting for the other shoe to drop and basked in the peace. I shouldn't have. One would think I was astute enough to see the patterns, six months of the good Danny, six months of the not good Danny. Give or take a few months here or there.

- FOUR -

Avalanche and Miracles

*"In the hour of adversity be not without
hope, for crystal rain falls from black clouds."*
—Persian Poem

My life is like an avalanche. First there are those little warnings - a few small rocks that tumble down - then a huge boulder pitches down the mountainside and crashes into my naïve unsuspecting nature.

There had been a boulder heading in my direction for several weeks, but I chose to ignore it, certain it would change direction. But boulders of that magnitude do not change their course, rather they build in speed and momentum. First Danny's late for dinner, then he's not home for dinner; half the paycheck, then no paycheck; gone for an hour, gone for the night.

The signs were so ridiculously obvious a child could have figured it out. I was told the cigarette butt I found in his car ashtray with lipstick on it must have been from his friend Barry who borrowed the car, probably was Barry's wife's; then a shirt with a smudge on it that hinted of lipstick, another answer - ink from his red pen. The best was the blatantly unmistakable hickey on his neck and Danny's incredible explanation that it was a bruise from a piece of lumber that scraped against his neck when he was unloading it from the truck. He had an answer for everything. He was a storage house full of stories

19

ready and available at the flip of his tongue. The sad thing was, I believed him. If I accused him and tried to prove I was right, he told me I was nuts. I believed that one too.

One week before my baby was born I was hit square in the heart from that runaway mammoth boulder.

I was on my way to school and something made me take a different route, one that was slightly out of the way. *This* was one of those gut feelings. I knew I was about to come face to face with my worst fear. I turned down a side street and saw Danny's car parked in Sandy's driveway. (Just to clear up any confusion, this Sandy had no similarities to the Sandy from Grease.) I had heard rumors that Danny had been seen with Sandy a few weeks earlier. I drove up and down the road a few dozen times not knowing exactly what to do. My stomach did flips. I swallowed the lump in my throat, my breakfast was ready to take a quick about face. I parked the car and made my way to the front door. The door was unlocked. Like a burglar, I slowly turned the knob and quietly entered Sandy's house. Apparently, Danny and Sandy were having themselves a good old time. Sandy's high-pitched cackle echoed off the bare walls at something Danny had said. I marched down the hallway and there in all their glory were the two of them playing 'house' in Sandy's bed.

Temporary insanity, that's what I called it. Blame it on my hormones gone wild. I attacked the two of them with my bare hands, slapping and punching anything within range. Danny escaped and ran out of the house leaving Sandy and me in a four-fisted dual. We yanked and pulled each other's hair and scratched at our faces. She kicked me in the stomach. A moment of clarity zipped through my brain: what was I doing to my unborn child? I made a dash for my car and practically fell to the ground. I struggled with the handle, tore the door nearly off its hinges and raced down the road wailing uncontrollably. Somehow I found my way home.

I stood in front of the bathroom mirror. The face that stared back wasn't the face of a twenty-three year old. It was tired and haggard, puffy and swollen, those eyes were blood shot and sunken, not sparkly and bright. *Who was this harrowed woman?*

I spotted Danny's prescription painkillers on the vanity that the doctor gave him for a back injury he got on the job. I opened the bottle and counted twenty-three pills and rolled them around in my hand. The texture was smooth, easy to swallow. For one fraction of a second, one millisecond, I contemplated the thought. *I could end it all here and now. He'd come home and find me dead. Then he would know how much pain he had caused.*

I dumped them in the toilet.

I dragged my swollen aching body to the couch. I was emotionally drained, numb. I was mortified by my behavior, my lunacy and what I might have done to my unborn baby. I wanted Danny to come home and beg me for forgiveness, to beg on his knees like a dog, so I could tell him to get the hell out, forever. I never wanted to see him again. I wanted him to suffer and be in pain. I fell asleep on the couch hugging Rachelle's Winnie the Pooh bear pillow clutched in my arms.

The screech of the sliding door opening woke me up. Danny shuffled in, his head hanging low in that forlorn forsaken way. He knelt down on his knees just the way I wanted him to. He covered his face with his hands and sobbed like a baby. I'm ashamed to say I didn't kick him out. I didn't spit in his face. I didn't say a word. Instead I patted him on his back and told him everything would be okay. He didn't have to beg me for forgiveness. With the unspoken word, I had already forgiven him. In my sick demented mind, what mattered was that he came home to *me*.

One week later after catching Danny with Sandy, I went into labor. I had been having slight cramps for most of the morning. The baby was coming at the expected time, so I didn't have to punish myself for my deranged behavior. I busied myself tidying up and doing some laundry. By the time the babysitter came for Rachelle and I tracked down Danny - who went into the extra good behavior mode, which at least gave the impression that he was remorseful - the contractions were coming quicker, lasting longer and getting stronger. I was in full labor when

Danny peeled into the driveway. My labor with Rachelle was so easy that I wasn't prepared for the gut wrenching pain. The ride to the hospital seemed to take forever; every bump caused me to clutch my distended belly. The woman behind the admissions desk was as slow as a snail. I thought Danny was going to sock her one. He stayed with me throughout my long arduous labor.

"Hang in there, you're a trooper," he offered. "You'll get through this."

I was a trooper all right, but I wasn't thinking in terms of my labor. My labor was akin to my life, exhausting and burdensome.

I had been pushing for a long time before the nurse finally gave me medication for the pain. By the time the medication kicked in I was too spent to press anymore. The baby's head was out of the birth canal and making its passage into creation. But I was too weary to react.

"Tam you got to push, the head is there. It's right there, you're gonna strangle it! PUSH!" Danny squeezed my hand frantically urging me on.

I bore down with what little I had left. This birth had no similarities to a slimy fish easily sliding out. This baby tore its way into the world with a fury of one who is determined to be born.

In the late afternoon in February of 1986 after four grueling hours, an almost nine pound baby boy entered the world, our baby Daniel. My prayers were answered. I had a son.

The way Danny rejoiced you would think he was the one who delivered the baby. He was as hyped and wound as a top. He stopped long enough to give me a kiss and whisper how much he loved me. He darted out the door and down the hallway bellowing he had a son.

When Danny's nervous and excitable energy was gone, the room quieted down. I had my son to myself. Whereas Shelly was petite with a delicate round face, Little Dan as he was officially to be called, had a globular face and two dimpled pinchable cheeks the size of a chipmunk's stuffed with acorns, and downy honey blonde hair. As Danny said, a boy would complete our family. I caressed his velvety soft newborn face. I had great expectations this sleepy baby boy would alter the course of his father's life.

By that evening Danny filled my room with balloons, flowers, stuffed animals, rattles, toys and a plastic stork announcing the birth of our son. On Valentine's Day, a day and a half later, boxes of chocolate candy added to the compilation of presents. Danny bought boxes of cigars and handed them out to every visiting guest that happened to walk past my room. To say Danny was proud is an understatement. To say I was hopeful was a simple fact.

Danny celebrated the birth of his son with a zealous gusto, so much so that no one knew where he was on the day I was to leave the hospital. It was my father-in-law who took me home. My mother, who had been visiting family in Florida, came home that day. She never knew about Sandy. The episode was dropped. I had a new baby to focus on, a baby that would create miracles.

Several months later there was no indication that Danny was going to make good on his promise. Having a son didn't change his behavior. The routine of our lives continued as before; a roller coaster of mixed emotions. As many times as Danny made me cry, he made me laugh. As often as I hated him, I believed it would work. As much as I wanted him to leave, I prayed he'd never leave. I saw the good in him, and closed my eyes to everything else.

I returned to school and completed my Associates Degree in Early Childhood Education with no further encouragement from Danny. The electric typewriter he had bought me as a token of his support had been flung across the room in a heated dispute.

On countless occasions I considered professional help, but there always seemed to be sufficient reprieve to take a breath and trust that Danny would have that turnaround I so desperately prayed for.

- FIVE -

Just For Today

*"Today is only a small manageable segment of time in which
our difficulties need not overwhelm us. This lifts from our hearts
and minds the heavy weight of both past and future."*
—One Day At A Time in Al-Anon

A few days after Little Dan's first birthday, my mother came into the kitchen holding some Al-Anon literature in her hands that one of the girls at her job gave her. I scanned them suspiciously. I didn't need to read through each one to know that was where I needed to go. I sank down on the kitchen chair and looked up at my mother.

"I'm scared." I said, but I wasn't sure of what.

Mom did her homework. She found a meeting for the following morning at a local church that had babysitting as well. When a look of terror came across my face, she agreed to come with me.

Danny hadn't left for work yet when my mother came downstairs in the morning to accompany me to the meeting. From behind Danny's back she mouthed to me, *'what is he doing home?'* If looks could kill - Danny would have been a dead man.

Mom chatted nervously, pretending we were off on a shopping spree and fussed unnecessarily with the zipper on Rachelle's snowsuit. I nearly dropped my son trying to give my mother the diaper bag in a rush to get out the door before Danny had the chance to question me.

We got to the church in record breaking time and followed a heavy set woman wearing a bright red parka and furry cap limp her way down dark musty basement stairs to a large room at the end of the hall. She was out of breath by the time she reached the bottom. She gave a wide toothy smile to Little Dan, revealing red lipstick on her front tooth. A small slightly built older gentleman with a sparse gray beard and a comforting voice greeted us at the door and pointed to the baby-sitting room across the hall. I followed along behind my mother like an obedient little puppy. All heads turned in our direction when we walked into the room. They motioned to some empty seats. I mentally tallied six people sitting around a rectangular table; all were much older then me. Thankfully the only man was the older gentleman who was at the door. I would not have felt safe if there were other men present. The table was covered with literature. A big coffeepot with cups, sugar, milk and cookies was set on a small table at the back of the room. Everyone at the table had a Styrofoam cup in front of them. My mother helped herself to a cup of coffee, but I refrained. I felt sick to my stomach. I found a seat behind a pole to conceal myself. I spotted an attractive young woman around my age sitting at the head of the table. She looked up, and with a bright cheerful smile gave a small nod of her head as if to say, 'welcome, you're in the right place.'

The meeting began with a few prayers, some discussion about a topic and then each person shared their own personal story. When it came to my turn, all I could croak was "I'll pass."

Mom briefly spoke a few words, thanked everyone and expressed her happiness that there was a place for her daughter to come to.

During the coffee break people milled about and chatted among themselves. Mom went to check on Rachelle while I stayed glued to my seat hugging Little Dan to me for comfort. The heavy-set woman with the lipstick on her tooth was hee-hawing with another full-figured lady over some funny movie she had seen the night before. I marveled at the gaiety and light-heartedness from these people who had just revealed painful experiences.

The pretty young woman at the head of the table glided her way over to me with a sprightly bounce to her gait. With an authentic smile and an effervescent twinkle in her dark brown eyes, she introduced herself as Carol. We were similarly built, she slightly taller, with short angular coffee colored hair and long dangling pink earrings to match her pink buttoned down shirt. She didn't ask me any personal questions or why I was there. She spoke briefly about her home life and told me unequivocally, if I keep coming back my life would change, as hers had. Carol wrote her name and phone number on a piece of paper and invited me to go to other meetings with her. She projected an aura of confidence and assurance. I wanted what she had.

The meeting resumed after the coffee break. After a few more people spoke the meeting closed with some more prayers. One by one each person came up to me and gave me a genuine hug and repeated Carol's words, 'keep coming back.'

And I did.

It was months before Danny found out I was going to Al-Anon meetings; he wasn't happy, but I continued to go anyway. The people I met there were kind and understanding, especially the older man, who I grew fond of. Instead of dragging my children scouring the bars for their father, I brought them with me to my meetings. Each time I went I learned something new. It was a long time before I had the courage to share some tidbit of my life, but I listened intently and soaked in what I heard like a dried sponge. One of the most profound things I learned, was I did not cause Danny to drink, I could not cure him and I had no control of his drinking. What a relief that was to discover it was not because I didn't keep a sparkling clean house or a meal was over cooked or I happened to say the wrong thing at the wrong time.

One day at a meeting, one of the 'old-timers', a frail elderly lady with silver blue hair and wire rimmed spectacles, shared the importance of taking care of ourselves.

In a shaky Katherine Hepburn voice she said, "Many years ago when I was taking a flight to Chicago, the stewardess made the usual announcement, she said if you were traveling with a child in the event we need oxygen, place the oxygen mask on *your* face first and then the child. I thought that was the most selfish thing I had ever heard. What kind of mother would I be to think of myself first? Naturally I would put the mask on my child before putting it on me. It was years later that statement made sense to me. What good are we to our child if we pass out; who will care for the child? For us to be available in mind, body and soul to those we love, we must care for ourselves, then and only then can we care for others."

It took some thought for this message from the wise old woman to sink in, but over time I came to understand the meaning of it.

Even though my home life remained chaotic, I found peace and serenity in my heart and kept coming to meetings to refill my empty cup with awareness, acceptance and love. I discovered a faith I never had and trusted that Danny would get help when Danny was ready, in Danny's time and in God's time. It didn't mean I loved him any less, it just meant I was learning to love myself.

The friendship with Carol rapidly evolved from meeting buddies to girlfriends. We spent hours on the phone and hours more at the park after the meetings. While our kids played on the swings we shared about our turbulent lives; secrets we kept hidden for years, even from our families. It was liberating to release my heavy burden. Inevitably, Carol and I became loving friends, closer than biological sisters.

I am grateful I had Carol and Al-Anon when Danny was arrested for driving while intoxicated. A thirty-day sentence was mandatory in the state of New York. It was believed by most people, primarily myself, that Danny's time at the county jail, and not at a rehab, would knock some sense into his hard head. He'd come out a new man, or at least come out a man and own up to his responsibilities. It worked – for a while.

He appeared humbled by his experience, quieter and maybe even a little mature. Mr. Patton, the father of one of Dan's friends who knew Danny since he was a kid, took Danny under his wing and became a second father to him and gave him the opportunity to learn a trade, as an apprentice electrician. For the first time in our marriage Danny earned a decent income, we were able to save enough money to move out of my parent's home and rent a lovely house with a great view of the bay. We even got a couple of dogs to complete the almost perfect picture, Ben and Lou, two Labrador Retrievers.

It wasn't exactly heaven, though Dan had stopped drinking, *again,* and the bills were paid, *again.* But he still was out at night until the wee hours of the morning. The way I looked at it, at least he wasn't drinking and we didn't fight as much.

On Mother's Day he bought me flowers, not just a bouquet of roses, as most men would do, but over thirty flats of annuals and perennials. Dan did do things in a grand style. It's not the unusual abundance of flowers that stand out in my mind as much as the memory of us planting the flowers together. By summer we were enchanted with a magical garden full of life and color; blossoms of pale pinks and deep purples, bright yellows, and indigo blues. In the fall the Montauk Daisies popped up their white faces and dozens of rich colorful chrysanthemums covered the entire entranceway.

It was indeed a magnificent garden, but it was only a façade. While the outside portrayed cheerfulness and light heartedness, inside my heart was despondent and hopeless. I often cried myself to sleep, lonely, confused, aching for Danny to be home with me. This was one of those nights. I lay in bed alone, listening to the night sounds of a balmy summer night; the soothing rhythm of the water lapping up against the shore, the symphony of crickets, the gentle whir of the overhead fan. Hugging Danny's pillow to my heart I dozed off to sleep.

I was startled awake by a bright light shining in my bedroom window. I slid out of bed and crawled over to the side window and peeked behind the curtains. I saw some cars in front of the house and men in suits. The dogs began barking and running through the house. Their racket woke up my son. Crouching down, believing I was under some sort of an attack, I scurried to my son's crib and soothed him with his bottle.

There was a pounding on the front door. I was immobilized by fear.

"Open the door, this is the police." They pounded some more. I threw a robe on and opened the door a crack, but one of the men pushed the door wider.

Ben nearly bit him. I had to restrain him by his collar. Lou cowered in the bedroom. One of the men told me his name and flashed a badge in my face. He asked me where Danny was and if I was alone. He warned me I would be in big trouble if I withheld information on Danny's whereabouts. The whole time he questioned me his dark eyes peered around the room. He made lewd remarks about Danny leaving such a pretty wife by herself, *didn't Danny know what could happen when pretty wives were left alone*? I was nauseated with fear. I didn't know if these men were really police or not. They continued to intimidate and interrogate me; finally they left. I locked the door and shut off the inside lights and stood hiding behind the curtains. I waited there until I heard them drive away. My heart was beating so loud I felt it pulsating in my ears. From the corner of my eye I saw the back door creak open. I lost my breath - it was Danny. He was crawling in on all fours like a Marine in combat; his clothes were drenched and stunk of canal water. He writhed his way around and managed to pull down the attic ladder, grabbed a towel then stole his way up the rickety stairs as light and nimble as a monkey sailing up a tree, leaving a trail of water behind him. He told me to stay quiet. Danny stayed in the attic all night. I hid under my covers trembling. When he finally did come down it was almost daylight and his clothes were still damp. He made up an elaborate story about his truck breaking down and swimming across the canal rather than walking the distance to get home. I knew this wasn't the truth. I never found out what actually happened that night or if the men really were police. They never returned and I chose not to pursue it. Danny would only lie further. The event was dropped and life resumed.

Six months later Danny was arrested again for driving while intoxicated; his second DWI. This time he was away for four months at a prison farm for rehabilitation. We almost made it one full year living in the little house. But without an income I had to move back to my parent's and leave my home with the beautiful view of the bay and the enchanted garden behind. The kids were too young to understand why I was crying. Every box I hauled out to the car brought an onslaught of fresh tears.

When my two-year-old son asked in his squeaky baby voice if we were going to take everything, even his bedroom walls, I lost it. How do you tell your child that the walls are going to stay, and the house is going to stay and the garden and the beautiful view of the bay is going to stay and all we're taking is a few measly possessions and we're going to be crowded living in Nanny's house, and we can't live in the apartment because your uncle lives there now, and I'll have to sleep on the couch and you and Shelly will bunk in the back room and we'll have to add a space heater because that room gets very cold in the winter and we have to give Lou up because it's a small house and Nanny has her own menagerie of dogs and cats, but it's only temporary and daddy will be home soon and then we'll have another house and we'll be a family and everything will be okay.

Of course I said none of those things. Instead I had the kids pick a bouquet of flowers for their grandmother. We piled in the car and headed to my mother's.

From the rearview mirror I took one last look at the little house with the view of the bay and the Montauk Daisies in full bloom dancing around in the breeze.

Living at my parents was as arduous as I imagined it would be. Not because of anything or anyone in particular. It's simply difficult to have two families live together under one roof, especially when there are small active children and a house full of animals. It seemed someone was always cranky and irritable and someone who was the peacemaker.

Just for today.

- SIX -

A Glimpse of Happiness

"I want to grow in my willingness to make room in my life for good times, having faith in their arrival and patience in my anticipation.
—Living With Sobriety

My mother sent the kids and me down to Florida for a month for some R & R with my relatives. She hoped being away in the warmth of the southern sun would be healing. She pleaded with me not to have any contact with Danny; I heeded her advice. I was rested by the time I returned. Having no communication with Danny for an entire month undoubtedly had something to do with feeling renewed. However, there was a stack of letters from him piled on my bureau when I returned home.

I wonder if things would have turned out differently had my mother thrown away his letters. But she didn't. Danny wrote a letter everyday going into detail about the farm's program and what he did from the moment he rose out of bed in the morning to the moment it was 'lights out.' The majority of his day was spent in therapy of some sort, whether it was group or individual counseling or participating in a twelve-step meeting. When he wasn't attending a therapy session, he would spend his spare time building up his body, eating peanut butter sandwiches to help him gain weight. On days when the weather was warm and sunny, he napped under the sun.

His letters demonstrated the daily progression of his recovery process. He had taken responsibility for his actions and behaviors and began to make amends to the people he had hurt. The words he spoke on paper were mature and sincere and not full of the line of bull from the past. I was confident Danny had reached his bottom and was prepared to turn his life around. I counted the days until he would be home. The past was the past. We both were committed to the task of accepting our mistakes and moving forward.

Danny came home on Memorial weekend of 1989. When I saw him after four long months, I fell in love again. He was fit and well developed from working out, his skin ripened to a rich golden tan, his hair was streaked from the sun's rays. His walk and his talk were confident and self-assured. He was in good spirits. Friends and family rallied around with encouraging words, and gratefully, Mr. Patton gave Danny his job back with advance pay to help us get on our feet *again*.

It was the first Memorial Day Parade we went to together in eons. We lived close to town and decided to walk rather than drive. We moseyed along holding hands enjoying the brilliance of the noon day sun. Dan strutted like a proud father, his small son's hand clasped in his, with Rachelle in her red, white and blue outfit merrily skipping along beside us. We looked like the perfect American family.

When you live in a small town everyone knows everyone's business. They surely knew our business and the reason Danny was away. It's the type of small town that remained more or less the same since my childhood. The hardware store, the delicatessen, the restaurants, still had the same owners. In fact if you lived in the town long enough, chances are your children could have some of the same teachers you had.

Most of the folks were happy to see Danny on that fine Memorial Day toting his family to the parade. Friends and acquaintances shook Dan's hand as if they were pumping water up from the well.

"Hi Dan, good to see you!" someone yelled across the

crowd.

"Hey man, heard you were home," his old drinking buddy Bruce said.

They chatted briefly. They each nearly fell over when they discovered they were both sober for the first time in their lives.

"Keep it simple, ya hear. Ring me if you want to bum a ride to a meeting." Bruce said.

Danny was stunned that Bruce was straight. Chances are Bruce thought the same about Danny. I thought the same about both of them.

After the parade Danny went to an AA meeting with one of his pals who had also made his way to a twelve-step program. He was lively and animated and in great spirits when he got home. He told me that many of our high school friends were also in the program. I offered a silent prayer of gratitude. Every person that wasn't out there drinking anymore would be one less person to influence Danny.

Over the weekend we moved out of my mother's home and rented a lovely, spacious three-bedroom ranch house that I found while Dan was away. It had everything to please everyone. Rachelle and Little Dan had their own rooms. I had a washer and dryer. Dan had a good sized shed to store his tools, a garage for the car, a cozy sun porch for some plants and even a four-foot above ground pool enclosed with decking, all nestled on a huge treed parcel of land. Top this off with a sober husband and a bright future. I found nirvana. This was the light at the end of a very long and dark tunnel that I had prayed for.

After spending the day moving furniture, hauling boxes, trying to figure out where to put what, bathing the kids and settling them into their new rooms, Dan and I collapsed on our deck squeezing together on one chaise lounge. It was a clear starry night, with a touch of an evening chill. Dan pulled me close, wrapping his arm around my shoulder. I rested my head on his chest listening to the gentle rhythmic beat of his heart. Some events in our lives remain in our minds and hearts forever, every detail so vivid you can even recall the faintest smells and the slightest sound; the fishy odor of the fertilizer newly dug in the field across the way, the silence of the night interrupted by the hum of a low flying plane, the whiff of Dan's after shave floating in the air. He was wearing jeans and a white tee shirt with his pack of Marlboros rolled up in his left sleeve. Ben settled down next to us, panting from the newness around him.

We discussed how we would decorate the rooms, where we'd plant a garden, whether we should clear the property some more or leave it more rustic, topics any couple would have. We avoided talking about events of the past, not necessarily on purpose, primarily because we were aware of the fact that the events of the past could not be changed. We hoped to learn by our errors, mine as well as his. We accepted we would live each day one day at a time and more importantly, we would do it together. I had no regrets. I was proud I stuck it out and I was proud of him. The future was promising.

That evening nuzzled in bed together, we made a conscious and sober decision to have another child. I felt secure and loved.

The children were thrilled to have their father around, particularly Little Dan. He'd follow him around like a puppy at his heels. Wherever Big Dan was, Little Dan was two steps behind. He wore little work boots and had his own tool belt, hammer and all, just like his dad.

On the evening of the Fourth of July we saw a spectacular firework show. Little Dan was perched on top of his father's shoulders, his pudgy hands wrapped in Danny's. Above the deafening booms of the fireworks, a little voice was heard, "I so happy Daddy's here waters coming out my eyes."

"I'm happy too, buddy," Danny answered. I know I saw water in his eyes too. I think that profound statement out of the mouth of a three-year old babe just about summed it up.

A year later Dan remained sober and active in his program. He was ambitious and motivated and started his own electrical business. He bought a good used truck, new tools and equipment;

the phone rang with customers looking for an electrician.

The one call we were hoping for finally came; the owners of the house were ready to put the house on the market and gave us first choice. We waited a year for this opportunity to purchase the house we had been comfortably living in and calling our home. We had saved every penny we could spare, but it wasn't sufficient to cover the down payment. When my grandfather heard about our dilemma he offered to help us. He believed, like many others, that Dan had sowed all the oats he needed to and left the rebellious teenager behind.

"Hey," my Grandfather said, "it happened, it's over, forget about what you did. Just don't do it again," he teased and wrote out a check for the amount we needed.

Throughout this time, I plugged away at school moving forward with my Bachelor's in Education. Danny took care of the kids when I had night classes. We came a long way from the days I hunted the local bars for him. Back then, not only did Danny not baby-sit his own children, he ridiculed my getting an education, telling me it was nothing but a waste of time. What a difference sobriety made, from an uncaring, loud-mouthed, egotistical and argumentative boy, to a supportive, kind and encouraging man.

About six months later I found out I was pregnant with our third child. It was a unique and gratifying experience to plan a child as two stable and responsible adults. This was a pregnancy the entire family enjoyed. Together we shopped for all the new baby's necessities. Rachelle wanted a baby sister and picked out dolls and Little Dan wanted a little brother and chose cars and trucks. The two of them bickered for months on who would get their wish.

My labor began early in the morning; Danny put Rachelle on the bus, and dropped our son off at preschool, then returned to transport me to the hospital. The contractions were so severe I thought I would faint from the pain. I nearly bit my tongue clenching my jaw closed. Danny drove like a maniac, frantic I would give birth any second. But a quick delivery wasn't in the plan. Danny was supportive throughout the nearly eight lengthy hours of strenuous labor. Close to exhaustion, I mustered up the strength for the final push that brought the birth of our third child wailing into the world. In a barely audible voice Danny murmured, "Oh my god, Tam, we have another son. I guess Little Dan got his wish for a baby brother."

The nurse placed the wet sticky baby in Danny's trembling arms.

"We have another son," he wept. "He looks like a baby bird, Tam. Look at his eyes, they're huge! They're as big as his head!"

We lovingly laughed at our scrawny 'baby bird' with enormous root beer brown eyes and fluffy chestnut hair. We were giddy with sheer happiness.

Our third child, Anthony, who was soon called Tony, made his grand debut on a cool fall day on October 21, 1990.

A few months after Tony was born, Dan added a second tattoo with his sons' names in two banners above an American eagle. This was Danny's way of sealing his commitment to his family, his badge of protection and guardianship.

We were a happy family for quite a while. One day in particular stands out in my mind as if it were yesterday. A snowstorm howled in during the night that created drifts over four feet high. In the morning the view in my backyard looked like a Hallmark card. The evergreens were draped in thick white wraps; the sun sparkled off the pristine snow. Danny had the kids out right after breakfast. I stayed in baking chocolate chip cookies. I wiped the steam off the window and peered out at them having fun. Danny was like the Pied Piper trudging through the snow with the kids and dogs following in his tracks. They were covered from head to toe in the soft white powder. For hours they frolicked outside in the giant sized igloo Danny built. All four of them crawled inside the icy dome, even our overweight Daschund. I could hear their muffled giggles from inside the house. Hot cocoa and warm cookies were ready for them when they came in. It couldn't have been anymore perfect than that.

- SEVEN -

Best Friends

Sharing laughter, sharing tears, sharing triumphs, sharing fears,
Growing closer through the years, true friendship is forever.
—Author unknown.

Carol and I had been friends for quite a while before we met each other's husbands. When Danny and Greg, Carol's husband, finally had the chance to meet, they hit it off as quickly and as comfortably as Carol and I. Soon whatever we did, we did as two families. With their three daughters, all within the same age as my three children, we'd pack our cars to the brim and head off for weekend vacations skiing in the mountains or spend the hot days of summer fishing off our small boat or digging our toes in the cool gooey mud for clams.

Carol and Greg and their girls became part of our Christmas Eve tradition at our home. Even in our poorest days, Christmas was always festive, especially Christmas Eve. It didn't matter if we were penniless or not, Danny would come marching in at the eleventh hour with bundles of lavish gifts for everyone. If you were there, you got a gift. One thing about Danny, he loved to spend money! It wasn't just the kids who eagerly waited for him to walk through the door with dozens and dozens of packages; the adults were anxious to see what the skinny Santa without the belly and the beard brought. We named him Danny Claus.

Best Friends

One year about a week before Christmas our two families set out to cut down our own Christmas trees. Carol and Greg came home with a beautiful and practical tree. Danny on the other hand chose a gargantuan blue spruce that took up the entire dining area and then some. It became the topic of conversation for years to come. Our meager trimmings were lost in the immensity of this huge evergreen. When Danny did things, he did them in a big way.

The best years of my marriage were the years of sobriety. It was during those years I had everything I could possibly want, a sober husband, beautiful healthy children and dear friends to share in my joy. No one can take these memories from me. They cannot be deleted and sent to the recycle bin as if they never existed. They are mine to cherish regardless to the fact that I probably clung to them longer than I should have.

My good fortune continued. Shortly after the Memorial weekend of 1989 that Danny had returned home, I ran into my friend Joy from school days. We had drifted in our own directions after graduation as most kids tend to do, but once we reconnected we developed the type of friendship that lasts forever regardless of distance or time. We soon came to learn that we led parallel lives.

As it turned out, Joy was married to Bruce, Danny's former drinking buddy. I had known Bruce through Danny, and Joy knew Danny through Bruce. But neither one of us ever imagined that we were the wives of the local 'bad boys.' We were thrilled to discover they were both on the straight and narrow.

"I always believed those two were joined at the hips," Joy remarked. "I knew when Bruce wasn't home that he was out with Danny. At least now the two goons are at an AA meeting and not hitting some bar."

While Bruce and Dan were off to their meetings, I introduced Joy to Al-Anon. The four of us plunged into our programs and lived our lives according to the guidelines of the twelve-step policies.

Life with Danny and Bruce during the early days of sobriety

was one hilarious adventure. If one of them wasn't plotting and scheming, the other one was. With or without the influence of alcohol, the two of them caused a raucous wherever they went. One summer weekend the four of us went white water rafting in upstate New York. The rapids weren't thrilling enough for these reckless characters. They convinced us the next day that what we needed was an action park. Unfortunately we found one. They were like schoolboys let loose from some strict military private school. They went wild! I nick-named them the exhibitionist and the showoff it didn't matter who was who; they were interchangeable. Danny wound up falling off one of the rides in some death defying stunt and getting hurt. Bruce who was as much of a loud mouth as Danny, had an argument with the ride attendant. We were all thrown out of the park. Joy and I wanted to crawl under a rock somewhere, but to the guys, it was the highlight of their trip.

Joy's not exactly a shrinking violet; she's a tough Italian from Brooklyn with magnetic Nile green eyes covered with thick long lashes and a head of voluminous dark hair. She has a sense of humor equal to Maxine, the character on greeting cards. She says it as it is.

"You know Bruce," Joy said in her dry wit on our way home, "I used to think you did these crazy thing because you were drunk. Well you ain't drunk now Honey, you're just plain freaking nuts!"

Her dry humor was often her defense mechanism and my salvation. We grew steadily closer. Her perky and exuberant personality was contagious; she could lift the spirits of the most down trodden individual.

The carefree fun days with Joy and Bruce didn't last very long. Bruce tumbled back into the dark and desolate ways of the drug world. Joy would call crying; Bruce wasn't coming home and money was disappearing out of her wallet. Danny often got on the phone with her and told her, "don't worry Kiddo, I'll find him and drag his big ass home."

Danny took it upon himself to be Bruce's savior, but Bruce

wasn't into being saved. He conned Joy into moving to Florida. He reasoned the geographical change would stop him from using. Desperate, frightened and not knowing what else to do, my dear friend agreed. At least her parents lived there.

The day Joy and Bruce pulled into our driveway with their car packed, was one of my saddest days. I was surely going to miss my funny high-spirited friend and Bruce's wacky zany ways.

Some months later Dan and I took a trip to Florida for a visit with our good friends. Joy wasn't her jubilant self and had added several pounds to her usually trim figure. Bruce kept his addiction under control while we were there. I was nervous Dan would join Bruce on one of Bruce's mysterious trips to town. We did some quick day trips to Universal Studio and Sea World and had the chance, even for a brief time, to relive the happy days. The day we were scheduled to fly home, Bruce decided that drugs were more important than friends were and wasn't around to take us to the airport as planned. With a very heavy heart, I left Joy behind.

While Joy had dark ominous clouds hovering over her, I was basking under white cumulus balls of fluff; Danny and I were enjoying the best times of our lives. I fought back tears and the old familiar fear that gnawed at me. If Joy's life could so easily flip like a coin, mine could as well. It was a scary thought and one I would find myself fretting over many times.

Joy and I spoke on the phone nearly everyday. We stayed in close touch regardless of the miles in between. We were and still are to this day, each other's lifeline. When one of us is down, the other is there with the life vest. Without question, Joy is one of my earth angels.

The roller coaster ride in Joy and Bruce's life continued for several years. During one of their good rides, Bruce found the courage to sign himself into a rehab and spent enough time there to come out feeling great about himself. It was as much of a relief to me as it was to Joy to have Bruce home and on the road to recovery.

The four of us planned a ten-day trip to Mexico for Danny's and my tenth wedding anniversary; it would be like old times again.

Joy and Bruce got to Mexico the day before we did and met us at the hotel. Joy was her sparkly self again and Bruce looked fit and rested. We were itching to get to the beach. We rushed to our rooms, plopped down our suitcases and hastily changed into our bathing suits. The four of us ran through the hotel lobby like four kids on the last day of school and shoved ourselves in the revolving door catching my finger in the interim and destroying my wedding ring. Bruce joked that I did it on purpose so that Dan would buy me a new ring for our anniversary. "No way, this is her anniversary gift." Danny quipped motioning to our surroundings. We spent the afternoon lazing on the white sand and wading in the aquamarine water. It was heavenly.

The next day we decided to do some shopping; however, the only way into town was by bus. If white water rafting was like floating in a pool for these two hotshots, a bus ride was about as adventuresome as watching a turtle creep across a dusty road. Neither Danny nor Bruce was known to be quiet for too long. They livened up the long boring ride with a two-man act.

Danny created a character named 'Appie', based on Dustin Hoffman's *Rainman*. 'Appie' was mentally challenged. Appie/Danny stood up in the bus, shuffled up and down the aisle repeating, "fifty seats, the bus has fifty seats, fifty people, there's fifty people in fifty seats." Bruce egged him on. It didn't take much. Danny was on a roll.

Appie/Danny sat next to passengers and said nonsensical things in a high pitched voice. We could not contain ourselves, but the people were scared. He kept this up until the bus came to a sudden stop, and military police with automatic rifles got on. The four of us froze. I know Dan and Bruce were looking for some excitement, but not in terms of sitting in a Mexican jail. One of the policemen wearing reflective sunglasses swaggered down the aisle, stopped, and looked at each passenger. He got two seats in front of us and grabbed a young Mexican boy about sixteen or so, dragged him off the bus, threw him on the ground and beat the hell out of him. No one dared to stop them. The police motioned for the driver to take off. We didn't look back. Not another peep was heard from the passengers, not even Dan or Bruce. Aside from that one hair-raising incident, the rest of the trip was enjoyable, peaceful, relaxing and fun.

Only a few months after our fabulous trip to Cancun, Bruce once again traded his sobriety for the desolate path of drugs and destruction. His addiction had progressed rapidly to the point that Joy had to lock her purse in the trunk of her car and then hide the car keys in an old Lipton tea box. Anything that wasn't bolted down found it's way to the pawnshop.

I took the kids down to Florida over the Easter holiday to spend some time with Joy and her children. Bruce picked us up at the airport; I witnessed for myself his erratic and unpredictable volatile behavior. His driving was reckless, bordering on dangerous; it was the ride from hell. Neither Joy nor I dared to open our mouths; white knuckled we gripped the seats and prayed. Bruce dropped us off at their house and disappeared – literally. He never returned again. Never. Joy filed an order of protection. Eventually she heard that Bruce was locked up, a drug deal gone sour. The cool dude decked out in gold with the pierced nose, turned out to be an undercover narcotics cop. It would be a long time before Bruce would see daylight again. Joy started divorce proceedings.

My heart ached for my friend, for her sadness and loneliness, for her confusion and for her fear of the future. I felt helpless. I could only offer paltry words of support.

"God works in mysterious ways," I soothed, "sometimes when we don't have the strength or the courage to do what needs to be done, God does it for us. Think of this as a blessing that Bruce is away from you. Now you will be able to pull your life together."

Although spoken from my heart, my words sounded flat and meaningless. I felt guilty that Danny had chosen a different path. I wanted to kiss the ground he walked on for turning his life around and providing a secure and peaceful life for his family. I could not imagine having the man I was married to in prison. How dreadful it was for Joy and her children to have to go through something so painful. I made a silent vow to be there for Joy as much as is humanly possible.

Who could have known that not that many years down the road, Joy would vow the same for me. The words I spoke to her, she would recite back to me.

- EIGHT -

Visions for a Better World

"Think the unthinkable and do the impossible!"

In 1991 Carol and I attended an inspirational three-day nationally recognized drug and alcohol prevention program for children. The workshop was presented by a beautiful blonde, vivacious and spiritual woman named Patti, who immediately became our dear friend. The program utilized colorful hand-sized puppets to teach children the necessary skills to cope with life's challenges. Because the disease of alcoholism affected both our families we hoped to find a way for our children to break the cycle of addiction and guide them into a healthy alcohol and drug-free future.

We needed $400 to purchase the programs' kit in order for us to get started. We began with a yard sale that, even though it poured like the dickens, raised exactly the amount of money that we needed - $400.93! Our mission was underway.

We carted our mobile puppet program to libraries, community centers, scout meetings and anyplace that would have us. Danny didn't take what I did seriously; to him it was what mothers did in the afternoons when the kids are at school.

Before long we progressed from visiting facilities to renting some space in a church basement where we could offer more programs for youths and their families. One of our specialty workshops was a ten-week presentation we gave to a group of troubled teens that to some degree were affected by HIV/AIDS. We were greeted on our first visit by a dozen intimidating mixed ethnic kids with bandanas wrapped around their heads and gold chains strung around their dark-skinned necks. These kids could have easily chewed us up and spit us out without so much as an after thought. To them we were nothing but two dumb white bitches on some good-will mission to save their hard-ass souls. It took several weeks for these kids to accept us and gain our trust. Two African-American brothers who were over six-foot tall and towered over us like massive football players grew particularly close to us. They had lost both of their parents over the years to the dreadful disease and were living with their grandmother. When Carol and I met this frail aging woman with white cotton hair and skin as dry and cracked as old leather, we were warmly embraced and thanked repeatedly for helping her grandsons find a better way to live.

For years Carol and I worked without pay. Our reward was the hugs from tiny grandmothers and parents of the young suicidal teens who turned their lives around. Our good work spread rapidly throughout the community. The more we offered, the more calls we received. The demand for our programs progressed at an overwhelming rate. Soon we outgrew our limited space in the church basement; it was apparent that we needed a more permanent structure to expand our ever-growing programs. We realized also, the importance for us to incorporate for the additional funding that was needed and managed to collect enough resources to take care of the legal matters. Then we enlisted officers of our new organization. Since I was the one in charge of collecting the money from the workshops (a whole ten dollars that I carried around in a paper bag), I was elected the treasurer. Carol had taken on the responsibility of writing letters and designing flyers, so she was nominated secretary, and Patti who helped us through the entire process and was our main source of financial backing, was elected president.

Carol, Patti and I have always had tremendous faith; we not

only believed in miracles, we expected them, and trusted that God would continue to lead us where we needed to be.

After some extensive research and many prayers, the town granted us an abandoned dilapidated farmhouse on sixteen acres of private wooded land, all for the price of $1 per year. The property was magical; elegant trees lined the front yard, an ancient evergreen stood regally alongside the house and two towering holly trees with hundreds of bright red berries shaded the walkway. In the backyard was an ancient massive cedar tree that majestically guarded the land. Our prayers were answered above and beyond our wildest dreams. There was a catch though; the rooms were gutted, wires hung from the ceilings, dirty rotting musty smelling insulation was piled in heaps and there was a nauseating stench of a decayed dead cat. But it was ours.

We spent weeks making calls for assistance and received a tremendous out-pouring of help. Hundreds of volunteers from plumbers and carpenters to retired citizens and teens donated their time, energy and resources. Carol's husband Greg was there as often as he could be, pounding nails, painting walls, sanding floors and doing whatever was necessary to be of help. Few people knew I was married to an electrician; in fact, few knew I was married.

By the time Carol and I had a center of our own, and it became apparent that my work was developing into a full time career, Danny began to criticize my efforts and told me to go out and get a real job. It was my suggestion that we pay an outsider to do the electrical work rather than me asking Danny. I wasn't up to his sarcastic remarks that all I was doing was donating my time to charitable causes, which had a measure of truth in it. As long as I didn't infringe on his time, there was peace. While Greg supported Carol in every way, Danny never knew what it was I did or had any interest to ask. It was a constant challenge for me to remain positive when continuously being browbeat and shot down by Danny's callous remarks. It took me many years to realize that whatever success or accomplishment I achieved was a threat to Danny. My career was the one area where he lost control.

With or without Danny's help our center opened its doors in 1996 for our fourth annual summer program with a full registration of four hundred children. Carol, Patti and I created a place of recognition within the community. Over the years the center's walls were covered with plaques and proclamations from the town honoring our services and scores of pictures of the three of us shaking hands with the town's politicians.

We were a success in every way, except one, our resources. We never knew where the next dollar was coming from. Like my personal life, we ran in the red for years. We were working over forty hours a week and wearing a dozen different hats, but we were never able to raise enough money for us to draw a decent salary. It was frustrating to all of us, but Carol and Patti had their husbands to depend on. I on the other hand had to listen to Danny tell me to *get a job that pays*. We depended on miracles to support us, but the center was sinking financially. Patti, never one to give up on her faith, was sure we would pull through, and of course we did.

One autumn day an attractive woman in a tailored suit with a recent degree in marketing approached our center. By the end of the afternoon, Diane signed on as our personal financial consultant, pro bono. As a shrewd businesswoman, Diane taught us how to make the most use of what little money we had and how to make that money work for us. In a matter of months she had our sorry affairs under way and soon we were actually able to draw a decent salary, but not enough. I still had to grit my teeth and confront Danny for money to cover the household bills. He despised the fact that I had a career and would make me squirm for the measly dollars I needed for *our* bills. Needless to say as the center evolved to a self-supporting financial and professional organization, Danny's pillory intensified.

It had become painfully obvious to me how much Greg was involved in our business. The center's photo albums were filled with pictures of Greg posing as Santa, or Greg climbing up the tree to hang spooky ghosts for our Halloween Walk, or Greg holding a golf club ready to tee off for our annual golf fundraiser. Carol's husband was an attentive listener especially when either of us would go on about something that had to do with our business; he would calmly offer practical suggestions. I never asked Danny his opinion or shared anything about the center. He wouldn't have understood and would only poke fun and belittle my efforts. He was nothing more than a phantom in my professional life.

NINE

Shady Confession

A friend can tell you things you don't want to tell yourself.
—Francis Ward Weller

It was around 1993 when Danny had been doing some electrical work on one of the homes in the new development not far from our home. He became friendly with the owners, a couple around our age, and wanted me to meet them. Dan made the arrangements for the four of us to get together for dinner. I nearly fell over when I was introduced to Beth. She was the most stunning woman I had ever seen. Taller than average, string bean thin, sleek shapely legs, long slender neck, ivory skin dotted with tan freckles, icy blue eyes and a mane of wavy carroty red hair that fell carelessly around her oval face; clearly super model qualities. To say that I was somewhat intimidated is putting it mildly. I was relieved to discover that Beth was down to earth and not the least bit pretentious. Her husband Tom was about a foot shorter, stout, muscular and macho. Dan and Tom had much in common, both were in the line of construction, both had Italian backgrounds, and both were raised in Flushing near the same neighborhood. Beth and I had less in common, but became very friendly. After the kids went off to school we'd call one another and chat about nothing in particular. Beth was curious about what I did at the center and eventually confessed she envied what she perceived as my independent life and my determination to continue with my education. Tom was from the old school; no wife of his was going to be trotting off to some school, work was definitely out of the question. According to Tom, the only life his wife needed was caring for their home and their children.

"Tom's a good man," Beth would say as if to make up for what was lacking, and added, "he's a good father and a good provider." Beth was not happy. Our conversations grew more intimate and Beth opened up about Tom's possessiveness and jealousy and the times he was rough with her. I gradually mentioned about Danny's past drinking episodes and his run-in with the police.

It was during my friendship with Beth when Dan and I began the slow but steady tumble from the peak to the valley far below. Dan became distant, he'd jump down my throat if I asked him a question, such as, 'did you see Little Dan's baseball bat?' That simple question would set off an unexplainable explosion, "how the hell do I know where the damn thing is," he'd scream and kick the dog's food bowl across the room. "If you put the freaking thing where it belonged you wouldn't have to always be looking for it!"

I didn't know it was my job to be in charge of baseball bats.

I was concerned Dan had started drinking again, although there was no evidence confirming that. He was angry about everything. He never talked, just argued or I got the silent treatment. For several weeks this odd behavior continued. I could not approach him on any matter. I avoided him as much as possible and buried myself in my work. When he moved himself out of the bedroom and took up residence on the living room couch, I confided in Beth. She suggested the possibility that there might be problems with Dan's business. She said Tom always acted weird when a customer was giving him a hard time.

One morning while Dan was in the shower, his beeper went off. Normally I would ignore it figuring it was probably one of his workers. But some little voice told me to pick it up. In bold

letters the message read – "THINKING OF YOU!"
Thinking of you? Thinking of you!
At last the pieces of the puzzle fit. Of course, that was it. He was fucking someone!

I didn't wait for Dan to get out of the shower; I barged in and threw the curtain back, ripping the hooks right off the shower rod.

"What the hell is this?" I shoved his beeper in his face.

"How should I know, did you ever think it could be the wrong phone number?" He was quick with an answer; never raised his voice or uttered a four lettered word. He grabbed his beeper from my trembling hand, stepped around me as if I had some dreadful oozing skin disease, got himself dressed, and out the door he went, muttering over his shoulder that I was nuts.

With a quivering hand I dialed Beth and told her about the mysterious beeper message and my suspicions that Danny was screwing around. She assured me it had to have been a wrong number; Danny wouldn't have been stupid enough to give out his beeper number.

I had become convinced that Danny had the phone tapped. He seemed to know too much and was always one step ahead of me. Like the time Beth and I planned on attending our boys' preschool play. I had a commitment at work that I couldn't get out of so Beth went without me. I had no intention of telling Danny I didn't go. But the next day he criticized me for being an unfit mother and going to my ridiculous job that I didn't get paid for. How could he have known I didn't go? He also knew about the credit card that I had received and hid in Rachelle's bureau drawer. How could he have had access to this information if the phone wasn't tapped? And why? Why would he spy on my phone conversations? Was he checking to find out if I knew what he was up to?

The next time I spoke with Beth on the phone I asked her in a chippy happy-go-lucky, everything-is-peachy-creamy voice to go for a walk with me.

We decided to meet at the corner halfway between our homes. I arrived before Beth, speed walking like an Olympic athlete, jaw set, eyes focused, arms pumping and feet pounding the blacktop.

When I saw Beth coming around the corner, I ran up to her.

"I know Danny's cheating," I huffed, "he's even tapped the phone."

I didn't give Beth the chance to ask the questions I saw on her face. I rattled off my suspicions and ended with, "how would he know these things?"

The wheels were turning in Beth's head too. She was dubious, but agreed we shouldn't talk on the phone anymore.

"All right, if this is true, who would Danny be with?"

I had never told Beth about Sandy, but this was as good a time as any. Beth was speechless.

"Danny *cheated* on you in the past?"

She was having a hard time digesting this juicy piece of gossip. Beth was as furious as I was and maybe even more determined to find out who the person was.

"That bastard! That son of a bitch! How could he do this?" Beth shrieked.

We saved our verbal slaughter of Danny for our walks. I didn't breathe a word of this on the phone to anyone.

The rug was being pulled out from under me, knocking me off my feet, not in a fast, fall-and-hit-your-head-be-unconscious way, but slow and steady, inch by inch. I couldn't stop it. And I couldn't stop my mind from spinning like a whirling dervish, around and around beyond the brink of sanity. I was driven like an addict on the search for a drug, any drug that could satisfy the desire. I was haunted by the need to find some shred of evidence that could prove I wasn't going off the deep end. I asked a friend to check if the phone line was tapped. It wasn't. If the phone wasn't tapped, how was Danny getting the information? I was drawn back to the days of being obsessed. I probed and spied and couldn't let this go. Aside from Dan's abrupt change of attitude, I had nothing to go by, no lipstick smears, no mysterious bruise on his neck, nothing, nada, zilch. But I knew. I just knew.

Joy came up from Florida in May of 1997 for my son Tony's communion, but I had a sneaky suspicion she had other ulterior motives for being with me. She was in the process of picking up the pieces of her own shattered life and knew first hand what my situation would be like if Danny and I broke up. She became my personal aide, cook, housecleaner, decision-maker, chauffeur and anything else I needed her for. I knew she was worried about me, especially the night she caught me crawling on the dining room floor in the middle of the night.

Joy heard a bit of a commotion and came into the dining room to see what was going on. What she witnessed was me underneath the dining room table scooting around on my hands and knees in my pajamas; what she didn't know was that I was trying to catch Tony's ferret which escaped from its cage. She thought I had gone over the edge. If nothing else we had a good laugh.

After the communion ceremony everyone came back to our house. Danny was his usual life of the party, telling jokes and being the funny man. I painted on my everything-is-great face. To see the two of us no one would have guessed the turmoil our lives were in.

I was happy that Beth and Joy finally had the chance to meet in person. But I was shocked by Joy's instant dislike of Beth. Joy couldn't have talked with Beth for more than twenty minutes when she grabbed me by my arm and dragged me into the bedroom.

"I don't trust that skinny bitch Tami, she's got something up her sleeve. I feel it in my bones, she's the one Danny's seeing. I just know it. You better watch that one."

"You're crazy, Joy. She wants to know who it is too, she's even more angry than I am."

"Tami, I know this is hard for you, but mark my words, it's her. Don't you see the way the two of them are giving each other those cutesy flirty looks? Makes me sick. I'm telling you, Tami, don't trust that anorexic redheaded bitch. I'm keeping my eye on those two, first gaga look I see, I'm gonna slap the shit out of her."

I couldn't imagine why Joy felt that way unless she was jealous of my friendship with Beth, but that wasn't Joy's nature. She didn't let up and every so often she poked me in the ribs. "See that Tami? Look at the two of them, all giggly and falling all over each other. Ugh!"

Joy told me that when she had gone into the kitchen to get some soda, which I had suspected she did on purpose, she accidentally walked in on Beth and Dan in a near embrace. I didn't believe her. But mysteriously Beth left right after that.

"I'm not letting Danny get away with this one, Tami. Maybe he can pull the wool over your eyes, but he's not fooling me. I'm gonna make him squirm."

As soon as the last person left my house, Joy ripped into Danny.

"You know Dan, you and that anorexic frizz head were a little cozy in the kitchen, don't you think? I know a bitch in heat when I see one."

Danny attempted to laugh it off, "what's the matter Joy, ain't had any since Bruce left ya?"

"Maybe I ain't had any Dan, but your goddamn thing is running on overtime."

The two of them continued to jab below the belt.

"It's no wonder Bruce left you, you're nothing but a jealous nagging bitch."

"Guess I hit a sore spot, hey Dan? You ain't fooling me none."

Danny grabbed his car keys off the counter and without so much as a 'see you later', left.

"You can't tell me, Tami, that wasn't guilt written all over his goddamn face. He couldn't get out of here quick enough."

Joy went home the following morning, pressing me not to trust Beth, to keep my eyes and ears open and to call her anytime night or day. I was grateful I had my job and my schoolwork to occupy my mind. I didn't dare allow myself to think about what Joy had said. I trusted Beth and would not believe she would be capable of being so underhanded. She was my friend.

After some weeks of Danny living on the couch and Joy prodding me to kick his sorry ass out, I was finally ready to muster up the courage to tell Danny to leave. I was just waiting for the right time. I first thought about putting his things in his truck while he was sleeping and then locking the door when he left in the morning, but I realized that wouldn't work. He'd have a fit and I'd have to put his crap back. I considered writing him a letter. That wouldn't have worked either. I would still have to face him. If I wanted him out I would have to be bold and tell him to his face. The right time wasn't coming and months were slipping by. It was an odd arrangement with him on the couch, but I adjusted to it. At least I didn't have to confront him. In the meantime, Beth and I continued with our friendship.

Out of the blue or it seemed like out of the blue, Danny came home one night and said he was leaving. Not exactly leaving because he couldn't afford to actually move out and rent someplace, he'd move into the garage apartment that he had built for my mother some years before when she finally found her inner strength to divorce my father.

I didn't think Danny's idea was a bad arrangement. He would be out of my sight, more or less. I wouldn't have to see him, cook for him, do his laundry or listen to his lies and his bullshit. And in my demented mind, I could still keep tabs on him and know when he was out and what time he came home. It became my nightly routine before going to bed to look out the window and check if Danny's car was in the driveway. If it was, I could fall asleep, if it wasn't I'd jump out of bed every time I heard a car. Crazy thoughts would race in my head. I'd imagine myself going into the apartment and finding him screwing some bimbo like I had years before. Eventually I'd fall asleep from sheer exhaustion. This was how I allowed myself to live.

I fell into the mundane routine of Dan in the apartment and me in the house and went about my everyday life. Sometimes he would eat dinner with the kids and me, other times I wouldn't see him for days. Every opportunity I had I'd spy in the apartment when I knew he wasn't going to be home in the hopes of finding something. I never let go of my insurmountable need to learn the truth.

There were some advantages not having Danny under my roof; I had the bathroom to myself in the morning, I didn't have to jump out of bed first thing and make his coffee and I could watch whatever I wanted on TV. Not much, I admit. But he still controlled the finances and I still needed to grovel like a low-ranking dog for a chunk of meat. I had to continue to play the game as I always did - by his rules. I'd ask him for money. He'd ask me what for. I'd tell him the bills. He'd tell me he's getting a check. The same old script.

The bills were due and I needed money. This was always a great excuse for me to go to the apartment and see what he was doing. Sometimes I'd listen at his door before knocking in the hopes of catching him doing something. Danny seemed to be a little too cheery and a little too willing to give me money without me having to go through the customary groveling routine. He was in the middle of writing me out a check and announced in a matter of fact way, as if he was telling me he bought new tires for the car, that he had been seeing this girl Mary that he met one night while he was out. I ignored him, figuring he was just saying this to get a rise out of me and waited for him to give me the check. But he was telling me the truth or the truth as Danny knew it. He even went so far as to tell me Mary was a nice person and I'd like her when I got to meet her.

I stormed out of the apartment, basically calling him a fucking idiot and called Joy.

"Look at it like this Tam, at least it's not Beth." Joy hadn't brought her name up for some time, but evidently she still believed there was something between Danny and her. "This Mary person, whoever the hell she is, if she really exists, will keep Danny from bothering you. He'll have somebody else to abuse."

I didn't feel much better when I hung up.

I decided to call Beth even though it was nine-thirty and I knew Tom didn't like it when Beth got calls in the evening. I begged her to take a ride with me and use the excuse that we forgot to pick up some supplies for the kids' art project.

"Danny has a *what*?" Beth screeched.

"A girlfriend," I answered in a dead non-human voice. "Mary, her name is Mary. I guess this is the bitch that left the message on his beeper. He wants me to meet her, says I'll like her."

"Are you sure Danny said it was his girlfriend, I mean.... *we....I...*"

I was so caught up in my own fury I never noticed Beth's voice trail off or the blank stare on her face.

A few days later Danny actually had the audacity to bring Mary to the apartment. I watched her trot along behind him. His new puppy.

I was frothing at the mouth, furious beyond words. How dare he bring that slut on my property. I speed dialed Joy; she wasn't home. I was too irate to leave a message. I needed someone at that very moment before I exploded. .

Beth answered her phone on the first ring.

"She's here, that bitch is here! How dare she violate me, how dare she step foot on MY property! *HOW DARE SHE!*"

There may be some women that might be wondering around this time why I didn't just fling the slime ball out on his ass as my good friend Joy suggested. But I'm sure there are others who see themselves in me. It's not that I wasn't angry. I was angry all right. I ranted and raved to Joy, to Beth and to my mother. On occasion I even called Danny a few choice names to his face. But I placed the blame on Mary. How dare *she* violate me, how dare *she* step foot on my property. Really though, what did that woman know about what was going on? No doubt Danny gave her some cock and bull story and made *me* out to be the villain.

In fact, I did come to like Mary as Danny said. She was like me. Pathetic.

In truth I didn't direct or acknowledge my anger toward the real person that violated me - Danny. I waited until the next day to tell him that I didn't want his girlfriend on my property again. That was the extent of it.

I played the role of martyrdom to the hilt. As my mother had said years before, we come from a long line of Joan of Arc's; the women simply stood back and accepted whatever was handed to them by their husbands. It took my own mother twenty-six years to divorce my father. The apple didn't fall far from the tree sort of thing.

Life resumed as before with Danny. I didn't kick him out. It stayed pretty much the same, except for one major difference. I wasn't only living in the insanity - I became the insanity.

TEN

Shot in the Heart

*"Truthful lips endure forever, but a
lying tongue lasts only a moment."*
—Proverbs 12:19

The week between Christmas and New Year of 1997, I went
to the movies and saw the romantic yet tearful, *Titanic*, with
Rachelle. I noticed Danny's car wasn't in the driveway when we
got home, but heard him a few minutes later.

My fifteen year old daughter and I were both feeling weepy
and downhearted from the sad movie and plopped ourselves
down on the couch with a box of tissues when Danny called me
on the phone and asked me to come over to the apartment; he
had something he wanted to talk to me about.

My stomach went queasy; I didn't like the tone in his voice.
I knew whatever it was; it was not going to be good.

I stepped into the apartment and found Danny sitting on
the chair with a newly lit cigarette in his hand; I caught a whiff
of sulfur from the match. He pointed to the chair across from
him for me to sit. I sat. I didn't like the pinched look on his face
or the tightness in his jaw.

Danny took a long drag on his Marlboro. He let the smoke
come out slowly, tapping his cheek to create smoke rings.

"Well," I said impatiently.

"I have to tell you something. It ain't easy for me to tell you this, but I gotta do it."

About a half a dozen things raced through my mind in less than a fraction of a second. None of them good.

"I've been seeing Beth."

"*What?*" I didn't believe him. He was sicker than I ever imagined.

In the middle of my screaming at Danny, calling him a liar and accusing him of trying to ruin my friendship with Beth, Rachelle came over to the apartment. I totally ignored her and continued shrieking. I never noticed she was crying.

"You're nothing but a jealous bastard." I spit my words at him.

"Ma! *Stop* screaming!" Rachelle screamed back at me.

Danny was yelling at me for screaming at Rachelle who was crying because Little Dan threw a fork at her arm and she was bleeding.

The entire household was insane. The boys had been off the wall since Danny moved into the apartment; they were either having yelling matches or worse, punching each other. I would usually hide in the basement for some privacy, ignoring the chaos around me. My teenage daughter became the peacemaker and caretaker.

I refused to listen to any more of Danny's bullshit. I stormed out of his apartment, called Beth and told her I was on my way to her house, without explaining why. I sped to Beth's like a fireman called to a burning building, not even slowing down for the stop sign. I screeched into her driveway and blasted the horn. I have no idea what Beth told her husband, but she raced to the car in her slippers throwing her coat over her pajamas as she ran.

"My god, Tami what's wrong? Has something happened to Danny? To the kids?"

"Danny said he's been having an affair with you." The words stuck in my throat.

"Is this true?"

"Tami you can't possibly believe him. I would never do anything like that. He must be crazy."

We sat for over an hour in the 7-11 parking lot sipping coffee trying to figure out why Danny would have made up such a horrible lie. I believed her. *She* was my friend. *He* was the low-life slime.

Danny was gone by the time I got home. He didn't come home that night. I didn't see him until the following night when he again called me and asked me to come over. He was standing at his door waiting for me. I pushed my way past him.

"What are you going to tell me now? That you're having an affair with my mother!"

"Tami, I'm telling you the truth, I can't hurt you anymore. It's true, Beth and I have been seeing each other for years."

"*Years?*"

"She's not what you think."

"Why are you doing this to me Danny? Haven't you already drained what little life I have in me? Why are you making up something so hurtful?"

"I'm going to prove to you that I'm telling the truth."

Danny dialed Beth's phone number. It didn't register in my brain that he knew her number. He clicked the phone on speaker and put his finger to his lips, signaling for me to stay quiet.

"Hey, it's me. I told Tam about us, but she doesn't believe me."

I heard Beth's voice clearly. "Why did you do that Danny? I thought we agreed not to let her know. What she doesn't know won't hurt her. I told you it's over with us, leave it alone."

"Yea, well it's too late. I've got you on speaker, Tami's right here listening to the whole thing. We ain't a secret no more."

"You're a fucking liar!" Beth's voice screeched over the speaker.

"I ain't lying. Tami's right here."

I might as well have been shot with a high powered rifle the pain was that severe; I felt as if my guts had been blown out of my body, splattered all about me. I stumbled out of the apartment and ran to the house, tripped on the back step and fell forward scraping my knees and hands.

"Where's the phone?" I shrieked like a mad woman.

Rachelle came out of her bedroom with the phone to her ear, innocently chatting with a friend. Her bubbly teenage light-heartedness instantly switched to fear.

"Gimme the damn phone." I snatched it away from Rachelle before she had the chance to say good bye to whoever she was giggling with. With a bloody quivering hand, I dialed Beth.

"Why Beth? *Why*? I can expect this from him; he's a piece of shit, but *you*? I thought you were my friend."

"I never meant for this to happen, Tami. I never wanted to hurt you." In between Beth's blubbering sobs she pleaded for me to forgive her. She didn't intend to fall in love with Danny, he was a great friend, it kept getting deeper and deeper, she knew it had to end. Blah. Blah. Blah.

I hung up before she could say anything more and collapsed in a heap on the kitchen floor. My young daughter bundled me up in her young arms and comforted me as if I was the child, just as she did when she was a two-year old. With my head on her bony shoulder, we cried.

Joy was right – I shouldn't have trusted the anorexic red-haired bitch.

Danny remained living in the apartment and continued his fling with Mary. I *never* spoke with Beth again. But I did find out why Danny *confessed* to me. It had nothing to do with his guilt. Nothing to do with his morals. And nothing to do with Danny not wanting to hurt me. Ironically, Beth ended their wanton affair when she discovered Danny was seeing Mary. Apparently Beth couldn't deal with the fact that Danny was cheating on *her*. And so to hurt Beth for breaking up with him, Danny confessed to *me*. So while Danny was cheating on *me* with *Beth*, he was cheating on *Beth* with *Mary*! They don't make soap operas this sordid!

Not more than a few weeks after my life was torn to shreds, Danny informed me that he and Mary rented a place and were taking up residence somewhere else.

I should have been grateful that Danny moved out. Certainly Joy and my mother were elated he was gone. Dan might have been out of the house, but he was by far not out of my life. Suddenly he became the good father and he *and* Mary would come over on Saturday mornings and take *my* sons to play baseball. Mary went out of her way to be pleasant with me. She seemed sincere and enjoyed having my boys with her and they liked her, which I had a difficult time accepting. I reasoned that the boys were young, only eleven and seven years old, and needed their father. I was thankful that Rachelle had no interest in being a part of the newly formed family.

What I couldn't cope with was the hard fact that Danny actually left me. The relationship he had with Mary wasn't an immature fling like he had had with Sandy, nor a sleazy affair like he had with Beth. In my mind this meant that Danny cared for Mary. Apparently he cared for many women. Apparently whatever he was looking for, he evidently couldn't get with me.

Interesting to note the females that Danny sought were women who were going through their own hell. Sandy's life from her childhood upward was filled with turbulence and upheaval. Beth was in an abusive marriage. And Mary was recently divorced and was getting on her feet from an alcoholic marriage. More than likely these women had little self-esteem; they were weak and ready for someone to take away their pain. I fit into their category.

As it turned out, Danny and Mary only lived together for a few months. In June of 1998 Dan went to jail for his third DWI.

- ELEVEN -

Avoiding the Issue

*"I cannot expect anyone to help me unless
I am willing to share that I need help."*
—In All Our Affairs

I foolishly stopped going to Al-Anon. I knew the steps that I needed to take and didn't take. It had gotten to the point that I was too ashamed to talk to anyone and admit that I never made Danny leave. I thought I'd try counseling, but it didn't work for me at the time. I was no more willing to talk to a stranger than I was with the familiar group at Al-Anon.

For the short time that I did try counseling I was at least honest about my childhood, because in my perception, it wasn't bad. In fact I thought we were a happy family. My parents were still married while most of my friends came from divorced homes. I didn't have a bad relationship with my father either; I simply didn't have one. He was the absentee father, a workaholic turned gambler turned alcoholic. He was a man of few words with unobtainable dreams, particularly to retire at a young age as a wealthy racehorse owner. He followed his dream until it eventually swallowed him whole and us along with him.

I grew up on a small horse farm, including not only the race-horses, but a few goats, sheep, a couple of pigs and a menagerie of dogs and cats. It was my father's fantasy to have a barn full of expensive and prized racehorses. But it was my mother that did all the work on the farm, from mucking stalls to grooming horses, tending the small livestock and maintaining a large farmhouse to boot. See any martyrdom here?

My father was one for starting things and not finishing them. A carpenter and mason by trade, and an intelligent and talented man, he could erect a building from an image in his mind, but could not complete the work on our house. We lived at the farm for years in a house that was partially finished. The downstairs bathroom never had a sink installed, the slate floor in the kitchen was incomplete, water pipes to the barn were never dug. If my mother wasn't happy, she did a good job of concealing it, especially from us kids, I never knew her to complain.

My memories of living on the farm were happy ones. I had my own horse and had won several ribbons at the 4-H Club events, I watched in amazement as our mare give birth, I fed baby pigs a bottle, I skated on the small pond that was in the back field that froze over in the winters, and I ate ripe apples off our trees. It wasn't a bad life for a child. In my senior year we moved to a smaller house closer to town and within walking distance to school and all of my friends; a move that I didn't find distressing. It wasn't until I was an adult that I learned my parents lost the farm due to my father's gambling. I wasn't aware how my mother suffered silently at the loss of the home she loved dearly and the animals that she cared for, some from birth that had to be sold or given away. My mother being the master of cover-up never revealed her sorrow; instead she did her best to make our new house into a home, even though this house as well, remained unfinished. For a while my father stopped gambling long enough to accumulate some money, he renovated the house and installed an in-ground pool, but par for course, once the gambling resumed whatever was not finished, stayed unfinished.

That was the basis of my childhood, a father who wasn't around much, a mother who hid her feelings; parents who didn't argue, but didn't communicate either. Happy holidays with relatives, but no family vacations. A mother who tried to do it all, a father who never noticed, a brother who acted out and me who stayed in the background. Not exactly *Father Knows Best*, but not horrendous either.

After three months of delving into my childhood and avoiding the real issues of my life, I stopped going to counseling and steadily progressed in my own disease; from living in the insanity, to being the insanity, to being in denial to being numb. One day rolled into another, day turned to night and night came back to day. The sun came up. The sun went down. That was the one consistent thing in my life. I plunged into my education and received my Masters Degree. In fact I had been working on my thesis when I was doled the crushing news about Beth and Danny.

Every day, regardless of what was going on around me, I went to work. I'd shower, put on make-up, and dress like the professional I was – at work. No one knew my guts were held together by a sheer Band-Aid, one wrong move and they'd spill out. Work was my refuge, my sanctuary, a place for me to hide. There I was looked upon as having it all together, a competent, confident, intelligent and sane woman. I could forget about me and reach out to others. It was my job and the center that Carol and I founded that kept me alive; it was my therapy. As long as I had my work I was functional, or so it appeared.

TWELVE

The "War-Hero" Returns

"You can't hold a man down without staying down with him."
—Booker T. Washington

I heard via the grapevine, or should I say gossip line, not sure if there is a difference, that Mary visited Danny in jail. I kept my distance. The one right thing I did for myself. The news finally reached me that Mary stopped her visits to her lover and in fact cut all ties with him. Bravo for Mary, at least she had some sense to get out before she drowned in the muck and mire of Danny's bullshit.

While Danny was locked up behind bars I could think with somewhat of a clear head and went so far as to initiate divorce proceedings. But Dan refused to sign the papers. Without Mary's sympathy and no one to cry to, Danny conveniently remembered he had a wife, and maybe even a small recollection that he had a couple of kids. Instead of signing the papers he began to write me long letters, pouring out his heart, his shame and his remorse. It didn't take long for him to snare me again. He was a desperate man at this point and I was making threats I had never made before. Dan reached deep into his bag of tricks and set his bait in a steel heart trap. It worked. I was tricked like the starved fox tempted by a morsel of meat caught in a steel leg device. Does it chew its leg off to escape or does it wait in fear to be released into the hands of the enemy? I grasped onto that morsel of meat and ignored my raw and bleeding heart and waited for the enemy.

In January of 1999 after spending six months in jail, Danny was back at home. I had done a superb job of placing every one of Danny's affairs and every disappointment in a neatly stacked folder labeled - "Don't Open – EVER." I knew everyone thought I was nuts taking him back again. But I thoroughly convinced myself that Danny finally came to the point in his life when he was ready to take responsibility for his actions and reached the threshold of maturity. I was certain he had come to his senses; after all he had plenty of time in jail to reflect on his life. I prayed so hard for him I forgot to pray for myself. I was completely incapable of seeing my own delusions and illusions and crazed way of thinking. I didn't need Danny's line of bull to sucker me in. I was fully capable of duping myself. My ridiculous dream of husband, family and white picket fence thrust its delusional head up like a persistent crocus pushing its way through the snow-crusted surface. Embarrassing as it is to admit, I was relieved that he was coming home to *me*.

Evidently I wasn't the only one wearing pink tinted glasses. My brother believed in Dan too. He suggested we take Danny out for a sort of welcome home celebration. Roger believed if we gave Danny our support and showed him we were behind him that Danny would give up his old habits. He took it upon himself to get Danny back on track and set up the celebration at a local restaurant with our immediate family members. My brother and my children might have been happy Dan was home, but my mother was another story. She did come to dinner, but I knew she would be chomping at the bit to make some snide remark. I sat near her at the table ready to poke her with my elbow or step on her foot the second a sarcastic comment sputtered from her tight-lipped jaw. Mom was suspiciously quiet all through dinner. She waited for the moment when everyone was happily gulping down their dessert to get her dig in. I heard her whisper to Roger, low enough so the kids wouldn't hear, but loud enough for Danny and I to hear. "You would think the way this family is welcoming Danny home that he was an honored war hero with a Purple Heart. I guess everyone has conveniently forgotten this man just got out of jail? *Again*, I might add." I gave her a jab and a threatening look. She rolled her eyes up at me and shoved another piece of pie in her mouth.

My mother was never one to mince words, especially when it came to Danny. She saw him for what he was and did her damnedest to get me to see it too.

The 'war hero' as my mother aptly began to refer to Danny, would cuttingly ask, "did the war hero get a job yet?"

We were in a financial mess, worse than we had ever been in. We had already filed bankruptcy some years before and had two mortgage payments because of it. Roger had lent a generous helping hand while Dan was in jail; he paid all my household bills and kept the house out of foreclosure. I was working but my income could not cover all the expenses.

Without ample cash on hand Dan couldn't return to his own electrical business. He had sold his work truck and many of his tools before going to jail to help pay for his attorney. Except for my brother, people weren't willing to rescue Dan out of another mess. He had to humble himself and work for someone. Eventually he found some odd jobs, enough to keep our heads above water and put food on the table. Danny was confident that we'd be back on our feet in no time. I wasn't anywhere near as positive and stuffed my fears deep enough to ignore.

The initial excitement I felt of him being home faded rapidly. I put on a good front and pretended so well that I actually fooled myself into believing him. I was grateful he wasn't drinking, we weren't fighting and he was home to take the burden off my shoulders of raising three kids alone. In time Danny's persistence and confidence landed him a good job as an electrician on the eastern end of Long Island. We caught up on the bills for the thousandth time.

Danny was in the 'good-Danny-phase,' which meant this

was the time I could get some of the things I wanted, like fixing up my outdated kitchen. Like many couples do on a weekend morning, we took a trip to Home Depot and bought new kitchen cabinet doors, picked out inexpensive, but durable kitchen flooring, and looked at new appliances.

For almost two years we lived as most ordinary couples. It was good long enough to fool me.

PART II

The Generosa Years

2000 - 2002

- THIRTEEN -

From Rags to Riches

"Whoever trusts in his riches will fall,
but the righteous will thrive like a green leaf."
—Proverbs 28:20

In the early spring of 2000 Danny came home from work excited about meeting with an old friend of his. The friend told him about a job that he was a working on in New York City, renovating a huge apartment building for an extremely wealthy woman. He also mentioned that the woman was in the middle of a nasty divorce and didn't care how much money she spent; whatever she wanted, regardless the cost, she got. In fact it was rumored her husband had allotted several millions of dollars to remodel the immense dwelling that was to be hers and their children's primary residence after the divorce. They needed a good electrician, Dan's friend said, and felt that Danny would be the perfect man for the job. Danny decided he would go into the city the next day to check this out for himself and meet with the wealthy Mrs. Ammon. The story sounded like an exaggerated tale to me. I would find out in less than twenty-four hours, it wasn't.

Danny called me on the way home from the city ecstatic that he got the job. He sounded like a kid let loose in a candy shop.

"Tami, this woman's got more money than God! You can't believe how she lives, she's got a chauffeur that drives her

75

around; she's even got somebody to walk her dog for *chrissake*. Tam, I'm gonna make a *lot* of money!"

I couldn't help but get caught up in Dan's fervor. This could be the chance to really get us out of a financial hole and do some much-needed work on our house. Dan quit his job and started his new employment in New York City that following Monday morning.

In a matter of weeks Danny was promoted from electrician to head electrician to Project Manager. According to Dan, Generosa Ammon was impressed with his work. He advanced from being paid by the hour to a yearly salary and was making more than he ever imagined he could make.

Dan traveled back and forth to the city like the hundreds of other commuters. But after a few weeks of inching along on the Long Island Expressway, he decided he was going to stay in the city, sleep in his truck and come home on the weekend.

I wasn't thrilled with this idea, and didn't make a big deal about it until I found out that Generosa Ammon took it upon herself to make the arrangements for Danny to stay at the same swank hotel that she was living in while waiting for her luxurious apartment building to be complete. I had already discovered that Generosa Ammon was not 'some dumb old rich broad,' like Danny said. Quite the contrary. Generosa was an attractive shapely blonde, only a few years older than I was. She was intelligent, cultured and used to getting her own way.

"It ain't what you think, Tami. Trust me. You can call me on my cell phone anytime if you don't believe me." He argued that it was a temporary situation. "Look at it this way, when I'm done with this job, we'll be living on the top of the world. Forget about Home Depot kitchen cabinets, we'll build a whole new damn kitchen, shit I may even add an extension."

I knew I wasn't going to win, so I didn't fight it even though little red flags were popping up all over the place. Generosa was a woman of wealth and power – and she was single. She had left Ted some time before after believing that Ted had been carrying on an affair while she was living in their castle in England

and he was working in New York. As the story goes, she went straight to her attorneys and filed a divorce demanding a huge chunk of Ted's reported wealth.

Even with knowing this I convinced myself this was the financial opportunity of a lifetime. I couldn't believe half of what Danny told me, but money did start coming in, not in the form of currency in my hand, but in lavish ridiculous gifts. Every weekend it was something else. Something extravagant and unnecessary. If Generosa was out to spend every last penny of Ted's money she found a bottomless pit in Danny.

Danny had always outdone himself on Christmas regardless of whether we had money or not. The Christmas of 2000 was beyond anyone's imagination. Danny must have made a half dozen trips to his car. Our family and friends stood at the door whooping and hollering like a bunch of contestants on a game show cheering Danny on with every armload of boxes and gift bags he carried in. He filled the entire living room and dining area with expensively wrapped packages. There had to have been at least five gifts for each person, from cashmere sweaters and suede jackets, to gold chains and wristwatches, perfume and leather belts, hats, scarves, gloves, wallets and an assortment of winter boots in every color and size. I received more jewelry that night than most women acquire in a lifetime; thick gold chain necklaces and delicate silver ones, some plain, some decorative, others with lockets. It was an excess of jewelry that I neither needed nor wanted. Rachelle was given five hundred dollars in crisp new bills, along with other expensive presents. The boys' gifts were delivered earlier in the day - two huge and what I considered dangerous quads. I said a silent prayer every time they got onto those perilous toys and was grateful when the machines finally broke down.

The kids unfortunately passed onto their father my desire to collect decorative indoor birdhouses. They should have never given him this information. I lost count after fifteen. Wooden houses, ceramic houses, glass houses, musical houses, I had more birdhouses on my shelves then a bird sanctuary.

After everyone said their good byes and happily carried out their mountain of gifts, Danny told me to come in the living room and sit down. He had something special for me.

"What, a birdhouse made of diamonds?" I joked.

He handed me an envelope with two roundtrip tickets to the Bahamas and reservations from December 28 through December 31 at one of the famous hotels.

"The *Bahamas?*" I was speechless. My mind leaped to a second honeymoon. It's incredible how many thoughts can flow through your mind in less than a second. This was surely Danny's way of making up.

"It's a surprise for you and Joy. Rachelle helped me make the arrangements….."

"*Joy?*" This was not sinking in.

I swear Danny was glaring at me like the cartoon character Tom the cat that was planning some fiendish end on Jerry the little mouse.

Danny was rattling off the details, "I'll take you to LaGuardia Airport…, Joy will meet you in Orlando…., a limo will drive the two of you to West Palm Beach where you'll hop a flight to the Bahamas………………"

My mind was rapidly working on clearing the cobwebs off my brain cells in order for this knock-me-off-my-feet information to penetrate.

Dan was planning on sending me to the Bahamas with Joy for the New Year?

"……and I'm giving the two of you five thousand dollars to spend."

"*WHAT!*"

This bit of whopping news was not little red flags popping up, oh no, this was colossal flashing neon lights. I smelled a fish, a big fat stinking, rotten fish.

"Aren't you excited, Mom?" Rachelle interrupted my racing suspicious mind unable to contain her own innocent excitement. My stomach flipped flopped and wasn't going to set itself right for quite a while.

"Daddy and I planned this whole thing. I bet you can't wait to call Joy and tell her."

You bet I couldn't wait to call Joy.

On Christmas morning I called my mother in Florida first where she had been visiting my grandmother. I wished her a happy holiday before I broke the startling news. I was hoping my mother could offer me some advice on whether or not I should accept Danny's outlandish guilt gift.

"Tami you might as well go, whatever Danny is up to, he's already doing."

The news wasn't quite as crushing to my mother. There wasn't anything Danny could do that would shock her. *Yet.* She continued in a matter-of-fact voice as if my being shipped off to the Bahamas was an everyday occurrence.

"Your staying home is not going to change Danny's course of action. He would probably leave you home alone for the New Year while he came up with some feeble excuse to be in New York City. Go. Have Fun."

My mother was right. She would be available to be with the kids while I was gone. I shoved the rotten dead fish on the back burner and called Joy.

- FOURTEEN -

Shipped Off to the Bahamas

"If you understand, things are just as they are;
if you do not understand, things are just as they are."
—Zen Proverb

I had three days to rush around and get my house and myself organized. I put away as much of the Christmas mess as possible, made sure the kids had plenty of clean clothes, grocery shopped so there would be enough food for the kids and critters and sorted through my summer clothes for something appropriate to wear.

I was up by six in the morning on the day I was scheduled to leave for the Bahamas. I haphazardly packed what I thought I would need for the four days in the sun. By ten o'clock I was on the train to spend the day in New York City with a group from my center for a holiday trip to Radio City Music Hall. Twelve hours later at a half past ten, on December 27, 2000, I arrived at the Orlando Airport, exhausted. Joy was waiting for me at the gate bright eyed and bushy-tailed. She pushed her way through the crowd and nearly bowled me over.

"We're going to the Bahamas," she squealed, leaping off the ground like a frog. We held hands and practically skipped through the terminal like two teenagers out on their first adventure. Which wasn't far from the truth; neither one of us had ever traveled on a vacation by ourselves.

We found our chauffeur, but was disappointed that we would be making the long drive down to West Palm Beach in a plain black Lincoln town car. We had expected royal treatment, white stretch limousine, champagne, the works.

We traveled for hours in the middle of the night, the two of us too wound up to close our eyes and catch a few moments sleep. We spent the long drive hashing over my surprise gift and Danny's ulterior motive for scooting me out of town, *way out of town*, on New Year's Eve.

Neither one of us were paying attention to where the foreign speaking driver with the mysterious dark eyes was taking us, not that we would have known the difference anyway.

Joy leaned to the driver and asked, "Are we there yet?" But the joke went over his head.

"We be dere zoon." He replied in a thick accent and winked at Joy in the rearview mirror.

"Holy geez, Tam. I think Danny sold us and we're on our way to some damn prostitute ring." We looked at each other and cracked up laughing. "That would be our freaking luck!"

We got to the airport so early it wasn't open. The driver dropped us off, gave us another wink and left us standing in the near darkness with our luggage.

"Well we weren't sold," my wisecracking friend half-joked.

"No we'll get mugged instead," I said looking around the eerie surroundings and purposely hooked my pocketbook carrying five thousand dollars over my shoulder.

"This must be some kind of a joke, Tami. What the hell kind of airport has no people in it? Are we on Candid Camera or something?"

The airport finally opened, but our flight to the Bahamas wasn't until seven, almost two hours away. Except for airport personnel, we were the only ones there.

I had been up for almost twenty-four hours; everything ached from my burning feet to my dry gritty eyes. We curled up on hard plastic chairs and the two of us fell asleep, clutching our pocketbooks to our chests.

At last, weary and bedraggled, we reached our final destination – the Bahamas. Alleluia!

It was worth the long day traveling to bask in the Bahamas sun, but it was freezing! Granted, freezing may be a slight exaggeration, but it was darn cold. Cold or not we wore our bikinis. Joy had lost several pounds and was fit and trim. With her olive complexion and light eyes, she looked stunning in her shocking pink skimpy bikini. I on the other hand, who would normally lose weight when under stress had gained weight and was heavier than I had ever been. A hefty roll of belly flab hung over my bathing suit bottom. My arms looked like a Samurai wrestler. I was shocked to see how much weight I had actually put on when I looked back at the pictures some time later. It was a sad indication of how miserable I was.

We wrapped ourselves in luscious white beach towels and lounged around the crystal clear pool with pina coladas in one hand and a magazine in the other.

"So this is what it's like to have money," Joy said slurping on her drink. "You know that saying, when life hands you lemons, make lemonade? Looks like you're going to be whipping up a big batch of lemonade, Tami! Gallons!"

We lifted our glasses and toasted. "Here's to lemonade!"

We settled down in the chaises, tugged our towels a little closer, sighed and closed our eyes. We ignored the reason we were there and were in bed and asleep by ten. The world travelers.

The next night we had dinner at the famous Atlantis resort. There were items on the menu that we'd never heard of.

Joy leaned over and whispered to me, "there's no prices next to anything, how are we supposed to know what to order?"

"Forget about how much the food costs, we have five thousand dollars, remember!"

"Holy shit, we do!"

Neither of us ever had that kind of money to spend. Joy had been struggling as a single parent to make ends meet and my finances were as erratic as Danny, here one day, gone the next.

We went ahead and ordered what we wanted; our eyes nearly bulged from their sockets when we got the bill!

We made our way over to the Atlantis's famous casino. The casino was a foreign world to us. We strolled around as giddy as two kids at a carnival gaping at the assortment of machines, flashing neon lights and the volume of people dressed to the hilt gathered around the various gambling tables with chips stacked high in front of them. No doubt we looked like the novices that we were. We sat at the first available slot machines. I broke open our one roll of quarters that we had between us and gave Joy a handful. I put in three. Joy put in one.

"You can't put in just one quarter," I chided.

Joy complained that was too much money and tried to hide her share in her hands.

"Put in three!" I bellowed at her.

She hesitated, saw me watching her and painfully released three quarters, plop, plop, plop.

"Here goes," she said as if she were plunging off a cliff and pulled the lever down. Instantly bells rang, lights flashed, sirens went off.

"Holy shit, I broke the freaking thing." Joy bolted from the chair, certain the casino guards were coming to get her.

I laughed so hard at my kooky friend's dumbfounded expression that I thought I was going to pee my pants. I could barely get the words out to let her know she won.

Joy was still in a daze when she collected her winnings - twenty-five hundred dollars! She sneakily stuffed her prize in her pocketbook, hid her pocketbook under her jacket, grabbed me by my arm, ushered me out the door and pulled me through the casino back to our hotel room like two thieves on the run. We collapsed on her bed doubled over in laughter.

That twenty-five hundred dollars was like a million dollars to Joy. She slept with her pocketbook under her pillow. She wasn't going to take any chances.

It took us over fourteen hours to get to the Bahamas to stay for only two and a half days, but it was worth it. It was the best medicine for me, even if it was only temporary and my dear friend came home with a hefty wad of much needed money.

In less than twenty-four hours a heavy dose of reality was waiting for me. It would be a long time before I would experience any gaiety.

We were back at Joy's house a few hours before New Year's Eve. Her kids were already at the door eager to dip their greedy little hands into the pot of gold. Joy pushed her covetous beggars out of the way and was on the phone with her mother before she set her bags down. I knew if she didn't get her story out to everyone and anyone, her lips would surely rupture.

I heard Joy on the phone in the kitchen erupting like a geyser relaying every detail of her big win. I was as caught up in it as she was and wanted Danny to hear about her incredible windfall at the slot machine, plus I thought it a considerate gesture to let him know I was back at Joy's safe and sound. Okay, the truth is, I wanted to know what he was doing and whom he was doing it with on New Year's Eve.

Danny answered his cell on the first ring. There was a lot of commotion in the background, a cacophony of assorted high shrilled and baritone voices were apparently speaking loudly over the blaring music. I had to tell him three times it was me on the phone, which I found extremely irritating since my own cell phone number should have appeared on his cell screen. I barely had a chance to say hello before he cut me short and put Rachelle on the phone. Rachelle was bubbly and chattered a mile a minute about this *gorgeous* hotel that they were staying at. In one long run-on sentence she told me Danny let each of the kids bring a friend, everyone had their own *gorgeous* room with king size beds, there were gold faucets in the bathroom and fluffy terry robes for all of them. Yada yada, yada. Whoopee do. I wasn't the slightest bit impressed. My mind drifted while she rattled on, but catapulted back into action when she mentioned that Danny's nice *boss* Generosa was *there* with *them* and that she was paying for everything.

84

Personally I didn't care a hoot who was paying for what. What I did care about was why *that* woman was celebrating New Year's Eve with *my* family! *Didn't she have a family of her own?*

The phone was passed around from Rachelle to Tony to Little Dan and back to Rachelle again. Danny never got back on; he yelled over the noise for Rachelle to tell me he would call me early the next day. Click. I was left standing with my cell phone in my hand. It didn't take but ten minutes for one phone call to puncture my exultant bubble flatter than flat.

I watched the New Year come in sitting around the television at Joy's parent's home, silently fuming.

When I spoke with Rachelle the next day she informed me in her child-like effervescence that Generosa gave her two thousand dollars for shopping. It took every ounce to control myself from not going ballistic. And if this outlandish information wasn't revolting enough, my daughter further went on to tell me that Danny actually offered our ten-year-old son five hundred dollars to take Generosa's dog for a walk! If heads could actually explode, mine would have at that moment. My blood pressure must have sky rocketed off the charts.

I wound up stuck in Florida for an additional day; all flights along the eastern seaboard were delayed due to severe weather conditions. I was glued to the weather channel, obsessed with getting home.

So - I did what most women would do under the circumstances – shopped. Joy and I spent a full day traipsing from one mall to another, filling our shopping bags to the brim!

- FIFTEEN -

Enraged

*"When angry, count to ten before
you speak; if very angry, a hundred."*
—Thomas Jefferson

Danny was waiting for me at La Guardia Airport looking quite spiffy in a new and rather expensive looking black leather jacket, black pants and a creamy beige mock turtleneck. His average brown colored hair, which normally stuck up or out like the straw man from the Wizard of Oz, was styled back and parted slightly to the side. This was not a small town barber-shop haircut. When Dan leaned over to give me a ridiculously spurious peck on the cheek, I got a whiff of an after-shave scent I was not familiar with. In a matter of days Danny had trans-formed from a blue-collar, dirt-under-the-nails electrician into some spurious manicured individual I did not know. Seeing him dressed to the nines and strutting as if he were a model for some sultry cologne advertisement, I was secretly glad I spent every penny of the money he gave me. My spiteful bitchiness may not have altered the rapid development between Danny and Generosa, but it did give me a moment of satisfaction.

Danny talked non-stop from the moment we left the airport, pretending to be interested in my trip to the Bahamas and Joy's triumph at the slot machine. He was good at flapping his lips about nothing of any importance, a tactic of his to keep me at bay. Whenever I attempted to switch the conversation to what I wanted to hear, such as what Generosa was doing with my family on New Year's Eve, he tip-toed around the question or completely avoided answering it altogether. He would have made a great politician. Dan had a knack of twisting the truth, double-talking and skirting any issue that might have put him on the hot seat. Usually by the time you were done speaking with Dan, you were apologizing to him for something he did.

I refused to let Danny railroad me. I knew something was going on between him and his boss and I wanted Danny to be up front and admit his guilt. I don't know why I expected that. He was never honest before. He only told me about Beth to hurt her, not to come clean with me. When I persisted in my pathetic interrogation, I was met with the usual response; 'it was all in my head.'

"Tam, I told you it's just temporary."

Yea, right.

"This woman's got loads of dough and she don't care how the hell she spends it."

Especially on clothes for you and two thousand dollars for my daughter.

"You know I gotta play the game, kiss ass. That's how it is."

No doubt you're kissing a lot more than ass.

"You don't have to worry about anything. I'm taking you to PC Richards for a new washer and dryer."

Now that should solve everything.

Danny bought the most expensive appliances in the store.

I had to let it go. I wasn't getting anywhere. And I really did need a new washer and dryer.

Each weekend Danny would come home with another elaborate gift, from a forty-inch television with surround sound to a brand new seventeen-foot fiber glass Mako speedboat with a one hundred and thirty five horsepower motor, all for the mere sum of twenty thousand dollars. The occasion – Little Dan's fifteenth birthday!

Enraged

Another weekend Danny insisted I go with him to see the 1992 Rodeo he picked out for me. I thought this was a practical gift. I needed a car and the Rodeo was in good shape and better than the 1980 beat up Oldsmobile I was chugging around in. I watched Dan dole out fifty, one hundred-dollar bills to the salesman. My mother brought to my attention the perceptible fact that my son's brand new boat, which was an unneeded luxury, cost twenty thousand dollars and my eight-year old car, which was an essential necessity, cost five thousand dollars; something was very wrong with that picture.

For three months I had been on a mental mission, possessed with finding something that would prove that Danny was having an affair with Generosa. It was the first weekend of March when I had the opportunity to search through Danny's wallet while he was in the shower. I found the mother lode - not one, not two, but three incriminating receipts from a few days before. One for firewood, one for wine, one for steaks, all purchased from shops in East Hampton where Generosa had her country home. In a matter of seconds I composed a cozy little scene in my mind for the cheating lovers, wood for the blazing fire, wine in long stemmed crystal glasses, and medium-rare filet mignon smothered in baby pearl onions and shittake mushrooms to boost their energy after they had non-stop sex on a plush white bear rug in front of a twenty-foot stone fireplace. It's a pity I wasted my romantic fantasy on two undeserving individuals.

I wanted to tear the shower curtain back and shove the receipts in his face as I had done three years prior when I found the message from Beth on Dan's beeper. But I didn't. I was more experienced now. I waited like a boxer in the ring, shifting from foot to foot, for just the right moment to land one solid jab between his eyes and lay him out cold.

The moment he stepped out of the bathroom, I attacked. If I were a pitbull I would have sunk my fangs around his throat.

"What are these, you lying son of a bitch?" I threw the receipts at him.

"Tami it's not what you think. Believe me. I told you before, I have nothing to do with her. I work for her that's all. She tells me do something, I do it. She wanted me to bring these things to her house in East Hampton. She was there with her kids for god's sake. Can't you just be happy? I'm getting you all these things. Just be happy."

Danny was a master at turning my mind around. He succeeded once again in making me doubt myself. Wasn't the story plausible? After all, she did have a house in East Hampton. He was her employee. He could have bought those items for her and delivered them to the house. Receipts didn't necessarily mean they were having an affair. My warped and battered mind questioned why I couldn't be happy. My friends added to my confusion by advising me to take advantage of Danny's outlandish spending spree. They argued that if I didn't take it, it would only go to someone or something else. What my dear friends didn't understand was it wasn't the material gifts I wanted. Nevertheless, the material things kept coming.

In April of 2001 my family, along with my brother's clan and another couple, took a trip to Disney; Joy and her kids would come the next day. We had rented cozy log cabins, a couple of good sized vans to transport the crowd and every kid had their own cart to zip around the park. What I envisioned as the perfect mini vacation, maybe even some time with Danny, turned out to be the trip from hell.

It began with Danny telling me he had business to take care of in the city; he would catch up with us in a couple of days. He tried to bullshit me that there were problems on the job that he just couldn't leave, but I knew his business was with Generosa. When he did arrive, one would have thought it was Bill Gates himself; Danny paid for everything for everyone. He wouldn't let anyone open their wallet. At every opportunity Danny flashed his wad of hundreds. The little kids wanted Mickey Mouse ears, so everyone got Mickey ears. He bought a video camera for over a thousand dollars and gave it to my brother before the trip was over. He showed off his Rolex and picked up the dinner tabs for all of us. We were told to order whatever we wanted. The sky was the limit. None of us drank liquor, but Danny ordered wine with his dinner. My son Tony had never seen his father drink, and Rachelle and Little Dan were too young to remember the troubled days of alcohol. But my brother remembered, and he was shocked. He knew it would be downhill from there, it was just a matter of time.

After a while the extravagance wore off, except for the kids who wanted more and more. For everyone else, it was purely obnoxious.

Danny spent an excessive amount of time on his fancy expensive cell phone whispering, murmuring and chuckling under his breath. When I had questioned him about the amount of time he spent on his phone, he answered that he was running the business in the city. I know that Danny had the ability to twist and distort my mind, but I wasn't a complete idiot. No one takes care of business by whispering sweet nothings to their workers. I knew he was talking to *HER*. I was jealous, resentful, bitter and down right miserable. I felt fat, old, ugly and pushed aside like a leftover piece of stale cake. The more time Danny spent on his cell the more his mood switched from the last of the jolly big time spenders to an agitated, disagreeable and ill-natured individual. I couldn't wait to leave. But once I got home, my stress only increased.

About two weeks before the trip from hell, I had come home from work and found my house gutted. I mean gutted - walls were knocked down, kitchen cabinets were broken to pieces, electrical wires hung from rafters, and the roof was *gone*. A huge blue tarp was tied down over the house like a deflated air balloon. I had asked for a new kitchen, not a new house. Danny told me he was building me my dream home - fireplace, front porch, skylights and all. I was horrified and too overwhelmed with the disaster to be happy. An enormous dumpster took up most of the driveway and was filled with piles of broken sheetrock, cracked studs with protruding rusted nails, and on top of the rubbish pile lay my sink and stove! There were piles of garbage everywhere. I had no idea what happened to my dishes, pots, pans and utensils. Sawdust covered the entire house, in the bedrooms, closets and even on the dogs. There wasn't a clean towel in sight.

I had hoped I would return to some progress, but the house was in the same disheveled and unsightly mess that I left. Light bulbs still dangled off wires, furniture was toppled over covered with dusty sheets of plastic, and my gutted kitchen remained gutted.

I lived like this for months, not able to cook a simple meal or even make a cup of coffee; the coffee maker was thrown out with everything else that was on the counter. I don't know if I will ever fully understand why I subjected my family to live the way we did, except to say that I was emotionally battered and numb to my surroundings.

Unlike other people that come home from their trip, relax with a cup of coffee and ponder the highlights of their vacation, I had to fight my way through the dust and dirt and the depression.

The kids darted off to their friends as soon as the car rolled into the driveway. Danny helped me bring the luggage in and said he had to get to the city; there were problems with the job.

"I'm leaving Tami, I gotta go."

My stomach rose up to my chest and then, like a roller coaster, plummeted suddenly. It wasn't what he said as the way he said it. Words didn't need to be articulated in fluent detail, a megaphone couldn't have been any louder or clearer. He was leaving and he wasn't coming back. I pleaded, literally down on all fours. I clung to his leg like a crying child. It's shameful to admit that I begged for him to change his mind.

My words fell on deaf ears.

"I gotta go, Tam."

And he left. Deserted me on the floor as if I were nothing more to him than a broken useless toy. He took his new suitcase full of name brand clothes and abandoned me like his old socks that he left behind in his bureau drawer.

I would like to believe that Danny felt some remorse. Whether it was remorse, guilt or arrogance, he called my brother to come over and check on me in case I did something drastic.

I was still crumpled on the hallway floor when Roger got to my house. He sat down on the filthy floor next to me, held my hand and offered his standard line of consolation that he recited to me over the years - that I was young, I had an entire life ahead of me, I'd get over it. Or words to that affect.

When you're in a state of despair there is very little anyone can say to lift your spirits. Maybe somewhere in the back of your mind you know that time heals all wounds, but when you're in the moment, there is no future time. There is only the present painful moment.

Roger stayed with me for over an hour, until he felt it was safe for him to leave me alone. I wasn't going to do anything to myself. I was more angry than hurt. Angry with myself for being a complete fool. I had had enough psychology courses over the years to know what I should and should not have done. I certainly knew what I might have suggested to someone else, yet I was trapped in my own way. It was the same pattern for almost twenty years of marriage, I would cry like a little girl and beg Dan to stay then sob some more and take him back. I knew this time no amount of crying or begging on my knees would keep Danny home. Generosa was a woman Danny would stick with; I could not compete with her wealth and her power.

I remained in my self-pitied stupor until the sun was nearly down. Eventually I removed myself off the filthy floor covered in sawdust and scattered with bent nails.

The gigantic blue tarp remained fastened to the house for several weeks, creating an eerie and spooky atmosphere. The wind howled and whistled through every gap and opening. The kids were frightened to sleep in their bedrooms, especially ten-year-old Tony, who didn't even attempt to sleep in his own room. The only television we could watch was in what was left of my bedroom. On most evenings all four of us would pile on my bed watching TV until we fell asleep.

One dark starless night Rachelle came home around ten thirty. The boys and I had fallen asleep watching a video.

"Mom," she whispered in my ear, "there's a raccoon on the kitchen counter."

I assured her in a half-sleep stupor that it must be one of the cats, but Rachelle insisted it was a raccoon. We debated back and forth until the boys woke up. I finally dragged myself out of bed to prove to my eighteen-year-old daughter that it was one of our own cats on the counter. The four of us peered through the clear plastic barrier that the workers had hung in the hallway to keep the back of the house warm from the front part of the house that was under construction. Rachelle was right, except it wasn't one raccoon, but a family of three contentedly munching on the cat's food. I panicked. I had heard stories of how mother animals can be aggressively protective of their young. I didn't know if the raccoons would attack my dogs, cats, or us. I made the kids scurry like little mice back to their bedrooms and throw some clothes on. I quickly packed a bag, locked my animals in one of the bedrooms, called my mother, told her we were on our way and all four of us crawled out of my bedroom window and escaped like a team of burglars.

I called Danny on my way to my mother's. This was the perfect excuse to disturb him from whatever it was he might have been doing. I knew there was nothing he could do at that time, but I wasn't going to let the opportunity go by to bitch and complain.

Danny was over early the next morning. He made a trail of peanut butter leading from the kitchen opening to the outside. He secured the rest of the house and was positive the raccoons would follow his peanut butter trail and vacate the premises that night; in the morning he'd come back again and repair any openings the raccoons might use.

In spite of Danny's certainty that the raccoons were gone, I was frightened to go back home, especially because there was a huge hole in my bedroom ceiling from one of the workers whose leg crashed through. I had tacked a large plastic garbage bag over the hole, as if that would prevent a hefty brazen hungry raccoon from getting in.

I would lie awake with one eye fixed on the plastic bag and one eye guarding my family from intruders, raccoon or otherwise. I should have insisted, or as my mother said demanded, that Danny put the kids and me up in a motel until my house was in order to live in.

"He's living like a king," my mother would remark, "in some swanky hotel probably being served breakfast in bed on a sliver tray and you're living with plastic garbage bags stuck to the ceiling."

I could always count on my mother to bring matters to my attention when I buried my head in the sand. Not that I ever followed her advice.

I began to see less of Danny. He had officially moved in with Generosa and her children at the ritzy New York hotel. A fact I had made slow adjustments to. What I could not adjust to, was Danny arriving at Tony's Little League game with *her*, her children and her dog in the *family* station wagon. I was outraged that that woman had the audacity to show up at my son's game. I know it takes two to tango and Danny was as much to blame, but I do believe that it was Generosa who took a mean delight in staking Danny as her claim and then flaunting it for all to see.

I resented that my children had begun to spend time with the little *Brady Bunch* family. On Father's Day Danny picked the kids up and they happily trounced off to Generosa's East Hampton home; the million-dollar estate that was to be hers as part of her divorce settlement. I was left alone in my empty broken house to wallow in self-pity. I forced myself to go outside and get some fresh air. I was sitting on my half-finished front porch attempting to enjoy the warm day when the two Rottweilers from down the road got loose from their property. They ran past my house and headed for my neighbor's tiny Maltese innocently bathing in the sunshine. I numbly watched that horrible unforgettable scene as they mauled the little dog and ran off with its lifeless body clenched in the jaws of the bigger dog's mouth. I spent the remainder of the afternoon talking with the police and consoling my elderly neighbor. The tragic event sunk me deeper into a dismal gloom. For several weeks I played the gruesome image in my mind like a remote stuck on rewind.

About a week or so after that dreadful day the Rottweilers viciously attacked the tiny Maltese, Danny brought me a taser gun, also known as a stun gun, for protection. I had never heard of such a device before. He told me to zap the Rottweilers or the raccoons if they came on my property. But the dogs were impounded the same day they mauled the little dog and the raccoons never returned. Even if the animals were still around I wanted nothing to do with this weapon and was terrified my sons would get their hands on it. I hid it in the basement and forgot about it, unknowing that the infamous stun gun would become a target of incessant questioning and harassment.

It infuriated me that my kids spent most of the summer of 2001 with Danny and Generosa; whatever Mr.Ammon thought of the situation, I had no idea. It angered me even more that my children were impressed with her wealth, her mansion in East Hampton, her castle in England, the nannies she had for her children and the way their father lavishly spent money. Each time my kids returned home from a visit they had another tale of extravagance to tell me, including it was Generosa that bought Rachelle her prom dress, which costs more than my wedding dress.

I know it's common to feel hurt and rejected when your children spend time with the opposite parent and that parent's new significant other. I've had many friends that have gone through divorces and have shared their stories with me, but I had no idea how jealous and bitter I would be. Maintaining my calm was a daily challenge. I had to grit my teeth and bite my tongue to keep from lashing out at my children.

Enraged

It wasn't long before their stories weren't about Generosa's money, but about her overt nastiness and their father conveniently ignoring her rude remarks.

Little by little my kids told me one account after another. When Tony stuck his finger in his glass of orange juice joking around, Generosa implied that *I* did not teach my children manners. I agree it was rude of my son to poke his finger in his juice, and I did find it embarrassing that he had done this while a guest in someone else's home, in particular because it was Generosa's house. But kids are kids and boys are boys. If reprimanding was needed, it was his father who should have been responsible for it. It was not Generosa's place to make derogatory remarks about *me* to my son. Admittedly, this wasn't that big of a deal and if this were the only incident it wouldn't be worth mentioning. But as the summer wore on, so did Generosa's ugliness.

Danny had invited our two sons to spend the weekend in East Hampton to do some fishing, which was and still is Little Dan's favorite sport. He had been looking forward to spending time with his dad, away from Generosa. He agreed to go only if they stayed in the boathouse and not in the main house. He was the only one of my children who was not taken in with Generosa's money and her grand lifestyle. But instead of taking the kids fishing as Danny promised, they had a bar-b-que with some friends and other members of Danny's family. Adding insult to injury, the kids were not permitted to enjoy the lobster or the steak. Generosa informed the kids that children don't partake in adult food; they were served hot dogs and burgers. At fourteen Little Dan did not consider himself a child; neither did I. Given the circumstances I found it understandable that my son was disappointed and angry with his father for not following through with his promise.

It was near midnight when Little Dan came home and told me what happened and the way that Generosa had spoken to him. He had wanted to leave much earlier in the day, but his father told him he'd have to wait for one of the other guests

96

to leave to get a ride home, and that he would have to thank Generosa for inviting him to her house, which he reluctantly did. According to my son, Generosa announced in front of everyone that she had hoped he had enjoyed himself because he was not welcomed back. I went ballistic with this piece of information. I know my son; he is a quiet and reserved individual. If he moped around it was because he was disappointed and probably felt rejected by his father, especially when Danny allowed his snooty mistress to rebuke his own son.

It was probably a blessing that I did not know where the East Hampton house was or I would have driven there in a blind fury in the middle of the night and snatched Tony away from that repugnant environment.

I called Danny repeatedly on his cell phone to give him a piece of my mind, only to have his voice mail pick up, which angered me more. He didn't have the decency to call me back until the next morning. I demanded he drive Tony back home, but he said Generosa had made plans and he couldn't get away for that long. If I wanted Tony home I would have to meet him halfway.

I had never known Danny to cower like a puppy with its tail between its legs, yet this woman had the power and the means to wrap him around her opulent little pinky.

Needless to say Little Dan refused to be anywhere near Generosa again, which made me happy; it also meant he wouldn't be seeing very much of his father.

The coup de grace involved an incident with Rachelle and Generosa. It was several months later before Rachelle had the courage to tell me what happened. About two weeks or so after Rachelle graduated from high school, Danny and Generosa had a small party for her at the East Hampton country home. I have no idea why they did this since my daughter had already had a huge celebration on the day of her graduation with about fifty people, a huge tent, a five-piece band and all the other trappings that go along with it. I suppose it was possible that Generosa was attempting to be nice and wanted to acknowledge Rachelle's accomplishment. Whatever the reasoning, Rachelle was allowed to invite some of her friends, one of them being her close friend Lynn, Joy's daughter who was up from Florida for a visit. In my daughter's words, the party had started out well, there were no restrictions of who could eat what or who could sit where. They were having a good time and Generosa appeared to be enjoying Rachelle and her friends. At the end of the evening when everyone left, Generosa, Danny, Lynn and Rachelle gathered in the family room and chatted about the party. Danny was sitting on the couch and Rachelle stood behind him massaging his neck like she used to do when he came home from work tired. She leaned over and whispered a thank you in his ear. She gave him a little kiss on his cheek and told him she was happy that he and Generosa did this for her. They all said their good nights and went to bed. In the morning Lynn and Rachelle helped Generosa set the coffee and bagels on the patio table for breakfast. It seemed that Generosa was in a good mood, there was no indication to the contrary. Soon after breakfast Lynn was in the kitchen with Generosa helping her put things away. Lynn asked Generosa if she had a tampon. For some unknown reason this question set Generosa off. She screamed at Lynn, called her a bitch and demanded that Lynn get Rachelle. Lynn was nearly in tears when she found Rachelle and told her Generosa wanted her in the kitchen immediately. Confused, the two of them did as instructed. Generosa was waiting for them, but pushed Lynn out of the room, stating this was a private conversation that did not include her and closed the massive kitchen door on Lynn's face. Generosa turned to my young daughter and basically accused her of sexually enticing her father. Pointing a long thin finger in Rachelle's face Generosa told my daughter that *she* was sleeping with her father and that Danny was *her* boyfriend and that she wouldn't tolerate Rachelle's disgusting behavior in her house. I imagine the disgusting behavior Generosa referred to was the kiss on the cheek my daughter gave her father. She told Rachelle that she was too old to be affectionate with Danny and

98

it was time she behaved like a lady. Generosa threatened that if Rachelle mentioned this to either Danny or me she would stop giving Danny money to fix up my house and she was sure that Rachelle wouldn't want to be responsible for that.

Eventually Rachelle told both her father and me. Danny didn't say much about it accept that he would have Generosa apologize. It's doubtful whether Danny ever mentioned anything to Generosa and if he had, Generosa never offered any amends. I don't know how I didn't, as the saying goes, blow a gasket. Probably the only reason I didn't was because there were so many other things going on at the time.

The one good thing that came from this episode was that Rachelle also refused to be around her father's girlfriend. In time none of my children ever went back to the East Hampton house.

- SIXTEEN -

Unhappy Birthday

*"Gradually I accepted the fact that my 'if only' wishes
were not about to come true. But I also learned that
I could be happy even if they didn't."*
—Al-Anon Faces Alcoholism

I had been feeling extremely lonely, depressed and worried
about finances throughout the entire spring and summer of
2001. Danny was giving me very little money to live on, bills
were mounting and worse, all work on my home came to an
abrupt stop. Danny had given me some song and dance about
the reasons why my house was left an uncompleted wooden
structure. It was several months later when I learned the truth;
Mr. Ammon put a stop to Generosa's expense account when he
discovered that she was spending an exorbitant sum of money
renovating her New York apartment. It's seems more likely he
put the kibosh on the funds because Generosa let her tool-belt
electrician boyfriend move in with her.

The terrifying attack of September 11th rubbed my already
fragile emotions raw. I was glued to the television like the rest
of the world, watching scene after scene of destruction and dev-
astation. In the middle of the world's suffering I found a pittance
of satisfaction that Danny left Generosa in New York City and
came home to spend the night with us. My woes were nothing in

comparison to the pain hundreds of others were experiencing, yet all I was able to focus on at that time was Danny being with us and not her. It is pathetic how my rancorous mind worked.

My son Tony's eleventh birthday came five weeks after the United States was savagely attacked, which was only five months from when Danny left. It was a terribly frightening time for everyone, especially for the children. Tony's young mind was still trying to compute why his father was gone. He was too young to understand the turmoil of his parents' marriage. Tony knew nothing of his father's mysterious periodic disappearances or his extramarital affairs. He simply knew his father as the person who taught him how to ride a bike and hook a worm. Dan was his dad, the man who strapped on his skies, tied his ice skates and fitted him for his first baseball mitt. When his father left, a big piece of my son went with him.

Tony was up early on the morning of his birthday waiting by the window for his father to come take him out for breakfast. Tony expected they would spend the whole day together, but when Danny dropped him off after their meal he told his son he couldn't stay because he had to attend his cousin's wedding. He promised Tony he'd be back later for birthday cake. Which I knew was one of Danny's lies to cover his guilt.

Tony pestered me all day when his father was coming back.

"When's Daddy coming? When's Daddy coming?"

I was furious that Danny would make a promise he couldn't keep. Unfortunately I took my anger out on my little guy.

"I don't *know* when your father is coming!"

It broke my heart to see this little boy run to the window every time he heard a car on the road. When the phone rang Tony grabbed it off its hook expecting his father to be on the other end. Danny finally called to say there was a delay with the wedding and he wasn't sure if he could make it in time for the cake. The only one that was surprised was Tony. I watched his little boy's face instantly change from hopefulness to sadness.

The one thing that helped perk him up a little was his newly painted and carpeted bedroom that my mother gave him for his birthday. While Tony was having breakfast with his father, Mom came over and helped me decorate the bedroom with the Yankee memorabilia Danny had bought for him some time before.

Tony stretched out on his new Yankee comforter, put his hands behind his head and crossed his lanky legs. That was his way of saying he liked it.

Later in the afternoon my brother and his family and one of Tony's friends gathered for a small birthday celebration. We ate pizza surrounded by wires hanging from open beams, plywood for floors and a temporary slop sink that my brother set up in a make-shift kitchen; not exactly a birthday atmosphere. Tony wouldn't let us have the cake until Danny got there, but by seven o'clock when it was evident that his father wasn't going to be joining us, we sang Happy Birthday as the birthday boy cheerlessly blew out his candles.

After my family left, I stomped around my gutted barren house, throwing paper party dishes in the garbage with a vengeance. By eight-thirty I needed to take Tony's friend home. I was half way down the road when Danny turned onto the street. I half-heartedly drove back to the house with an obvious chip on my shoulder. Tony's own eagerness to see his father had faded beneath his hurt and anger.

Danny carefully avoided eye contact with me and directed his conversation to his son. Tony brightened a bit when his father showed an interest in how his bedroom turned out. I overheard Danny comment about what a good job my mother and I did. In the same breath, in that patronizing tone he used when soliciting his authority, he questioned whether Tony remembered to thank us. That was just like Danny, divert the attention away from his own misdeeds and put someone else on the hot seat. It wasn't Tony that needed a reminder on manners.

Since Danny did manage to make it back to the house I asked him, none too sweetly I might add, if he could take a look at the leak in Tony's closet, the same leak he said he would fix a few weeks ago. When the upstairs addition was added on, water leaked in when it rained and it had been raining a lot. I had wedged a plastic bag in the crevice, but my handy work was not all that handy and the rain came in on Tony's clothes.

I left Danny at the house in his fancy suit plugging up the leak while I proceeded to take Tony's friend back home. To my surprise my son came with me. I had expected that he would want to stay with his father; perhaps he feared he would be chastised again. I assumed Danny would still be there when we returned, but par for the course, he wasn't. He slipped into the night without so much as a good-bye or a hug for his son. As I said, it wasn't my son that needed a lesson in manners.

When Tony came to the sad conclusion that his father was gone for the night, he plopped on his bed and refused to talk with anyone. Rachelle and Little Dan attempted to cheer him up making jokes about the hole in the wall my mother made trying to nail a picture up, but Tony wasn't buying their phony jabbering. It tore me apart to see my children trying to cope with something that had nothing to do with them.

- SEVENTEEN -

Murder, Media and Mayhem

*"Do not be anxious about tomorrow,
tomorrow will look after itself."*
—The Bible

The day after Tony's birthday Danny called me at work; Ted Ammon died, a day before Generosa was to sign the divorce papers. It was believed his death was due to an overdose of some kind. I had never met Mr. Ammon and I certainly was not fond of Generosa, but my immediate reaction was how horrible this would be for their children. Their twins were the same age Tony. It wasn't until the next day that it was reported that Ted Ammon was brutally murdered. I never considered Danny or Generosa as suspects, especially not Danny, but the law and the media had other thoughts.

The onslaught of the media began around Halloween. My father-in-law had stopped over while I was in the middle of painting the front door. He wanted to see the progression, or rather the non-progression of the construction on the house. We were inside talking when there was a knock on the door; my hands were full of red paint so my father-in-law answered it. A medium built man with light brown hair was holding a small notepad in his hand; he introduced himself as a reporter from the *New York Post*. He wanted to know if Danny was available and if he would mind making a statement. I asked the reporter what he wanted a statement about, but my father-in-law interrupted. He made it clear to the reporter that Danny was not there and no one had anything to say. He firmly closed the door with the reporter standing on the front porch, notepad in hand. Dan's father advised me not to talk to anyone until we found out what was going on.

What went on was a rapid progression of the media, scores of phone calls from TV stations and every newspaper, including one from London. They were all hoping for the same thing, that Danny would make a public announcement of his whereabouts on the night Theodore Ammon was murdered. Neither Danny nor Generosa ever made a public statement; Generosa's attorneys conveniently protected the two of them.

My children and I were not as lucky. I was in the bathroom putting my makeup on getting ready for an event at my job when Little Dan came running into the house out of breath. He told me there were men with cameras on their shoulders that followed him from the bus stop. I peered out the window and was astounded to see an entourage of reporters mulling around the front of my house, vans from CBS, NBC, ABC and Channel 12 News were parked along the road. I was looking out at them, and they were ogling back at me. The large front room window was bare of curtains or coverings because there wasn't any molding around the window to hang a curtain rod. I felt like a fish with no place to hide in my fish bowl. I was concerned that the newscasters would hound Tony when he got off the school bus. Little Dan and I planned to run to my car and speed off before the reporters could catch us so I could pick Tony up directly from school and hide out at my mother's. But the reporters stormed at me the moment I opened my door, clicking their cameras in my face.

"Mrs. Pelosi, can we have a statement?"

"Was Danny with you the night Ted Ammon was murdered?"

"Do you know where Danny was?"

"Do you think Danny murdered Mr. Ammon?"

I watched them from the rearview mirror taking pictures of my car driving down the road, shaking my head at their preposterous questions.

Almost every afternoon hordes of reporters were waiting for me. Cameras clicked and clacked non-stop as I ran to my house covering my face with my hands.

I called Danny's younger brother, a New York City cop. Thankfully he was at home. He was at my house in record breaking time and called the local police. I hid in the house trembling, nearly gnawing my fingernails down to the quick while my brother-in-law spoke to the cops. Unfortunately there wasn't anything the police could do. The reporters were shrewd enough to know that as long as no one was on my property, they weren't breaking any laws. Danny's brother, a big hulk of a guy but gentle as a lamb, asked them nicely to leave my family alone. They did on that day, but they would be back again and again for months to come. Neither my children nor myself stayed in our house any longer than we had to. Straight from work, I'd pick the boys up from school and drove them to their friends. Rachelle didn't even bother to come home; right from her job she went to her boyfriends' house. I took to hiding at my mother's.

"This is absurd," my mother grumbled. "These reporters have no right to be bothering you."

Right or not I'd wait until night came and the reporters were gone to pick up my sons. Rachelle would wait for us to return home before she left her boyfriend's. When we were safe within the confine of our home, the two older kids would close themselves into their rooms and Tony would fall asleep in my bed with the TV on. What little family life we had totally disintegrated. I was incapable of being a mother.

When the reporters discovered they weren't going to get anywhere with me, they invaded my neighbors. They swarmed the neighborhood like locusts, asking personal questions about Danny and our marriage. "Was he violent? Was he abusive?"

They picked the neighborhood clean.

For a while the phase of the media retreated, only to be replaced by detectives.

They started at Carol's house. Two detectives asked Greg to come to the precinct for questioning. Being one of Danny's closest friends, Greg had worked for Danny on Generosa's New York City apartment. He also helped to install an alarm system at the East Hampton house, the same alarm system that was mysteriously turned off on the night Mr. Ammon was murdered. The detectives questioned Greg for over three hours.

Later that day, the same two detectives knocked on my door. They also grilled me for hours, not at the precinct, but on my front porch so that any neighbor that was passing my house could witness the interrogation. They repeated the same questions over and over again. "Where was Danny on the weekend of October twentieth to twenty-first? Did Danny ever give me anything for protection? Who worked for Danny? Why did Danny leave me?"

Occasionally I caught myself stammering. I didn't want the detectives to think I was hiding anything. It wasn't as if I was accustomed to standing on my front porch being probed by two burly intimidating detectives about the possibility that my husband could have murdered another individual. This wasn't a scene from Law & Order and it wasn't the autumn cold that caused my body to tremble and my teeth to chatter.

The younger taller detective handed me his card. Under his name in bold print was the word **Homicide**. *Homicide!* The word alone was unnerving. He told me to call him if I remembered anything. I could barely recall what I had for dinner the night before. I waited until I saw the detective's car turn onto the main road, then zoomed to my mother's house.

I showed my mother the card and told her the questions the detectives kept asking me.

"They really think Danny did this, Ma." I said the words but they weren't connecting to my brain. Mom and I on occasion thought the unthinkable, but neither of us would believe it could be remotely true. It was inconceivable.

- EIGHTEEN -

Nothing the Same Again

"Today is only a small manageable segment of time in which our difficulties need not overwhelm us. This lifts from our hearts and minds the heavy weight of both past and future. "
—One Day at a Time in Al-Anon

Around the week before Thanksgiving my father-in-law treated the entire Pelosi clan, a grand total of twenty-six, to four days in the Bahamas for his seventieth birthday. It was an event that he had planned for over a year. Naturally I had been included, but that was before Danny and Generosa were an item. They had been living together for over six months, even though we weren't divorced yet. I didn't know whether an invitation had been extended to Danny's girlfriend or not; if it had I certainly wasn't tagging along. I think I would have drawn the line there. But Danny's father assured me that Generosa was not included in his family gathering.

I wanted to be part of my father-in-law's celebration. I had had a good relationship with my in-laws over the many years and didn't feel there was reason to detach from them because Danny decided to try out a new life. I justified that being married for nearly twenty years qualified *me* as the daughter-in-law with the privilege of attending his birthday festivities. Plus I felt my kids needed a break from the press, the publicity, the local gossip and time to spend with their father, *without* Generosa.

108

This was all true. But the real reason I wanted to be there was for the same personal satisfaction that I achieved when Danny came home to his family the night of September 11th. It was the one area Generosa didn't have complete power. Ninety-eight percent of the time she led Danny around by the leash. If all I could grab was two percent, I took it. If I were a child I would have stuck my tongue out and taunted, 'nana nana nana'. But as an adult it's simply referred to as passive aggression. I didn't care what my behavior would be called. In my mind I won.

It had been agreed by all of my in-laws to avoid any discussion relating to Generosa or the murder, Danny wasn't officially considered a suspect at the time. We wanted my father-in-law to enjoy his special day without being reminded of the mess that his son had gotten himself involved in. But the agreement was broken the first day, by none other than Danny. He flashed his expensive gifts from his rich girlfriend, a gold necklace, the Rolex, and his recently capped front teeth. One subject led to another and soon the topic of the murder was brought up. It was almost impossible to ignore the elephant in the living room. We discussed it, over dinner or sitting at the pool, the different possibilities of who might have broken into Mr. Ammon's home and why he was murdered. I think it might have been Danny's brother that reminded us we were there for a birthday celebration and not as a team of investigators. The subject was dropped and we enjoyed the gift that Danny's father gave to us.

It was a good trip while it lasted, not like the one to Disney. We laughed, we ate, we soaked in the sun; the kids had a ball. Twenty-six happy tanned Pelosis' arrived at Kennedy Airport. Small groups left with their families. Danny had a limo waiting for him; my gang caught a ride with my in-laws. And then it was over. Reality has a way of socking you in the face quicker than a left-hand punch. For a short time I was able to forget the media, the detectives and the long and lonely nights. My father-in-law's birthday was the last joyous occasion of the Pelosi brood. *Nothing* was the same again.

- NINETEEN -

Lily-Livered-Yellow-Hearted-Chicken!

*No one lights a lamp and hides it in a jar or puts it
under a bed. Instead, he puts it on a stand, so that those
who come in can see the light. For there is nothing hidden
that will not be disclosed, and nothing concealed that will
not be known or brought out into the open.*
– Luke 8:16 -17

Christmas Eve of 2001 was a sad replica of the previous year.
Carol and Greg's family and my brother's family were at
my house for our traditional holiday gathering. There was some
question as to whether Danny would show up, or if he would
find some excuse as he did for Tony's birthday. He strolled in
near midnight, not with the usual array of gifts, but enough
for everyone. The laughter and gaiety of Christmases past was
nothing more than a bittersweet memory. We gathered in the
half-completed den with building supplies piled in the corner.
Roger built a roaring fire in the grand twenty-foot high, five-foot
wide, river rock fireplace that my father built while I was away
in the Bahamas for my father-in-law's birthday. It was the only
source of heat in the large airy room. During the day the room
was brightened by the colorful hues from the sun that streamed
in through the skylights and double sliding doors, but at night
the room was dark and cold.

If you used your imagination and did not notice the plywood

110

floors or the exposed insulation in the walls, but focused your attention on the Yule logs burning in the massive hearth, the few festive holiday decorations and the Scotch pine tree lit up in the corner of the room, you might have thought this warm cozy scene was right out of an L.L. Bean catalogue. The fake homey setting was the stage to the characters in the room.

The relationship between Danny and his close friend Greg changed after the detectives interrogated Greg. That would put a damper on any friendship. Finding a subject that would not trigger questions about the murder was a challenge. My brother told a few jokes that lead to a few laughs, but most of the evening was awkward for all of us.

Surprisingly Danny stayed the night. I had expected he would have left after an hour or so and then head back to his new family. When everyone was gone he sprawled out on the couch as if he had never left and was snoring by the time I washed my face. I wrapped myself in a big comforter and curled up on the loveseat across from him and studied his face as he slept, trying to figure out what it was that kept me bound to him. An interesting analogy popped into my mind while I watched the fire gradually burn down - I was like those few stubborn embers that refused to die out.

Christmas breakfast was quiet and uneasy. Danny made small talk with the kids; every once in a while one of them chuckled at an attempted joke. I cooked bacon and eggs while Danny paced the floor. I knew from his nervous laugh that he wanted to leave but didn't know how to say it. I wasn't about to give him the green light. I let him squirm. He gobbled down his breakfast and handed the kids an additional hundred dollars each, his way of making up for the fact that he would not be having Christmas dinner with them. He wished them a Merry Christmas and left, not with his usual swaggering walk, more subdued I thought, even sad, or maybe I was projecting my feelings onto him.

The post holiday blues lingered well into January. I couldn't sleep and when I did sleep I couldn't get out of bed in the morning. I found myself not paying attention to what I was doing or where I was driving. I'd pass exits or slam on the brakes at a traffic light. Work wasn't my haven as it had been in the past. I was edgy and irritable and snapped at simple questions from co-workers. I wasn't able to focus and kept forgetting what I did with my paperwork. When I entered a room I couldn't remember what it was I needed. I exhibited the classic signs of stress, but the real stress hadn't even hit yet.

The year 2002 didn't appear anymore promising than the previous. And by far it wasn't. There's a saying that goes, 'what else can happen?' – don't say it. Don't even put the thought out there, because believe me, anything can happen.

I had dragged my body out of bed on that cold Thursday morning of January 24, 2002 feeling even more exhausted than usual. I hadn't fully absorbed the fact that my divorce was finalized the day before. It was my attorney who called to give me the startling news.

"I don't know how this got through so fast," he had joked, "someone must know someone of importance."

I can guess who that person of importance was. The entire divorce process from the initial submission of paperwork to receiving the stamped sealed documents took only four months, an unusually short amount of time in the state of New York.

Danny had been nagging me the week before for me to call my lawyer and find out the status of the divorce. I thought his pestering had something to do with his agreement to sign the house deed over to me, the one asset I felt entitled to, and was looking for a way to back out of his promise.

I discovered the reason Danny was badgering me before I had a chance to take a sip of coffee. I had shuffled from the kitchen to the dining area in my worn slippers and unrolled the morning newspaper. My eyes were still heavy from a sleepless night, but they sprang open as if I had stuck my finger in a live electrical outlet. On the front page of *Newsday*, in big letters

– DANNY AND AMMON'S WIDOW MARRY!

The fury and rage that rose up from my gut was indescribable. Enflamed, wrathful, livid are mere adjectives. I was shaking so much I could barely hold the paper to read the rest of the sickening story.

"That coward! That piece of shit! That lily-livered, yellow-hearted-chicken!"

I screamed at the newspaper. "How dare he let me find this out in the newspaper. And to get married a day after our divorce was finalized! *HOW DARE HE!*"

The newspapers had a field day with the story. They loved that Danny wed the wealthy widow twenty-four hours after our marital contract was terminated. For me to learn that Danny was honeymooning at Generosa's castle in England to protect *her* children from the media, nearly gave me a stroke. There certainly was no way I could protect my children from their father's thoughtless and selfish act; it wasn't just me that Danny was hurting.

I would have loved to bury myself in my blankets and never see the light of day again, but that wasn't possible. I was a mother of three children who were experiencing the same pain as I was, maybe even more.

Rachelle found me in the den staring out the back window. Not surprising my cursing and screaming rampage woke her; fortunately my sons slept through it. I handed my daughter the newspaper and watched her soft doe eyes fill with tears.

"Oh my God, Mommy," she snuggled next to me reading the upsetting news.

The boy's alarm clock went off, but I had no intention of getting them up and sending them to school. I didn't see how either of them would be able to concentrate once they found out their father had gotten married. I sent Rachelle to their bedroom to shut the alarm off. The longer they stayed asleep, the better. I had let the dogs out the back door to do their morning business, but instead of running to the backyard as they normally did, they ran toward the front barking wildly. I peeked out from behind the large sheet I tacked to the front bay window and discovered that the press had congregated like a lynch mob in front of my house. I knew that as soon as one of us opened the door they would attack like sharks on a fresh kill. I made a decision that all of us would stay home.

When my sons got up, the four of us huddled around the kitchen table. Tony, too young to understand the full impact, was happy for a day off of school, but asked as only an innocent child would ask, "does that mean Daddy's not ever moving back with us?" Little Dan on the other hand was angry. He felt his father lied to him. He took Danny's sneaky marriage as a personal betrayal. I couldn't provide answers for their questions or offer any means of support.

Within the hour the phone began to ring, first from family and friends wanting to know if I heard the stunning news. By lunch an overwhelming number of calls came from every newspaper, news station and magazine. They asked the same questions;

"Mrs. Pelosi, can we have a statement?"

"Mrs. Pelosi how do you feel about Danny getting married one day after your divorce?"

"Mrs. Pelosi what do you think about Danny moving to England?"

I finally stopped answering the calls and had to change the message on my answering machine. The new message stated that I had no comment to make regarding the current headlines and to please respect my family's privacy. I turned the ringer off. Throughout the day the light continued to flash on my machine. The kids and I hid in the house all day. I wouldn't let them answer the phone, go near a window or out of the house. No one came over in fear of being trapped by the press. We were prisoners in our own home.

I knew the tabloid mongers would leave by five. When they did we escaped to my mother's. She had dinner ready for us and put the TV on to find a movie for the kids. While searching the channels, the news flashed on – there was *my* house on the TV withmy cat Spanky sitting on my front porch!

The newscaster was showing the public the average-sized Long Island home that Danny left for the expansive castle he would be living at in England.

My family might as well have lived in a glass house, our every move was noted. Whenever Danny's name hit the press, and it hit the press often, reporters were at my door. It was up to me to protect my children and fight for my family's privacy.

The detectives were at my house every few days. They harped on the same questions, never letting up, persistent and unflagging in their relentless attempt to wear me down the way a constant drip of water eventually bores a hole through the dense stone. Their tireless pursuit didn't stop with me; they went so far as to track down a former job of my mother's. One of the women in the office that she remained close with knew what was going on and called to tell her two homicide detectives flashed their badges, asked questions of where they might find her and left their calling card. Unfortunately there were other women in the organization who weren't aware my mother had a connection, however slight, to the current headlines. I don't know if the detectives were embarrassed when they learned my mother hadn't worked there for over five years, but my mother certainly was.

"It's no wonder these cops haven't been able to solve the murder, they didn't even know I haven't worked there for years!"

My mother was understandably annoyed that near strangers were privy to what was going on in our family's lives. My mother didn't go around blabbing that Danny was her son-in-law, former or otherwise. It wasn't a topic that was discussed outside of family and close friends. Fearful that the detectives would pursue their search and show up at my mother's new place of business, she called the number on the card. They asked my mother several of the same questions they asked me, apparently convinced that Danny had confessed to me and that I in turn confided to my mother.

The steady strain had taken its toll on my family. The more Danny's name appeared in the papers, the more we retreated into our own worlds. The more the finger was pointed at Danny, the more we denied it. We slowly fell apart. None of us could sleep. We were like zombies roaming around the house bumping into each other at all hours of the night. We'd finally fall into a deep sleep as the sun was coming up. It had become a daily battle to get the boys off to school. Half the time I was successful, the other half they refused to get out of bed. I was too tired to argue with them. Naturally, their grades plummeted. Everyone was short-tempered; one wrong word and we'd attack one another like dogs in a pit. When my sons finally did wake up, they disappeared to their friends. They wanted to be anywhere but home. Rachelle stayed more and more at her boyfriend's. Thankfully his parents were kind and understanding. Except for the holiday meals, we never shared dinner together. We were like nomads, never in one place too long. We scattered in different directions.

Everyday I'd haul my body out of bed, mechanically dab on some make-up and drive to work. Regardless of the fact that I was close with the girls who worked with me, I was too mortified and embarrassed to speak with anyone and spent as much time as I could hiding out in my office. I ventured out of my safe little cubicle only when absolutely necessary. I feared that the parents who entrusted their children to my care would connect my last name to the one that continued to make the headlines.

I couldn't cope with the onslaught of publicity that caused my children and myself endless shame and disgrace. I began having panic attacks to the degree that I often needed to pull my car over to the side of the road because I swore I was having a heart attack. I'd cry endlessly whenever I was alone, whether in my car or folding laundry. My face was one continual puffy, blotched mess that I attempted to cover with extra layers of make-up. I wasn't fooling anyone. On the evening that I picked the kids up at counseling, (I at least made sure that they received some help), their therapist took me on the side.

"Tami, you have got to get help. Look at you, you're shaking, you have dark circles under your eyes. I can see you grinding your jaw. Your kids need you; *you* have to be their rock, their pillar. Without you they have nothing. I'm going to give you the name of a psychiatrist who can prescribe something to help you cope." She quickly added, "it will just be temporary, to get you through this."

A *psychiatrist*? A *shrink*? I cried some more. I had lost control of my life. I was a failure as a mother. I felt like a paralyzed person, able to see what was going on around me, but incapable of responding. I had never taken a drug of any sort in my life, except for the occasional antibiotic or Tylenol. I never dabbled in mind-altering drugs. Drugs terrified me. I didn't even smoke. The counselor pushed the psychiatrist's card in my hand and reminded me how much my children needed a mother. I stuck it in my purse. It was a full two weeks before I called for an appointment and that was only after I woke during the night with tightness in my chest as if someone was crushing my ribs in a vice. I was given a prescription for Xanex.

Miraculously, the pains in my chest subsided. I was nearly functional.

- TWENTY -

Pennies From An Angel

"That everyone who believes in him may have eternal life."
—John 3:15

On the morning of March 30, 2002 I was overjoyed that a repairman was at my house fixing the heat. There had been constant problems with the heating unit from the first day the ducts were installed. Of course given the fact that the main area of the house was only sheetrocked and the second level a shell, the house was more than drafty, it was downright cold. Although the thermostat registered less than sixty degrees, I was feeling pretty damn good. I think my daily dose of the little pink pills had much to do with the ability to function. I wasn't suffering from panic attacks or burying my head in my pillows crying. Not to say that life was a bowl of cherries. Detectives continued to show up at my door, and I definitely hadn't adjusted to Danny's disingenuous marriage to Princess Ta Ta, my nickname for Generosa.

But on that sunny Saturday morning I answered the phone with a cheerful voice. My lightheartedness was short-lived. My former sister-in-law was on the phone with dreadful news. Danny's younger brother, the police officer who did his best to keep the news reporters at bay, had been rushed to the hospital in cardiac arrest. She had no other information then that, but promised to call me the minute she knew something.

118

The phone barely rang when I grabbed for it. Danny's brother had died.

My legs buckled under, I slid, more like slithered, down the front of the kitchen cabinet, knocking the dog's water bowl over. Slumped against the cabinet, sitting in a puddle of cold water, I wailed for the loss of someone dear. The kids were woken by the mournful sobs that rose from deep within my soul. The repairmen made a quiet exit.

The news was shocking to everyone. He wasn't sick. He wasn't old. He was a strong hulking man, a New York police officer; a huggable big bear of a guy with a broad happy smile known for his easy going manner and his ability to get people to laugh. He was the stable one, the rock, the person other family members depended on, the mediator, the referee, the arbitrator, the hero. His death was a tremendous loss to the Pelosi family and to the community as well. A hundred or more uniformed police and firemen donning black armbands for their fallen comrade led a solemn procession of police cars, fire trucks and scores of vehicles from the funeral parlor to the cemetery.

The press remarkably kept their distance during that sorrowful time. Although a few days after the death, a story or two was printed in an effort to link Danny's brother in someway to the crime. There had been unfounded reports that he had obstructed justice in an attempt to protect his older brother.

The death of Danny's brother would become a major cause of contention within the Pelosi family and a shocking strategy that the prosecuting attorney targeted two years later at Danny's trial.

A few weeks after the funeral, around the second weekend of April I attended a weekend seminar with my dear friend Josephine at the Omega conference in New York City. It was an intense two days of lectures from well-known spiritual leaders that covered topics from healing to connecting to God.

With everything that had been taking place in my life, Josephine thought about me when she heard about the conference and made all the arrangements for the both of us to attend.

Josephine is a beautiful woman in body, mind and spirit. She has been blessed with an extraordinary gift only a few chosen people possess; Josephine is a psychic medium. Through Josephine's loving guidance and the incredibly enlightening weekend, I was able to understand that although my brother-in-law was no longer on the earth plane, in 'spirit' he would be my guiding light.

Coincidentally or not (I have since learned there are no coincidences), on Sunday night when I returned from the conference weekend, I received a call from a relative. She told me about a dream she had the night before. In the dream Danny's brother called her into a room where there was an old fashioned record player; he told her to play the record "Wind Beneath My Wings" by Bette Midler. In the dream he said, "tell Tami that song is for her." In the months following his death, whenever I was feeling down, frightened or overwhelmed, Bette Midler's 'Wind Beneath My Wings,' would *coincidentally* play on the radio, confirming what Josephine told me. I'd often find myself "talking" to my brother-in-law, asking for his help, but I didn't trust that he heard my prayers. I asked him for a sign, some assurance that he truly was there. A little voice suggested that whenever I would find a penny, I could trust my prayers were being heard.

Not three days after I made this little agreement with my deceased brother-in-law, I arrived at work one morning and found a jar filled with pennies that had been left anonymously on the center's doorstep! Eighty dollars worth! An inordinate number of pennies have continued to mysteriously pop up in the oddest places and at the most needed times.

I came to learn that my experience with pennies wasn't as unique as I believed it was. When I shared the connection pennies had for me I was surprised at how many others had similar tales to tell. I related to one story in particular about a woman who when worried or fearful inevitably finds a coin, not necessarily a penny. She believes it's a message from God since all coins have *In God We Trust* inscribed on them. For her it's a time to take a moment to pray and to acknowledge that God is always with her. I like that story.

I was fond of Danny's brother, everyone was. He was a wonderful caring individual who was often a source of support during some of the difficult times of my marriage. Ironically, it was through his death that I felt most connected to him. Each time a penny magically appeared I could envision my brother-in-law's warming smile and feel a sense of peaceful comfort settle around me.

When we take notice, messages of encouragement come to us in the most unusual of ways.

- TWENTY-ONE -

Interrogated, Intimidated

*Though I walk in the midst of trouble, you preserve
my life; you stretch out your hand against the anger
of my foes, with your right hand you save me.*
—Psalm 138:7

Tony and I were relaxing happily on the couch one warm
Saturday evening in mid-June watching a video. With my
older kids out it gave me the chance to spend some time with my
youngest son. We sat with a huge bowl of popcorn in between
the two of us, taking turns shoving our hands in the mound of
hot buttery popped corn and stuffing handfuls in our mouths. It
was one of the few occasions that I almost believed my life was
as normal as any other American family. Like other American
families with teenagers, a knock on the door at nine thirty sets
your heart pumping. Terrified that I might open the door to an
uniformed police officer asking if I was the mother of such and
such, I switched the dim overhead porch light on with my heart
in my mouth.

I was relieved on one hand that it wasn't police officers with
some dreadful news, but shocked to find the same two detectives back on my front porch at that hour of the night. I took a
quick look over my shoulder to see if Tony had followed me,
then stepped outside and quietly closed the door behind me.

The detectives kept their voices low, whether out of consideration or intimidation I'm not sure. Hastily they went through their formal preliminaries, and immediately went about shooting questions at me like a loaded automatic rifle.

"Did Danny ever give me anything for protection?"

"Did he leave the house with any items on that Sunday night?"

"Did I leave Danny in the house when I left?"

"Was he alone in the house?"

"Was anything missing after he left?"

They demanded I go over every detail of the weekend of Tony's birthday. The detectives insisted I knew more than I was telling them and that I was purposely withholding information. They threatened that I had better realize what I was doing and get out of my denial and face the fact that my ex-husband was a murderer and I had better tell my kids.

I heard a little noise behind me and turned to catch my eleven-year old son's face pressing against the window screen. I had no idea how much of this interrogation he had heard.

"Nanny is on the phone," he whimpered.

Believing that was his excuse to be eavesdropping, I urged him to go back to watching the movie and assured him I'd be inside shortly. But I was not. My young child's frightened face at the window did not deter the plainclothesmen. They continued where they left off without regard for my child, warning me that my house could be taken for forfeiture. For what seemed like hours I was tormented. When they did leave, they forewarned that they would be back as often as they deemed necessary.

In the middle of this impromptu interrogation, I saw my mother's car slowly drive past my house, go down the road and not return. I found out later that she had called and when Tony told her I was outside talking to some men, she rushed to my house. Unsure of what she should do when she saw the three of us on the front porch, she parked across from my neighbor's house and waited until she saw their car turn the corner before coming to my house. We sat outside on the porch step for a few minutes. In a low whisper I briefed her on what the detectives had threatened. Other than that, we were silent. After my mother left, still shaken by the evening's event, I managed to get to the bathroom in time to vomit. I did my best to compose myself before going into the den with my son and answer his questions without lying but also without frightening him. Tony might have only been eleven years old, but he wasn't an idiot. Children are a lot wiser than adults give them credit for. I could have lied until I was blue in the face to shield him from what was taking place in his father's life and in our lives, but all he would need to do was look at a newspaper, turn the television on or have some half-brain make a stupid comment that his father was a murderer. There was no way to protect my family from this horrible mess. I was at least grateful the two older ones weren't around to bear witness to that particular daunting event.

Early the next morning my mother called.

"I've had some time to think," Mom said in her I'm-in-charge voice. "You need an attorney. You don't need to be talking to these detectives without a lawyer present."

"I have nothing to hide, why would I need an attorney?"

"Because they are harassing you, that's why. They badger you because you let them. They think you are the weak link and that you will eventually break down."

"I don't have anything to break down about."

"They don't know that. And they will continue to plague you. You need an attorney, right away before they're back at your door. And next time they may come and arrest you!"

"That's ridiculous. They're not going to arrest me."

The thought of being arrested seemed too far-fetched; even so, I called the lawyer that I used for my divorce later that day. He contacted homicide and informed them he was representing me. He explained I had nothing to hide and that I was willing to speak with them, but in the future he would be representing me.

Miracles of miracles, they stopped coming to my house. And they never asked for me to come in for questioning. But every couple of days they would drive up and down the road, just to let me know they hadn't gone away. They were watching.

- TWENTY-TWO -

A House Renovated and Investigated

*"You cannot create a statue by smashing
the marble with a hammer,
and you cannot by force of arms release
the spirit or the soul of man."*
—Confucius

By the end of April my house was under full construction just as it had been the previous April. Money was flowing from Danny's hands to the several different tradesmen who regularly showed up bright and early everyday. Carpenters, masons, electricians, plumbers, you name it. Craftsmen were hanging kitchen cabinets; tile men were laying the twelve by twelve tumble stone tiles throughout the kitchen and dining area; spacklers were sanding the approximately eight hundred square feet of sheetrock; landscapers were planting over fifty shrubs, men were leveling the three-car driveway and preparing it for red brick Pavers, including a brick and cement border around the driveway with recessed lighting every eight feet. Other professionals were busy installing fencing, and more men were working on the underground sprinkler system. My house looked like the North Pole with dozens of Santa's elves scurrying about in preparation for Christmas. I couldn't even begin to guess how much money Danny was spending. I never saw a bill or was given a receipt; no transaction ever passed through my hands. When I opened my mouth to protest at the extravagance, Danny responded with his usual, "Don't worry about it. Your job is to pick out colors."

It was mind boggling how quickly and efficiently the men worked. I had waited over a year to have the simplest thing done, like a kitchen sink, and suddenly without my asking, jobs were completed in record speed.

One afternoon I came home early from work to check on who was there and what was going on. I was in the middle of a conversation with one of the electricians who was explaining to me how the lighting that would cover the perimeter of the property was going to work, when I was distracted by a loud noise that sounded like a bulldozer coming from the backyard. I excused myself and walked through the house to get a better view of what was going on out there. I nearly fell over when I saw a bulldozer digging out mounds of dirt in the middle of my backyard.

I screeched! *"What are they doing?"* I was informed by one of the workers that gargantuan hole was a pool.

"A pool? Who asked for a pool?" They shrugged their shoulders and went back to whatever it was they were doing. I had taken to shaking my head and wringing my hands. Xanex or not, this was too overwhelming for me.

That colossal hole in the ground turned into a twenty-five by fifty, Mountain Lake heated pool, eleven feet deep in the middle, with an attached hot tub. In the hot tub made out of peacock blue tile was a full sized dolphin. At the deep end a magnificent waterfall cascaded down a mountain of rocks.

I often noticed my neighbors gawking at the impressive transformation that took place in less than two months. My friends would stop over and stare with mouths agape as if they were looking at the Aurora Borealis. Those who didn't know me believed I was in seventh heaven. Those who did knew I would have been content to receive steady child support, to me that was luxury. I had requested a remodeled practical kitchen, not an outlandish extravagance. A lavish house meant nothing to me if there was no family, no husband to snuggle with on a cold winter's night, no father at the dinner table asking his children how their day went. Of course that was my dream, it never was a reality. The times Danny and I had snuggled were usually when he was guilty about something, and discussions around the dinner table were more like meals in an Army mess hall with Danny shouting out commands to his kids – "clean your room," "do your homework."

Anyway, the lavishness was Danny's way of compensating for the pain he had caused, his idea that the bigger the gift the better. But for me it was not the cure all for our ailing family. It was too much, too soon. The tragedy of September 11th was still fresh in my mind. I hadn't even grieved the loss of my brother-in-law, not to mention Danny's marriage, the murder and the law literally on my doorstep. I would have gladly traded every material item to have my children free from the glare and ridicule of the public and a safe, peaceful house to come home to.

The downstairs of my house was three-quarters complete. The walls were painted a soft ecru, oak molding and trim was in place, solid oak doors were hung for all the closets and light oak flooring covered the living room and down the hallway. With new over-stuffed furniture, a large custom-built cabinet for the television, pictures on the walls, and my collection of birdhouses, it started to look like a home. The upstairs was another story and wouldn't be finished for some months to come. The back portion of the house remained untouched and outdated in comparison. The kitchen cabinet doors that Danny and I bought long before remained in the basement.

By the end of June a cluster of workers were at the house everyday finishing up the final touches on the outside. There was one delay after another getting the pool filter to run properly and the unit to heat the pool. A smattering of landscapers replaced some of the ripped up sod and planted additional shrubs and trees. There were still workers milling around, or coming and going, but not as many as before. One of the landscapers I knew personally told me a couple of electricians had come to the house that morning and needed to go into the basement to check on some wiring. He told me he let them in and that they were in the basement for several hours. I called Danny pissed that he was giving strangers permission to go in my house when I wasn't home; we had had an agreement that he would let me know when workers would be at my house. But Danny said he didn't send any electricians and swore that he didn't know who was in my basement. He told me he would look into it. I didn't like that Danny seemed nervous and decided it might be best to contact my attorney. My lawyer was concerned that it might have been undercover cops planting listening devices in my house and advised me to be careful of what I say on the phone. *Listening devices!* I was outraged that the detectives would go to any length to try and 'catch' me in a lie and prove themselves right. This was a total invasion of my privacy! I was more than angry, it was unsettling what the law could do and get away with. When the kids came home from school I took them outside; we went for a walk down the road, away from my house, far away from the listening devices so I could tell them what was going on. I felt like a criminal, like I was hiding something. The kids were terrified. We were afraid to talk on the phone; frightened we might say something that may sound incriminating. We nearly tiptoed around the house. We searched for anything that remotely resembled a microphone. I didn't feel safe in my own home. I lay awake at night wondering how my life had come to this. This wasn't what I had envisioned when Danny took my hand and we walked down the church aisle as a young hopeful married couple.

The next day the same 'electricians' returned, but this time they left a card with the landscaper. The card claimed them to be investigators for Long Island Power Authority (LIPA); they asked the landscaper to have me call them. I called my attorney. He called them. A LIPA official explained to my lawyer there were reports of meter tampering and stealing electric and LIPA investigators would need to inspect the premises. He made no mention of anyone being in my house, in my basement, for hours the day before. My lawyer called me back and suggested I give LIPA permission for them to come back, which I did. Arrangements were made for the investigators to come the following afternoon when I would be home.

They arrived with cameras and a clipboard full of notes. They took several pictures while they were in the basement, and more pictures inside the house and of the outside meter. I did not follow them around. The heavyset investigator told me there was a dangerous illegal meter bypass, which they fixed. They would be back the next day to monitor the meter. None of this made any sense. I was suspicious of everyone and everything and was certain the detectives were out to get me.

I was grateful Joy came the following day to attend our twentieth class reunion on that weekend.

"Just in time," Joy said, "to follow those investigators around. I'll be damned if they're going to be walking all over the place with no one knowing what the hell they're doing. I'm gonna keep my eye on them and see what the hell they are up to."

Joy has always been gutsier than me. Wherever an investigator went, Joy was two steps behind. She followed them around and pumped them for information. But they had little to say except, "we know Mrs. Pelosi has nothing to do with this, only an electrician would know about the bypass."

When they left Joy and I tried to figure out what they were talking about. We were baffled. I was on a monthly budget with LIPA, at the end of the year they would adjust the rate for the following year. I might have paid my bill late, but it always got paid. Yet these investigators insisted Danny was responsible for this bypass, but no one could say or would say who was in my basement for six hours two days previous.

The third time the LIPA inspectors came, Danny was there with his own attorney. Danny's lawyer spoke with the investigators and said if they needed further information to contact him. The investigation was between Danny, his attorney and LIPA. I was out of the picture. As far as I knew this matter had nothing to do with me, was out of my hands and was being taken care of by Danny's attorney.

PART III

The Shameful Years

2003 - 2005

- TWENTY-THREE -

Arrested!

You gain strength, courage and confidence by every
experience in which you really stop to look fear in
the face. You are able to say to yourself, 'I have
lived through this horror. I can take the next
thing that comes along.' You must do the
thing you think you cannot do."
—Eleanor Roosevelt

Once or twice a week, the girls from my job would come over after work with their kids for pizza and swimming in my movie star pool. It was open house. If it was hot out, bring your suit and take a dip. Five or six of Tony's friends were there on a daily basis, swimming, and hanging out. With a heated pool and unique colorful lighting, the kids could swim until late in the night. Most weekends my backyard was a regular adventure land. And it looked beautiful. My mother had busied herself planting a picturesque array of impatiens around the pool and tall beach grass on both sides of the waterfall. All things considered, the summer wasn't bad.

Summer folded into fall and Tony's twelfth birthday. It had been a rough year for my young child. Paint ball was the current fad and Tony was looking forward to his father playing on the opposing team. Danny was on the phone with him every couple of days, teasing about which team was going to be the loser. I guess you could say Tony won by default, if you can call having your father not show up a victory. Danny never made it to the game. He sent a friend in his place, as if a friend could take the place of his father. Tony's twelfth birthday wasn't much different than his eleventh, with a few major exceptions – his father was remarried and a suspect in a brutal murder.

I had little enthusiasm for the holidays. I had no idea whether Danny would come to the house on Christmas Eve or not. He had a wife now, a rather possessive and controlling one. I didn't think she would want him spending too much time with me and my children and too much time away from her and her children. Who knows what steps Danny needed to dance in order to see his family for the holiday, but he did manage to break loose and arrived around nine in the evening bearing small gifts for whoever was there. It wasn't the same hullabaloo of Christmases past. In fact when Danny arrived everyone else began to leave. Greg didn't come that Christmas, Carol said he wasn't feeling well, but I have always wondered if there was more to the story than that. The Christmas tradition of our two families together was over. Danny stayed for a few hours and came back on Christmas morning with the gifts for the kids, expensive useless jewelry for each of them.

The winter months were long and dreary. Danny found himself back in jail again in March of 2003 for another DWI he got while living in East Hampton the summer before. While he was behind bars, it was Generosa who made the decisions regarding my alimony. *She* was the one who decided I would re-ceive only child support, not maintenance. I hated that Princess TaTa governed my finances. I forced myself to acknowledge the fact that Generosa didn't have to give me a dime. She could have said 'screw Tami.' It wasn't her responsibility to support me while Danny was locked up, even though in reality it was her money that was supporting me when he wasn't locked up.

I never did receive another maintenance payment again. One year later all means of support came to a screeching stop.

Danny had a new wife for over a year, but still thought of me as his possession, to which I achieved my sick little glory. When he was in jail he'd call *me* up. He'd shout orders, expecting me to jump when he snapped his fingers. Usually I did, but not without a yelling match. The only way I knew how to assert myself was to yell louder than him. We had been at each other's throats for several days because Little Dan wanted to quit school. He had just turned seventeen and did not need my permission. I was at my wits end and ready to give in.

Dan and I had battled on the phone early in the morning of Friday, April 4, 2003. He screamed, "what kind of mother are you to let your kid quit school?" I screeched back, "you think it is easy raising these kids after you walked out on us?"

I slammed the phone down, grabbed my car keys and headed to work cursing at myself for letting him get to me.

I was driving along on the Long Island Expressway preoccupied in my thoughts wondering how I was going to get my son to stay in school; a former A student, yet failing in every subject. I knew he was rebelling over everything that had happened. Leaving school was his way to lash back. I was frightened he'd take the alcohol-drug route so many kids did under lesser circumstances. He was genuinely a good kid. I never had any problems with him. I felt guilty that I would let him quit. Danny's words rang in my ear. It was my fault. I was a failure as a mother.

I pushed those thoughts from my mind and focused on more pleasant things – like leaving work early that day to attend a retreat with Carol at the lovely little church she and I had started to attend at the beginning of the year. From the very first Sunday I knew this was the place for me. Even though I don't think of myself as a religious person, at least not in the traditional sense of religion, I immediately felt uplifted by Pastor Lydia's real-life approach to her sermons that always seemed to relate to my life.

Thinking about what a great weekend I was going to have surrounded by loving individuals, I looked up to see a cop behind me with his light on; I pulled over. I realized I didn't have my seat belt on.

The cop swaggered over to my car, glared in at me with ice blue eyes and recited the official memorized spiel.

"License and registration, Ma'm."

I handed over my papers and asked what I did wrong, irritated by the interruption. He informed me that I had failed to signal when I changed lanes. I hadn't given much thought to what he had said at that moment, but realized later, I *hadn't* changed lanes. I was still in the right lane having just gotten onto the LIE from Exit 68.

"Step out of your car, Ma'm and stand behind it."

"*What?* What for?"

"Normal procedures, Ma'm."

I had one traffic violation in my life and that was years before for not coming to a full stop at a stop sign. I was not asked to step out of my car then. I had never heard of such a procedure. I was leery and not sure of what to do. But I did as I was told. He ran my license to check for warrants while we were standing outside. He towered over me and radioed to headquarters with one of those walk-talkie contraptions they wear on their shirt. Within seconds a report was back - there *was* a warrant out for my arrest!

"I have no warrant. There has to be some kind of confusion." My stomach went into a spasm. I assured him this had to be a mistake.

"What could the warrant be for?"

He talked with his jaw shut, muttered a cocky, "I don't know, Ma'm. I have to take you in."

"*IN?* In where?"

He snapped back with a curt, "the precinct."

The minor irritation I felt escalated into major fear. I attempted to explain to him that there *must* be confusion with my insurance company. I had switched from one company to another and the motor vehicle department had notified me that my auto insurance had lapsed. I had immediately gone to the DMV and had the matter taken care of and received the proper documents stating this fact, which were in the console of my car. The police officer would not let me get them. He repeated in that locked-jaw gruff voice that he did not know what the warrant was for.

"Lady, you are under arrest. Put your hands behind your back." (He did not read me my rights.)

"What for?" I was stymied.

"Because I have to cuff you." My ignorance wore thin on him.

"I'm not getting cuffed." Ignorance manifested to anger.

"Lady, then you'll be charged with resisting arrest."

He would not hear me out or allow me the chance to retrieve the papers. He pulled my arms behind my back and snapped the cuffs on. I pleaded with him to let me drive my car to the precinct. Instead he shoved me in the back of the police car, like a dog. I feared I was going to be raped, or worse. I knew there was no warrant for me. And there was no way out of that car. I was handcuffed in the back of a police car, powerless. Being taken somewhere I did not believe to be the police department. I had recently seen a TV talk show about women who were raped by police officers, or men who pretend to be officers, the show emphasized - never get to the second location. I cried, silent salty tears that trickled down my cheeks and dropped onto my blouse.

This can't be happening, oh my god, this can't be happening.

"Please," I begged. "You don't understand, there is a mistake. Please.......my daughter...she'll be concerned......She'll see my car on the expressway. She works with me. She'll think something terrible has happened to me."

Something terrible is happening to me!

The officer's cold blue eyes peered at me from the rearview mirror, "What's the matter, never been in a police car before?" He seemed to find pleasure in my terror. "We don't put warrants out for no reason, you know. What are you lying about, huh?"

Fight or flight. My old psychology courses came to mind. For a fraction of a second the body freezes in motion. Shuts down. Shock. Immobilized. Fear so great, it's paralyzing. Pupils dilate. Muscles tighten, ready for action. Adrenals kick in. Rapid short breaths.

This is not happening!

But it was. We arrived at the 7th precinct on William Floyd Parkway in Shirley. I was relieved that I wasn't taken to some deserted wooded area. I was at a police station and trusted someone there would help me.

But help was not coming then or at all. I was yanked from the car, pulled by my arm and escorted to a back door into a windowless 8 x 8 cinder block concrete cubicle. It was not an over active imagination or too much television that convinced me I was about to be raped on the cold cement floor where no one would hear my screams. In fact I believed that other officers would one by one violate me and they would all get away with it. Why wouldn't my mind go in that direction? I knew I had no warrants out on me. Frightening, unbelievable events had already taken place in my life.

Gratefully, I was not raped. I was told to sit in the chair. The cop menacingly joked that he was going to shackle me to the floor. I pleaded like the captive that I was. Crying, blubbering. I wiped snot on my blouse.

"Please, don't shackle me. I won't go anywhere. I promise." I wondered how many times the officer heard those feeble words from others, *those* criminals.

"I have to call …call….my job. I'm a…..a teacher; I need to open the school. If I'm not there…. they'll worry." I stuttered, the words caught in my throat. I let him know that I had my cell phone in my bag; all I wanted was to make one call.

Just give me my bag!

This tall cop with silver hair and those icy blue eyes had a moment of compassion. He assured me he would notify my job, went so far as to take the phone number down. As he walked out of the room, he turned back to look at me, and in a kind voice he said, "don't worry, I'll find out what the warrant is. I'll be right back."

I was left alone, my hands cuffed behind my back, sitting under a glaring fluorescent light. I prayed.

Dear God, please let him tell me there was a mistake.

I don't know how long the officer was gone, maybe fifteen to twenty minutes. I jumped when I heard the door open.

"Did you ever leave a restaurant without paying a bill?"

"*What* are you talking about?"

"Your warrant is for Theft of Services. It could be an accident, maybe you left a restaurant without realizing you didn't pay." He was being suspiciously nice.

"Absolutely not." Thoughts raced through my mind trying to recall when I had been out to dinner and who I was with. Usually we would split the tab evenly. Even if there were the remote chance that one of us forgot to pay the bill, how would they have gotten my name? Did that mean that whoever I had dinner with had a warrant out as well? This was beyond bizarre.

The police officer looked as confused as I was. He left again saying he'd find out what was going on. All of a sudden he was my buddy!

Not ten minutes later he was back; the warrant was from LIPA. I sighed a breath of relief. Now I knew this was a misunderstanding. Attorneys were handling the case; all I needed to do was give the officer the lawyer's phone number and the matter would be resolved. But he left again before I had the chance to explain this to him.

The door opened again, but it wasn't the mean-officer-turned-nice-officer, it was the two homicide detectives who just happened to be at this particular precinct at the same time I was there! The same two detectives who had previously been informed that my attorney would need to be present if they wished to question me. But I had forgotten about the verbal agreement and never thought to ask for my lawyer. They sat their suited bodies across the table from me not caring I was handcuffed like a convict. They briefly flashed a legal looking paper before me that stated "LIPA Against Pelosi." I have no idea whether it said Tamara Pelosi or not.

The older stocky detective pointed his thick stubby finger at the document. Not caring that he was basically bribing me he told me this was a felony; if I want a-get-out-of-jail-free-card, I should give them the info they want.

"I've already told you everything. I don't know what information you want, in fact I don't even know when Mr. Ammon was murdered."

The same detective with obvious years of badgering and terrifying people, slammed his fat fist on the desk, "on your fucking son Anthony's birthday!" Foamy spit flew across the room like a rabid dog.

I was stunned by the rage of this man in a gray suit and tie. His shocking behavior spurred my own fury.

"You are disgusting!" I don't know where I got the courage to assert myself and demanded to be spoken to with dignity. "If you want to continue to talk to me, you better use a different tone." I finally remembered to ask for my lawyer. But they denied it.

They switched their tactic to the good-cop, bad-cop role. While the rageful older one yelled at me, called me names and accused me of withholding information, the younger slimmer one spoke in a soft voice, suggested it would be best if I cooperated, otherwise I could spend a long time in jail.

My temporary bravado dissipated quicker than a puff of smoke; the weak-kneed captive was back.

"Please just let me call my daughter and let her know I am safe."

'Good cop' said he would check with the arresting officer if a call had been made to my job. Two minutes later he was back with a phone in his hand. No one had called. He placed the phone on the table, plugged it in an outlet, mercifully removed the cuffs, and leaned his face over mine, close enough that I could smell coffee on his breath. No longer the 'good cop,' he threatened "if you know what is good for you, you will not say you are being questioned by homicide detectives. You will tell them there is a mix-up with your license and you will call them back when you get the chance."

Amazingly I remembered my work number. Even more amazing I was able to compose myself and recite the instructed script to Carol, although I desperately wanted to scream for help. I lied to Carol and told her I had been mistakenly arrested for a mix- up with my driver's license, I was at the seventh precinct and everything was okay.

Carol wanted to come to the precinct, but I quickly hung up telling her I would call her later.

I knew Carol would not idly sit and wait for me to call her back. I found out much later that day she had immediately called my mother and the two of them set off on a quest to find me and solve the mystery.

I was interrogated for several hours; grilled and drilled endlessly on the same questions I had already answered dozens of times at my house. These two men who dressed meticulously in business suits - they could have been bankers - browbeat me, intimated me and threatened me; they could take my house, they could put me in jail and basically throw away the key, how would I feel leaving my kids alone because their mother was locked up in prison. They boasted they had clout, if I knew what was good for me I'd open my mouth and spill the beans. If I gave them what they wanted they had the power to drop the Theft of Service charges. They played games with my head, from bullying me to pacifying me, to bragging what nice guys they were, so nice they would drop the felony charge to a misdemeanor. Their goal was to wear me down and they did, but not in the way they hoped. I finally told them I had nothing more to say to them. They could go ahead and charge me with the felony, I was too emotionally and mentally exhausted to care.

They joked back and forth between each other on what they could do with my charges, settled on the misdemeanor, then informed me they would be transporting me to the Fifth Precinct in another town, where supposedly the charges would be processed. This made no sense to me, but nothing that had taken place that morning made any sense. Handcuffs once again were locked tight around my wrists, formalities they said. I was escorted to an unmarked car, with a detective on either side of me holding on to my arms, as if I was going to make a mad dash to freedom.

Squinting from the bright sun after being closed in the dungeon for what must have been hours, (I had no conception of time), I spotted both my mother's and Carol's cars in the parking lot. I was more baffled than before. This was like trying to put a thousand piece jigsaw puzzle together with half the pieces missing. There was no logical reasoning for anything. None at all.

The detectives ushered me to their car, mumbling that my mother and Carol had only arrived a few moments before *(How did they know that?)* and would be meeting me at the Fifth Precinct to bail me out. That was the first I heard about being bailed out.

However, this was not the case at all. Carol and my mother had been at the seventh precinct for over an hour getting the run-a-round from the police. They were told conflicting stories; first that I was not there, then no one seemed to know what precinct I was at. To top it off, the two detectives questioned my mother for about a half an hour. They pumped her for information and gave their "we have clout" lecture and *suggested* she *encourage* me to cooperate with them, otherwise her daughter was facing a felony charge. Neither my mother nor Carol knew I was there the same time as they were; they were told I was at the Patchogue station. They were not going to the fifth precinct to bail me out, *but to find me.* In the meantime, my mother contacted my attorney who had also been given the run-a-round from the police. He called several police stations before anyone admitted where I was and had the chance to speak with me.

I was transported to the Patchogue station in the backseat of an unmarked car, and taken in handcuffs to a side door at the fifth precinct. A uniformed officer was sitting at the desk.

"You've got to help me," I cried. "Something is terribly wrong. I should not be in cuffs. Please help me." The older detective made some snide comment to the young officer regarding how he loved his job, they all laughed, obviously a sick sense of humor must be a job requirement.

The detectives led me down a bleak gray hallway. To the right of the hallway was dark, almost black looking cells and to the left were tables with glass dividers for criminals. The room began to whirl, the dismal grays and blacks spun before my eyes, my knees gave way and I slumped to the floor. The terrifying reality of the sinister looking cells and the frightening inter-rogation room brought on a full-blown panic attack. I began to hyperventilate and was not able to breathe; sharp pains stabbed my chest. I had had other attacks before, but nothing compared to this. With an ounce of humanity, the detectives helped me to my feet, removed the cuffs and from somewhere a cup of water was given to me. They each held me under an arm and walked me to the table. I was told to sit on the criminal side of the table, but I refused.

"I am not a criminal," I sobbed. "Don't you understand, I didn't do anything wrong. Why are you doing this to me?" My chest tightened to the point that I needed to gasp for air. Water was brought to my lips. They sat me on the other side of the table, not the criminal side. A small moment of victory. In a low voice the younger detective spoke to me as if I were a child or mentally disabled.

"Okay, I know this has been rough on you, but it's almost over. I need to take you over for fingerprinting............" He caught the terror in my eyes. "It's procedure. Then you'll be out of here." He neglected to mention - purposely or not, I don't know - the other demeaning procedures that would follow the fingerprinting.

I was taken to the area where the fingerprinting was set up in the back part of the building. The officer grabbed one finger at a time, rolled it on an inkpad and pressed each finger on some sort of machine. My hand shook so much it annoyed the police-man who had to go through the procedure several times to get a decent print. After that degrading experience came a more shameful one - the mug shot. I was ordered to place my feet on top of the shoe prints that were painted on the floor and look into the camera. A flash went off. My mug shot was on record.

When they were finished putting me through this mortify-ing ordeal, I was brought back to the interrogation room and sat at the same seat as before. I was told I would be released in a few minutes once some paperwork was completed. A phone was handed to me that appeared from nowhere; it was my at-torney. After a quick inquiry about how I was doing, he gave me a brief encapsulation of what it took for him to finally locate me. He advised me not to speak to anyone until he got there; *(Too late!)* he would leave his office right away. Since it would take approximately forty minutes for him to drive across the Island, I told him it wasn't necessary for him to come. I would be out before he could get there. (It was about another hour before I actually walked through the doors to freedom.) I promised to call him as soon as I could.

For a few moments I was alone. I don't think I was ever as exhausted as I was then. With my head on my arms on top of the table, I sobbed quietly. My body began to tremble uncontrollably, more from nerves than cold, but someone did bring me my jacket. I urgently needed to use the rest room. I thought I could wait until I was released, which I believed was any minute. But after another half an hour of sitting at the table, nature was screaming, I couldn't contain my bladder a moment longer. A female officer escorted me to the ladies room and stood in there with me. When I came out of the stall she told me she would need to search me.

Search me!

I was directed to lower my pants. There was a knock on the door; the timing couldn't have been more perfect; there was no need to search me. I was being released!

Thank you, God!

It took another half an hour to finish the processing. I bailed myself out for $50 cash. I was given a desk appearance ticket to appear in court on May 23, 2003. I had no idea what my charges were for.

I don't know what I looked like, but after six tormenting hours of emotional and mental badgering, by the expression on Carol's and my mother's face, I was not a pleasant sight. The two of them embraced me, all three of us in tears. They bombarded me with questions I refused to answer *in there.*

"Get me out of here before I get sick." My stomach was nauseous; I gulped down an acid taste in my mouth. A sip of water made me queasy. I was guided out the door like an invalid to Carol's car, which was parked next to mine.

"How did my car get here?" The three of us looked at one another, another puzzle piece missing. We did our best to put the pieces together, but there were way too many missing. When was my car taken from the Long Island Expressway to the Fifth Precinct and who drove it? When someone is arrested, aren't their vehicles towed away? Or left at the site? Was it a planned set-up for the police officer to arrest me? Why were my mother, Carol and my attorney not told where I was? The questions were endless and to this day, most are unanswered.

My kids nearly bowled me over when I walked in the door. Rachelle knew something serious had happened when I didn't show up for work, but it wasn't until much later in the day, after Carol and my mother located me at the police station, that she learned of the arrest. She and Little Dan had been extremely worried, leaning on each other for support. Tony was quiet and withdrawn. They huddled around me on the couch asking questions I couldn't answer. How could I explain what had taken place when I myself was mystified?

When I finally got to speak with my attorney he was outraged by what was done to me. He had spoken with a representative from LIPA who knew nothing of a warrant or of any charges against me.

"They basically broke the law. You were protected with an attorney; no one was to speak with you without me being present."

He encouraged me to file a lawsuit, as well as a civil suit. "Someone needs to be held responsible for this atrocity!"

A few days after I was arrested, I learned that my arrest was apparently a complicated 'sting' that was carefully executed. Within the next twenty-four hours three of Danny's friends and his cousin were pulled over by unmarked cars while on their way to work, hauled to the police station and interrogated for hours regarding the murder of Mr. Ammon. I was their first target and the only one arrested on the pretense of a false charge.

- TWENTY-FOUR -

Utter Humiliation

"May the Lord give you peace."
—The Greeting of St. Francis of Assisi

Eight hours after I was yanked from my car, handcuffed and carted off to the police station, Carol was back at my house encouraging me to attend our women's weekend retreat that I had been looking forward to that morning. But I was too emotionally drained to move myself off the couch and pack a few things and I didn't want to leave my kids – or my home for that matter. Both Carol and my mother convinced me that a weekend of rest was what I needed. While I was in the shower my mother threw some clothes together in an overnight bag and reassured me my kids would be under her care.

I had originally planned to take my car, but both Carol and I were suspicious the police had 'bugged' my car, so we decided to use Carol's. If the car had been wired, all they would have heard was me sobbing. I cried the entire weekend. My eyes were swollen little slits; my voice was hoarse. No one but Carol knew what had happened. By the end of the second day I found the courage to speak with Pastor Lydia. I told her about my life and what led up to the arrest. She held my hands and prayed over me. Instantly a calming sensation penetrated every cell. The tension in my face and jaw slipped away. My shoulders relaxed. There was a sense of peace that I couldn't get with Xanax.

Pastor Lydia told me a story about how Jesus had to rise above his pain. She vowed that one day God was going to use this experience in a way I could never imagine. She suggested I pray for Danny; pray that he could find peace in his life.

"You have to let go of him," she said kindly. "In order for you to do that you need to forgive him. That doesn't mean you have to accept the things he has done, but you cannot go on with your life if you hold onto him."

I cried healing tears throughout the weekend until there were no tears left to cry. I was grateful for the two days away and for Pastor Lydia's compassionate words of wisdom. I was actually able to smile by the time the retreat was over on Sunday afternoon.

Heading to work Monday morning, feeling a sense of calm, I received a call from Mrs. Marcus, Tony's school guidance counselor. She told me she had tried to contact me several times on Friday to let me know Tony had a 'melt down' while in school. For no apparent reason that she knew of, he started to cry in the classroom and was sent to her office where he continued to cry non-stop for hours. When she asked him what was wrong he answered he didn't know, but could not stop. Eventually his tears subsided and she allowed him to take the bus home.

When I learned of my son's distress I was furious with the detectives who kept me locked away at the police station while my son needed me. And guilty that I had gone away for the weekend unaware of the pain my young son was experiencing. I was so enmeshed in my own misery I never noticed how troubled he was. My mother reported he was sad and gloomy over the weekend, but she attributed his quietness to my arrest and my being away; he never mentioned anything to her or to me when I returned home Sunday night. According to Mrs. Marcus, Tony was sent to her office at ten thirty and calmed down around two; around the same hours I was being harassed.

Coincidence? I don't think so. Tony may not know what made him so upset on that Friday on April 4, 2003, but I have no doubt my son picked up on my distress.

On Wednesday, the ninth of April, five days after my arrest, a professional TV recording company was coming to the center to help us create a videotape for parents interested in our programs. I had a terrible case of laryngitis, but to cancel would mean waiting months again for another appointment, so I creaked and squeaked through the interview and came across as cool, calm and composed. I cleverly concealed my shameful degrading experience from a few days before with a phony smile and a chic pearl-gray linen suit. A skilled professional to the public eye.

The next few days passed without any major disasters, allowing me some time to catch my breath for the next catastrophe.

I had taken my attorney's advice and was going ahead with the civil suit. He had recommended a young lawyer who would represent the five of us who had been taken in for questioning. Unbeknown to me, the lawyer decided to hold a press conference. The media went into a crazed frenzy when they learned that my name was part of the suit. Somehow the reporters discovered where I worked and raided my job like a pack of famished canines. A half a dozen or more news people arrived on the property of my center within a half an hour from the press conference - unfortunately at the exact time parents were picking their children up. The reporters grabbed every parent they could and gorged on each bit of information they could get their teeth into.

"Are you aware of the charges against Tamara Pelosi?"

"What kind of person is Mrs. Pelosi?"

"Is Mrs. Pelosi here?"

They brazenly knocked on the center's door looking for me.

I hid upstairs in my office wishing I could crawl in a hole for the rest of my life.

The Program Director told them I was unavailable for comments and asked them to leave. They lingered after all the children were gone. Eventually they got the message and vacated the grounds in the same rushed mania they arrived in.

Carol sat with me for a while to be sure I was all right to

drive home. We discussed what this incident might do to our center. We thought it best to immediately send letters to the parents explaining what had taken place, rather than waiting for them to read a distorted version in the newspapers. I decided to take two weeks off work for things to calm down. I did not want to put the school or the center in jeopardy. Driving home in a stupefied daze I wondered what the parents would think of me. I was prepared for parents to sign their children out of the school. After all, who would want their child to be around a *criminal?*

I turned into my road and there they were – *reporters!* I made a quick U-turn and headed to my mother's, my stomach locked in cramps.

Carol called me over the next several days reporting the outpouring of letters that came to the center, letters from the parents expressing their support, how much they admired me not just as a teacher, but as an individual. Many sent personal handwritten notes offering words of encouragement along with bouquets of flowers and thoughtful gifts. I was overwhelmed and deeply touched by their response. But no acts of genuine kindness could eradicate my embarrassment.

On Friday, May 23, 2003, the date of my first court appearance, I was terrified I was going to be convicted for a Theft of Services charge, simply stated – stealing electric. I spent the night curled in a fetal position with horrific stomach pains and a pounding vice-like headache. By the time morning arrived I was weak and debilitated. My former partner Patti from my center, who is also a court advocate for women, came with me for support.

There was some confusion when we got there. My name wasn't on the court calendar, there was no docket number, nor proof of warrant for my arrest, yet I needed to appear before the judge. My attorney felt certain the case would be dismissed that day, but to his surprise it moved forward regardless. The motion to dismiss was denied. I was informed I would have to face a jury of my peers and plead not guilty. That was it. Two days of stress, two hours of court, and another court date for June 21. My lawyer did his best to reassure me that the matter would be dropped once the judge read the thick folder he had prepared in my defense. However, this drama went on for two years, every month a court date, every month a postponement. Every month I'd be sick for days prior to court. No one seemed to know what was going on, except I was told to be prepared for a weeklong trial. My attorney decided not to represent me since he was going to be one of my witnesses, so another lawyer took over. Each time I appeared before the Judge it was the same humiliation I experienced on the day I was arrested. I was obsessed with shame – what if I ever had to fill out a job application and write a conviction? No matter how much I primed myself emotionally and mentally, no matter who came with me, no matter what the attorneys believed, I was petrified.

Ironically, a warrant for my arrest was never produced, yet every month I had to appear in court for the Theft of Service charge, only to have each appearance postponed.

Two weeks after my arrest, right after Easter, Little Dan quit school. He simply didn't return after vacation. He had no interest in anything and my arrest didn't help matters. His escape was to hang out with his friends; they were his safety net. I couldn't argue with him, I knew how he felt. If I didn't have to support my family I would have quit my job and buried my head under my pillows.

I had a lot on my plate; in fact it was so overloaded I could barely distinguish one day from the other; one calamity from another. There were rumors that prosecution had called for a grand jury to gather sufficient evidence to arrest Danny for the murder of Mr. Ammon. The grand jury was scheduled to begin sometime in July. There was some speculation as to whether my name was on the list - as it turned out - it was. The District Attorney called my attorney who notified me. This new and alarming information was up on the *Top Ten Things I Do*

Not Need In My Life, Now Or Ever. I was already ravaged with anxiety over my own trial - and now a Grand Jury as a witness *against* Danny! If I were a drug addict I would have zoned out on some mind-altering narcotic. Instead I delved deeper into my church, attended as many inspirational workshops that I could and trusted my life in God's hands.

I also took a break from the sheer madness and spent the first week of July in Florida with my bubbly friend Joy. She wasted no time and immediately got down to business – funny business. She had me laughing before we pulled onto I-95 heading for her home in Melbourne.

"You know," she said in her normal dry humor, "you're like that damn Eveready rabbit, you just keep on going!"

"That's easy for you to say," I joked back. "Indefatigable, I'm not. I may keep on going. I may appear tireless, but unlike that Bunny my batteries do run out."

"I've got it," Joy said excited with a new idea that popped into her mind, "You're more like a prizefighter."

"A prizefighter?"

"Yea. The bell dings," she said simulating a boxing match, "you're sent to your corner. I'm your trainer," she added pleased with giving herself a notable role, "I squirt some water around in your mouth, I dab your wounds with some medicinal numbing spray, I give you a little back rub, a little pep talk and zap – you're back in the ring for another round." I couldn't have described my life any better.

Round One-Hundred-And-Ten. I returned from Joy's on Sunday the sixth of July. I did have a week of rest, some much needed laughing therapy, soaked up the sun, and felt recharged. I went back to work on Monday as regenerated as was possible under the circumstances; summer camp at the center was in full force with kids participating in one activity or another. The weather was as sticky and humid as it was in Melbourne. By Wednesday I was dragging my feet. After a long, hard hot day, I was grateful for a cool shower and a relaxing evening. The kids were out and about doing what kids do on summer evenings. The house was blissfully quiet in comparison to the energetic exuberance of fifty little kids. Feeling content and peaceful I sat down to eat a light dinner and browse through the *Suffolk Life*, a local newspaper. A story about the Guide Dog Foundation on the front page caught my interest. I placed one forkful of food in my mouth, turned to the page where the story continued and DING! The bell went off. I was back in the ring for another grueling hellish round I was not prepared for! Across the page from an adorable picture of a Golden Retriever puppy was my *mug shot*! Along with Danny's and some strangers and a lengthy article of the LIPA investigation and the Long Islanders who were arrested for *stealing* electric. *My* face and *my* name in connection with these total strangers for all *Suffolk Life* subscribers to read, including the parents whose children attended my center!

I leaped from the table, knocked the chair over and coughed up a piece of lettuce I had gasped down my throat. *This is outrageous!* My fingers zipped across the phone buttons dialing my attorney and left a message on his machine. Then I called Danny's attorney who was handling his LIPA case. I wailed to him, '*how did THAT picture get in the newspaper?*' He responded in a mechanical, not very sympathetic tone, something about free press, nothing he could do, it was within the law for my mug shot to be printed.

The round was over. A knockout. Defeated. Total and complete humiliation.

I spent my days tucked away in my office, far from the pitying glares, too shamed to see anyone. I refused to participate in the kids' programs in fear a parent might see me.

Two days after my public condemnation my lawyer called me – I was due to appear before the Grand Jury on Monday, July 14.

I was at the Riverhead courthouse with my mother by nine Monday morning after a long fretful sleepless weekend. I've learned over the years, if you want to present a confident persona, dress in a manner to support the illusion. With my blonde hair neatly pulled up and back with a clasp and a tan business suit, one would have thought *I* was the one to boldly defend some unfortunate soul. Instead I was the unfortunate soul. Wisely, my mother brought her book and waited for me in the small area, anxiously watching the clock tick minute by minute.

Appearing before a Grand Jury is unlike anything I have ever experienced. I was seated in a hard-backed chair, which was almost in the middle of the room, surrounded in a horseshoe shape by thirty or so jurors. There is no judge or legal representation at a grand jury. You are on your own with thirty pairs of unrelenting eyes glued to you.

The DA sat at a rectangular table to the right of me, accompanied by her assistant who continuously shuffled through a stack of folders laden with a copious supply of investigative materials. I learned in a matter of minutes not to be fooled by the diminutive size of the slightly built District Attorney; after all a stick of dynamite is not very large.

After the prefatory swearing in, the DA hammered away posing the same questions as the homicide detectives, "Did Danny give me a stun gun? Why did Danny give me a stun gun? Where was Danny on the night of the murder? What was Danny wearing when he came over my house on Sunday morning October 21, 2001? How was he behaving? Do I know where the missing hard drive is? Did Danny deposit huge amounts of money in my personal bank accounts? Did Danny ever admit to me that he murdered Mr. Ammon?"

As per my attorney, I answered only what was asked; I followed his instruction even though I wanted to explain why I said what I did. Occasionally I caught a few jurors nodding their heads in agreement or maybe in understanding. But one juror in particular, a gray-haired older woman in her sixties or so, rolled her eyes up as if she couldn't be bothered listening to me, as though she believed I was lying. I am convinced it was no accident my mug shot was displayed for open criticism five days before I was to stand in front of a grand jury.

For brief moments the interrogation subsided as the DA and her assistant sorted through their myriad of papers. Then as if they hadn't heard a word I said, parroted the same questions. On and on and on for an hour and a half.

I had hoped that I had hoodwinked the jurors and perhaps the DA as well, by masquerading as a secure undaunted witness. Obviously not. One month later on the thirteenth of August, I was again called to the grand jury. Dressed in yet another business suit, a crème colored silk scarf around my neck clasped to my suit with a delicate gold Angel pin and my hair falling loose, whatever false bravado I may have exhibited the last time, was flushed down the toilet with my breakfast. For the District Attorney to want me back could only mean one of two things, either I said something important enough worth repeating or this DA planned to abuse and denounce my statements in the hope of bringing me to my knees and spilling forth whatever the prosecution needed to seal their case against Danny.

A half an hour into the interrogation with the DA repeating the queries she had asked for over an hour four weeks ago, and which were harped on repeatedly over the course of a year by the homicide detectives, I came to doubt if I had divulged anything new or of substantial significance. And since I was *not* concealing any information, she diligently pressed on. I became agitated by the monotonous repetitious rhetoric, which if nothing else, dispelled my fear. I wanted to lash out at *her,* question *her, 'who* issued my arrest? *Who* manipulated my mug shot to appear in a widely read newspaper quite *coincidentally* a few days prior to my appearance at the grand jury? *Who?*

The diatribe continued for another hour. Whether I provided the prosecution with anything different than the last time, I didn't know, but mercifully, I was not requested to appear before the Grand Jury again.

However, the grand jury resumed for some months to come, collecting evidence and ample testimony for Danny's intended arrest. I kept the kids away from their father as much as possible. No one could ascertain when the time would come that he would be apprehended and under what conditions; it could happen at a family evening bar-b-que, or fishing with the boys off the dock in Danny's backyard. Whatever or however the arrest would take place, my kids did not need to witness their father being handcuffed and roughshod away by a swarm of broad-shouldered men in business suits.

Everyday the newspapers, both local and national, reported some story regarding "The East Hampton Murder" and whatever current situation there was.

The new headline that grabbed the interest of the masses in August of 2003 wasn't about the murder per se, but about Generosa – *"Ammon Widow Dies of Cancer".* I had heard a rumor that Generosa had been diagnosed with breast cancer some months before, but in all honesty I thought it was one of Danny's stories. Even when he told our children that Generosa had made him move out because she didn't want him seeing her deteriorate; I still thought it sounded a bit too dramatic to be true. But on August 25, Generosa succumbed to the disease, taking with her the possible link to who murdered her former husband. To my children, her death meant freedom for their father. They, in their innocence, blamed Generosa for taking their father and keeping him away. I understood their happiness to have their father back in their lives, but brought to their attention that two young children were now without a father and a mother. My heart went out to the twins who had become close stepsiblings to Tony.

The following day on the cover of the *New York Post* was a picture of Danny sitting bleary eyed at the Stanhope Hotel's lounge with a cigarette dangling from his lips, a drink in front of him, and a shopping bag with Generosa's ashes sitting on top of the bar. Next to her ashes were her favorite drink and a lit cigarette burning in an ashtray for her. The story titled, "To You, Generosa – Pelosi Toasts Ashes of Wife In Bar Where They Met."

The story described how Danny snatched Generosa's ashes

from the funeral home and how, at her request, wanted Danny to have a drink for them after her death in memory of when they first met.

All I could do was shake my head in disgust.

- TWENTY-FIVE -

Glory and Grief

*"Whatever hour God has blessed you
with, take it with grateful hand."*
—Horace

I took a break from the daily 'Danny headlines' and flew down to Melbourne in September to celebrate my fortieth birthday with my zany pal Joy and her jaunty fire department buddies that she worked with. These compassionate and courageous men whose job it is to save lives, helped in saving mine. They sent me home with an overdose of a super-duper laugh fix strong enough to last a good long while.

In the meantime, while I was away, my mother and Rachelle planned a surprise fortieth birthday party for me. In less than a week they managed to put together a gathering of twenty-five of my dearest female friends. My mother asked if each one of the girls would give a little speech on why they chose to celebrate my fortieth birthday with me. Halfway through the tributes all the women were bawling! My mother wrote me two poems and saved them to the end. The first one was a comical litany on how we differed as mother and daughter and the second a reflection of my life from birth to present day as seen through her eyes.

Twenty-five emotional, peri-menopausal women gathered in one room could be a dangerous thing! In between tears, there were giggles, from silent sobs to hearty guffaws, screeches and screams. Laughter really is the best medicine. I am grateful for these interludes of mirth that replenished my soul and helped to soften my facial muscles that had begun to take on the appearance of a chiseled face of stone etched with a permanent scowl.

A miracle of sorts took place at the beginning of the school year, Little Dan decided on his own to return to school. I met with the guidance counselor and the administration to determine what options he would have and if he could graduate with his class as scheduled. Mrs. Mulvaney, the high school counselor, put a program together for my oldest son. She arranged for him to double up on his classes, combining what he missed the previous year with the necessary credits for his senior year. He was only lacking a few credits and since he was an intelligent being and maintained high grades in the past, Mrs. Mulvaney felt confident he could pull this off with a little effort and motivation on his part.

It was a glorifying feeling to have Dan back in school, but it required much effort on my part to get him up in the morning. It was psychologically exhausting keeping him propelled in the direction of graduation.

On the other hand, I received a letter from Tony's school stating he wasn't able to focus in the classroom due to his high anxiety and was advised he was a candidate for home tutoring. Tony was released from the public school system for the remainder of the year and put on anti-anxiety medication. The tutoring solved the school's dilemma, but it added to my stress. I had to schedule the tutoring when an adult was home, which meant adjusting and readjusting my schedule and any other adult who could volunteer their time. Tony may have been relieved not to face the pressures of school, but he didn't relish home tutoring either. He bucked me every step of the way. In his own words he said he felt like a 'freak.' He was already singled out as the kid whose father was thought of as a murderer. Home tutoring set him further apart from his peers.

The morning struggles with my sons continued. I didn't have to wake Tony up for school, but I was subjected to his daily protests and refusals to cooperate. This was the on-going scene in my home everyday, compounded with the chore of getting his older brother Dan out of bed.

I had one son who was emotionally incapable of attending school, another son who was indifferent about graduating, and a twenty-one year old daughter who was attempting to live a normal life. By the time I arrived at work I was an exhausted bundle of nerves.

It didn't help matters any when the holidays rolled around to have Danny show up on Christmas Eve bearing ostentatious gifts. He bought Tony an adult sized high-priced CR125 Honda dirt bike, Rachelle enough cash for the cruise she was planning with her friends and dazzled Little Dan with a Christmas stocking filled with one thousand one-dollar bills.

I shuddered to think what the New Year had in store.

I had been contemplating whether or not to resume my education. With everything that was going on in my life I didn't see how I could manage more stress. But I had discovered that delving into my studies was therapy for me; it kept my mind off of the daily pressures and what I couldn't control. My books were my salvation. I had applied for the Doctorate Program in Education and was accepted in January. It was a good way to begin the year, something positive to look forward to.

March was another story. It is the month of the Spring Equinox, it can either come in as a lamb and out like a lion or in like a lion and out like a lamb. This spring was the latter, only the lion never left, and I don't mean the weather.

It was the month of dichotomies from extreme highs to irreversible lows. A month of pride. A month of grief. A month of facing realities.

Into the third week of March, Carol, (who was also working on her Doctorate), and I needed to fly down south to the university for a few days for our doctorate orientation. When we had done this in the past for our Master's, it was an exciting and exhilarating experience. We had behaved like giggling nervous schoolgirls on our first day and left feeling a sense of determination and pride, giving ourselves a big pat on our backs for our courage and fortitude. This trip, however, was anything but exhilarating.

The day I left for Florida, March 17, 2004, Danny phoned me to say there were rumors of his indictment, which could be as soon as the next day. For over a year I had anguished over this day, worried about how my kids would handle their father in jail for murder. I was going to be a thousand miles away and felt powerless. I knew I could count on my mother to help them cope, but felt I should be there. But since it was a rumor and not a fact, I had to sit back and wait on pins and needles for the next phone call. I half listened to the professor giving the doctorate students the run down of what it was going to take to obtain their degree.

"You might as well kiss your life good bye, say *adios* to your social calendar", the professor joked, "tell your husband, your wife, your friends, you'll see them in two years, because every moment you breathe will be devoted to study. You'll sleep with your books, you'll eat with your books, you'll ...."

I didn't take the professor's words as a threat; not having to think about anything but my books was a relief.

The following day, Thursday, March 18, Danny and his attorneys, accompanied by an entourage of reporters and cameramen, showed up at the Riverhead Courthouse with the understanding an indictment would be issued. Danny's lawyers thought it best he turn himself in, rather than take the risk of a surprise arrest. But when they arrived at the courthouse no one seemed to know anything about an indictment and Danny was sent home a public spectacle. I spent the night on the phone with Rachelle and my mother keeping me posted of the outlandish events, feeling completely helpless.

I was back home by Saturday, happy about the prospect of my doctorate and also concerned over the mystery of Danny's indictment. It was a frustrating and bewildering dilemma with no explanation. Every day we'd wake wondering if this could be the day. Not that I wanted to see him put in jail for murder, but the suspense was taking its toll on my family.

Whatever the reason for the lack of an indictment on Thursday the eighteenth, by Tuesday March twenty-third, one was issued; three days after the lion roared the announcement of spring. The morning before Danny was to turn himself over to the authorities he came over to the house to say good bye to the kids. I said a quick emotional farewell and left him alone with them. He took each one privately on the side and told them, "I love you, you listen to your mother, ya hear. I'm gonna be okay. I didn't do this thing and one day I'm gonna prove I'm innocent." To Little Dan he added, "you're the man of the house now, you gotta take care of your brother. Be an example to him, graduate from high school. Stay out of trouble, don't wind up like me." Rachelle's sobs echoed through the house. The four of us watched him leave from my bedroom window. I kept the kids home from school. Who could concentrate on a textbook?

Danny was indicted one hour later for a second-degree murder charge without the former fanfare and the ballyhoo of the week before. He was handcuffed and escorted to the Riverhead jail where he was held without bail. As far as Danny was concerned, this was not a supine, pusillanimous surrender, but a statement of his innocence. He gave a brief, but exhorting speech to the press expressing his itchiness for his trial to begin and his confidence of the outcome.

In contrast to Danny's cockiness and self-assuredness, I was frightened at how brute reality was sinking in, like quicksand that sucks you deeper and deeper into the earth. I had bore witness to the DA's canniness. She would not be a shrinking violet to Danny's bumptious big league attorneys.

In the middle of Danny's on again off again publicized indictment, my center held their Parent-Teacher conferences. I had no choice but to meet with the parents; escaping to my office was not an option. I often felt like I led two lives. On cue I could snap a finger and like a genie could magically transform from a frightened, humiliated, embarrassed woman, to the professional competent co-founder and director of a private non-for-profit preschool; shame and fear kept neatly tucked away behind a forced and simulated smile.

- TWENTY-SIX -

Angels in Action

The eye which I see God is the same eye which God sees me.
—Meister Eckehart

Three days after Danny's indictment, Carol and her friend Lisa picked me up on Friday afternoon for a weekend women's retreat in Montauk with Pastor Lydia. The weekend with the women from my church was just what I needed to help me sort through my emotions that were on overload, see-sawing up and down, juggled back and forth and spun round and round until I couldn't identify what I was feeling. Part of me was sad for Danny, saddened by the choices and decisions he made in his life, but a bigger part was furious with him *because* of those choices and decisions. My heart ached for my children and their innocence. They loved their father and believed *he* was the victim of this damn mess.

Carol and Lisa chatted quietly with each other while I sat in the backseat numbly watching the scenery whiz by. My situation was uncomfortable for most people; it was as awkward to talk about my current affairs as it was to remain quiet.

We stopped at a local pizza parlor for a late lunch, but I didn't think I could eat. While they were ordering a slice of pizza and soda, I looked down at the newspapers in the stand. Glaring up at me was Danny's picture on the front page. In large bold letters it read:

ELECTRICIAN INDICTED FOR MURDER OF WEALTHY
FINANCIER

There was no escape from the fact that the man I was once
married to for twenty years would be on trial for murder. No
snap of the finger could alter my overwhelming sadness or
lessen my shameful feelings. By the time we got to the retreat I
was wishing I were home in my cocoon. Thankfully I wasn't.

The three of us shared a suite at a beautiful resort on the
tip of Long Island. We dropped off our things and met Pastor
Lydia and the other women at the restaurant for the orientation.
The lively chatter of a hundred or so women filled the large
room that was set with a dozen round tables. Lisa, Carol and
myself made our way over to an empty table and were joined
by five jolly sprightly women that I recognized from church. It
was immediately apparent these jovial women, all around my
age, were close friends who had that special bond women have
when supporting one another through hard times. Smiles went
around the table and heads nodded in recollection of seeing one
another at church.

Pastor Lydia called the women together and asked everyone
to find a seat. She opened the evening with prayers, a short
sermon and a few moments of quiet reflection. Except for an
occasional cough, the room was quiet. The pastor gave a brief
synopsis of the weekend activities; we were to meet back at the
restaurant the next morning by eight o'clock for breakfast. After
breakfast we were to divide into groups of eight, return to the
resort and gather in one of the women's suite. Before leaving the
restaurant that evening, we needed to discuss among us whose
room we would use for our workshop. Since the five of them were
friends and had been on Pastor Lydia's retreats in the past, Carol,
Lisa and I left the decision up to them. There didn't seem to be
any question between them that we'd congregate at their suite.

After light refreshments of coffee, tea and cookies, we went
back to our rooms. I was relieved the evening was over and
happy to retreat to the sanctity of my room. It had been a long
emotional day.

We were up with the roosters and ready for breakfast. My stomach was growling. I hadn't eaten anything substantial for two days. The 'happy five', as I dubbed them, met us at the restaurant. I don't think I have ever seen such glowing bubbly perpetually merry women; they laughed at everything. There wasn't a trace of despair in any of them.

After prayers, a hearty meal, and some further instruction from Pastor Lydia, we headed for the suite, the 'happy five' leading the way, with Carol and Lisa in tow and me lingering behind. We formed a circle in the spacious room. The gaiety of the 'happy five' was momentarily put aside as each woman shared their personal tragedy. One of the women spoke calmly about the death of her teenage son, killed in a car accident the year before. She spoke of the earth shattering pain, the tremendous loneliness and the deafening stillness in her home. And her faith that helped her survive.

I was last to speak. I did not want to talk about my personal life and wanted nothing more than to escape the ongoing shame I felt. Yet I was tired of pretending I was strong and capable. If this woman who endured the greatest tragedy a mother can experience, the death of a precious child, could still find the courage to rise out of bed every morning, find beauty in a sunset and joy in her garden and remain steadfast to her faith, than I could as well.

I told them everything spilling forth my entire scandalous story. For the first time I revealed to strangers my terrifying arrest, the public shame and embarrassment, and the criminal charges against me. I paused, waiting for their response. One by one they came and embraced me. The weekend was more than I ever hoped it could be. For the first time in more months than I could recall I felt freed from the dark secrets that weighed heavy upon me.

Carol, Lisa and I were asked to join the 'happy five's prayer group. Every Thursday evening I made sure I was there. It was *their* prayers, *their* constant faith, and *their* devotion to God that moved mountains in my life. Their endless courage and faith and the sense of peace that surrounded them were a continuous source of inspiration to me.

At the beginning of the New Year, Carol and I had been informed that we were handpicked, along with ten other women, to be honored for the first annual "Women of the Year" award. We, like the other women, were offered the award in recognition of our dedication, our supreme efforts and the difference each of us made within our community.

We were a diverse and varied group of ages, shapes, sizes and color. We ranged from the woman who devoted her life to saving the teenage druggies on the streets of New York City, to the woman who devoted her life to saving the stray and abandoned cats in Nassau County. Whatever the cause, each woman gave of their time and often their personal resources. Carol and I were acknowledged for our efforts to educate children on the prevention of drugs and alcohol abuse, for offering a number of support groups for families in crisis and because of our hard work and tenacity of not giving up when faced with adversity.

The date of the function, March 30, was sandwiched in between Danny's indictment, and two days before my next court date, and on the second anniversary of Danny's brother's death. It wasn't until the day before the event that I discovered the theme of the ceremony was none other than, "The Wind Beneath My Wings."

The event took place at a prestigious restaurant in Westbury. It was an impressive extravaganza with delectable appetizers, an elegant entrée, and scrumptious desserts.

After mingling with our guests during the cocktail hour, the twelve honorees were asked to stand in a circle around the dance floor, our loving families and friends gathered behind us. Rising from below a portable floor in the center of our circle, drifted an ethereal mist and a lovely human angel. The woman was adorned with magnificent celestial white-feathered wings, in a melodious voice she sang Bette Midler's touching tune. The angel floated around the circle gazing at each woman as she sang. She lingered a second or two more when she reached me and lightly brushed my hand with hers. A roadside billboard could not have delivered a more a powerful message; my *guardian angel* was undeniably watching over me.

When the heart-rending tribute was presented to me I'm sure the spectators believed the muffled sobs from my family and dear friends were in response to the emotionally charged atmosphere, but those close to me knew the significance of this poignant evening.

During the last two weeks of March I was filled to capacity with a huge lump of contrary emotions all squeezed into one averaged-sized human being. The exuberant high at the acceptance into a doctorate program; the depressing shameful low of Danny's indictment; the pride of being one of twelve women hand-picked for "Women of the Year" award; and the inspirational gift of the 'happy five'. *Whew!*

- TWENTY-SEVEN -

Plugged Into Robot Mode

Worry Never Robs tomorrow of It's Sorrow;
it Only saps Today of It's Strength
—A. J. Cronin

April is usually the month that people either love or hate. Why? Because they either receive a hefty sum of money from the United States government or they need to pay a hefty sum out. I couldn't care less about my taxes that year. I had an accountant to take care of that. I was concerned about the first day of April - back to the courthouse for the LIPA charge. Would the judge know I was honored for an esteemed award two days before or would she appraise me as an unscrupulous pilferer of the Long Island Power Authority? Would she associate me with the Danny Pelosi indicted a week before for the murder of Mr. Ammon? If so, would that affect me? It didn't matter what she thought; the court date was postponed until the end of June.

With Danny in jail and no Generosa to see that I received child support, I was left with the responsibility of caring for my children and carrying a home whose monthly expenses were triple my monthly income.

After speaking with a financial advisor who was younger than my daughter, I was told I had no choice but to sell my home.

That was not what I wanted to hear. I did not want to stress my kids out anymore. Our home was the only form of stability any of us had in our lives.

There were slim pickings for other options. I could look for another job that would pay more, but that was easier said than done. I wasn't mentally, emotionally or physically capable of taking on such a giant challenge. And who would hire me, the ex-wife of an accused murderer? The filcher of electric? How could I start a new job with what I had going on in my life? Conclusion - that was not an option. Or I could refinance my house. That was a more logical solution, but not one that would put money in my pocket when I needed it.

I wound up making the decision to refinance, (really the only decision I had), to bide some time to figure out my life. To hold me over for the refinancing to be complete, I borrowed money from relatives and good friends. I detested being placed in that position. My blood can still boil when I think of the mess Danny left me in.

I had too much going on all at once; I didn't know which way to turn. I was thoroughly exhausted.

One evening while sitting in my mother's living room as I had done thousands of times, I looked up at a picture she had on her wall. Under this Native American picture of a wolf and an eagle was a quote from Chief Joseph from the Nez Perce,

"I am tired, my heart is sick and sad.

From where the sun stands.

I will fight no more forever."

That was how I felt. I was ready to surrender, wave the white flag. Give up. Call it a knockout. There was no energy left in the Eveready Bunny.

I plugged myself into robot mode and mechanically got through the days. A dim flicker of light made its way into the darkness when Little Dan's teacher called to tell me she believed that he could graduate. He needed to take on some extra assignments to boost his grades and pass every test with an 85

171

or better. The teachers were confident he would pass his finals with flying colors. It was the most hope I had had for quite a long time. My women's prayer group prayed diligently for my family and in particular for Danny to graduate.

I was due back in court, where a jury was to be selected and a trial was scheduled to take place, exactly the same week as my son's finals. In fact, I was told the trial would more than likely end on the same day of Danny's graduation, Friday, June 26.

Running on remote mode, I hastily planned my son's graduation party. I wanted to have every last detail taken care of in case I was in court everyday. My mother even suggested I plan a victory party along with Dan' graduation, but I was not all that confident.

My case was postponed again. I had a brief moment of relief knowing I wouldn't be facing a jury of my peers while my son was taking his finals, but panic quickly set in when I found out the next date was set for September – the same time Danny's murder trial was scheduled to begin. The thought of having the two of us on trial simultaneously terrified me. Besides what it would do to my children, I didn't think having my name on a court roster when Danny's name was making headlines would be beneficial to my case. I was worried that if the judge hadn't figured out that I was Danny's ex-wife at that point, she certainly would have by September and no good would come from that knowledge. My lawyer told me not to worry, go home and relax. He was sure he could get the judge to change the date. But I didn't go home and relax; I went home and collapsed.

There is a sun and it does come out from behind the clouds. On June 26, 2004 my son graduated from high school. Many of the graduates received honorary awards for exemplary grades and outstanding work within their school community. As far as I was concerned it was a miracle to see my son in a cap and gown. For him to reach that goal under the circumstances that he faced was more of an achievement than any award. When my son walked across the stage and was handed his high school diploma by the superintendent of schools, I think it was my family that hooted the loudest cheers in the auditorium, and there were plenty of happy hooting parents.

For a moment I detected sadness on my son's beaming smile. I know it was hard for him to turn his tassel to the other side of his cap without his father's baring witness to his momentous accomplishment.

I had a small party at my house to celebrate Little Dan's graduation, nothing like the grand festivities I had for Rachelle. Danny's absence hovered over the meager gathering like a dark gloomy film.

July and August were ultra quiet months, which wasn't necessarily good nor was it bad, just peculiar. It was the first summer I did not work at my center's summer camp, which was the first time since Carol and I began our programs for children ten years before. That in and of itself was an odd feeling, but the time away from work did allow me the opportunity to focus on my doctorate studies. My backyard was void of the activity of the previous summer, an empty abyss without kids splashing around in the over-sized eleven-foot deep pool until their lips were blue and their skin pasty and shriveled. Occasionally Tony would splash around to cool off on a hot stuffy night, and maybe I'd take a quick dunk in and out. There were no pizza parties, no bar-b-ques, no friends stopping over after work. The media took a break. And I wasn't due back in court until September. It was the summer to plug in my Eveready battery and recharge for the next set of events.

For a short while, and I mean a really short while, the burdens that weighed heavy on my shoulders were slightly lifted. With the help of my fully charged battery and a new set of boxing gloves, I was as ready as I was going to be to get back in the ring and face my opponents. My first victory was the postponement of my trial until November 8, grateful that I wouldn't be alongside my ex's public trial. The second victory was Tony's return to school in September. I had high hopes that he would follow in his big brother's footsteps and make it to the finish line, but he had years to go before that might be a possibility. I learned to live in the present, and for the present, my son was in school and I wasn't in court. But Danny's trial was quickly approaching and there would be no postponements.

- TWENTY-EIGHT -

A Father Takes The Stand

"Each man's life represents a road toward himself."
—Hermann Hesse

It took over three weeks for the opposing attorneys to sift through over five hundred prospective jurors to narrow down to the twelve that would serve on the "Danny Pelosi Murder Trial." The final choice included nine women and three men that would one day seal Danny's fate and the fate of my children's lives. The trial was set to commence on September 27, 2004.

My children felt it was their duty to be in court for their father. I thought it best that I wasn't. To see Danny sitting in a room accused of a brutal murder would have been more than my raw unsettled emotions could handle. I knew I would wind up feeling sorry for him, that out of all the human emotions, pity would be the one that would rise to the surface. I would have preferred my children didn't go either, but I allowed each one to make their own decision. They could not understand my reasons for not going and argued with me in defense of their father, but I stood by my conviction.

The press had hounded me for over three years; I was sure my presence at Danny's trial would open a Pandora's box that I preferred to keep sealed, for my children and for myself. As a possible witness for the prosecution I was told I would not be allowed to be present during the trial. I didn't know if this was a fact or not, but it was the excuse I needed to stay out of the courtroom.

I watched my kids get themselves up and ready to spend the day in the courthouse. They looked grown-up, the boys in sport pants, button down shirts and leather shoes, no sneakers. Rachelle's petite frame in a smart suit, her hair pulled up. But to me they were just children. Rachelle gave me a quick kiss with a quivering lip. They walked to her car with shoulders hunched, one following the other in a somber little parade. I worried if it was the right decision to let them go. With Danny being in jail since the day he was indicted, I wondered what effect it would have on them to see their father for the first time in six months - in a courtroom - on trial for murder.

When they arrived at the Riverhead Courthouse they were overwhelmed by the amount of TV vans from all the major stations that were lined up in the parking lot. Reporters from the various stations were conducting interviews on the courthouse steps. The press was everywhere.

As it turned out, my children didn't see their father that day, nor did anyone else. They milled around outside the courtroom with a horde of reporters, attorneys and curious on-lookers. For undisclosed reasons everyone was told to come back the next day. It wasn't until the third day that the court officer opened the courtroom doors - with a warning to the impatient mob. There was an orderly system in entering the room - first the court artists, then the press, followed by attorneys, assistant attorneys and law students and last - family members. The crowd elbowed their way into the small courtroom. The first two rows of seats were reserved for reporters and attorneys. Standing was not permitted. If you didn't have a seat, you were asked to leave. The kids were shoved to the back of the packed room and had to squeeze their three bodies into two seats in the last row. Rachelle was irate that family members, meaning her, would have to sit in the far back while gawking strangers had front row seats.

My children witnessed two officers, one on each side of their handcuffed father, escorted to the table where his three attorneys waited for him.

The bailiff announced the arrival of the jurors. From where Rachelle was sitting she couldn't get a good look at the twelve people who would judge her father. From what she could see, they looked nice enough.

Everyone was asked to stand when the judge entered then the kids squeezed back in their seats. The trial was about to begin – or so they thought. The District Attorney and her assistant shuffled through a mound of papers. With a stack of papers in her hand the DA walked to the podium. Instead of presenting her opening statement, she made a jolting announcement that Danny had a list of sixteen counts against him, from witness tampering to an alleged forty hours of confession on tape, and threatening the safety of her own children. The spunky DA claimed investigators came to her house the day before the trial and installed panic alarms, checked for listening devices and inquired about her children's bus schedule. Danny's attorney jumped from his seat, insisting this was a charade, and demanded to know from the prosecuting attorney why she advantageously waited until she had the attention of the press to reveal this information when she could have disclosed it in the privacy of chambers. He believed it to be an act of dupery, purposely to set the mood for the trial.

The judge pounded his gavel; court would be adjourned until the attorneys settled the matter. The courtroom was buzzing like bees in a hive. The judge left, the jurors filed out. The kids remained in their seats while Danny was handcuffed and led away. He peered over his shoulder, with a bogus smile he gave a wink as if to say, 'don't worry guys, everything's okay.'

The trial was postponed until the matter could be resolved. Tales of a mistrial were circulating faster than a tornado spinning across an open field.

That night Rachelle cried about the weight Danny had lost,

and how horrible it was to see her father in handcuffs.

"Mommy they made him wait until he was in his seat before they took his handcuffs off. Why couldn't they just let him walk in with some dignity? He's not a criminal. They haven't proved anything. I thought people were innocent until proven guilty. He should be allowed to come into the courtroom without handcuffs on." Little Dan echoed his sister's outrage, and Tony went to bed early. I knew they shouldn't have gone.

A mistrial was not called and the long awaited 'East Hampton Murder' trial was finally underway, almost three weeks later, with opening statements from both attorneys. The additional charges against Danny were taken up at a later date.

Rachelle made it her business to be present at the trial as often as possible. Knowing that news reports are often exaggerated, or at least not completely factual, she wanted to be sure to hear first hand what was being said in the courtroom. Like a court stenographer she took detailed notes, and in the evenings would relay the day's events to me.

Occasionally Little Dan would go with his sister, but needing to work and help out with expenses was his excuse not to go. Tony didn't need an excuse; he simply refused to return.

At first the reporters didn't know who Rachelle was, when they discovered her identity, she was chased like a fox in a hunt.

"Mom you can't believe what it's like! They run after me, clicking cameras in my face. They ask me a hundred questions. 'How do you feel having your father on trial for murder? What's it like seeing him in the courtroom? Do you think your father is guilty?' How do they *think* I feel? It's horrible. I hate those people! "

Each time Rachelle entered or exited the elevator on the fourth floor of the Riverhead Courthouse; the cameras clicked in rapid motion. She learned to walk with her head tucked in toward her chest facing the opposite direction of the cameras. They persisted to hound her anyway. Rachelle discovered an escape route, a staircase that the press was not allowed to trespass, a temporary safe place. But once she was in the parking field, the game of cat and mouse continued.

Rachelle listened day after day to one inflammatory testimony after another against her father. She heard and saw things no child should see or hear about their father.

"These people are lying, Mommy. They're twisting things around." Rachelle protested the day she returned from hearing one of Danny's former co-workers testify that a year before Mr. Ammon was murdered, Danny told him he would kill Ted to get his money. "How would Daddy know a year before that he was going to drive out to East Hampton and kill Mr. Ammon? He just met Generosa. That's ridiculous! How could the jury believe that?"

I let her rant and get out her frustrations. While she worried about what the witnesses were saying about her father I worried about the possibility of being subpoenaed. Word was out that Greg would be called to testify by mid October. If things followed course, as they did three years before when the detectives went to Greg first and me later the same day, I would be called shortly thereafter.

In the end, I was never called, to which I was grateful.

My mother began to attend the trial for the same reasons as Rachelle, to personally hear what was said and not what was printed in the newspapers. She agreed with her granddaughter that the reports were highly fabricated pieces of information based on a few actual statements, then written for the sensationalism that this trial was generating.

She too found it upsetting to see Danny bound in cuffs. Not that she hadn't wanted to tie him up to a post herself throughout my marriage and especially now.

"It's a shocking dose of reality that smacks you in the face," she would tell me later. She avoided eye contact with Danny as much as possible, mainly because she wanted to remain anonymous, but also she didn't want him to believe she had forgiven him for the heartache he caused her family.

Mom became one of the 'regulars', sometimes sitting off by herself, other times with Rachelle. The reporters were puzzled as to who she was, and on a few occasions attempted to find out. One reporter asked if my mother would like to read the papers while waiting for session to begin again, he offered his hand and said he was from the *New York Post*. My mother shook his hand back and with a big smile answered, "Hello, nice to meet you." My mother never disclosed who she was and remained the mystery woman to the end.

On a warm autumn afternoon when court was finished for the day, my mother sat outside the courthouse waiting for Rachelle. One of my mother's long time friends from high school days happened to be exiting from the courthouse and spotted her. She was there for jury selection for another case. The two stood chatting, each relaying why they were there. Rachelle met up with my mother and her friend and the three of them started to walk to their cars. Within thirty seconds reporters and cameramen pounced on them, even clicking their cameras on my mother's friend! Thereafter, whenever my mother left the courthouse, she made sure she left the building alone.

Rachelle found most of the financial testimony from both Generosa's and Ted's accountants monotonous and over her head. But my mother's ears would perk up like a dog detecting a bird in the bush when my name was mentioned, which she reported was way too often for her comfort. For more than two days the tedious financial statistics were reviewed. Prosecution clearly wanted to present to the jury the amount of cash that flowed through Danny's hands, which was a substantial amount. What was also brought up was the money that was deposited in my bank account, which was under both Danny's and my name. Danny had his name on Rachelle's account as well. According to Danny, his name was on the accounts, as per Generosa, so she could keep a close eye on where her money was going. However, this gave the impression that Danny was using my accounts to stash money and that I was in cohorts with his activities. Here my mother had to sit back and grit her teeth.

Danny had made arrangements to automatically transfer money from his bank account into mine to cover his monthly child support. The figures deposited were accurate, but there was no investigation of where the money went once deposited. The reports neglected to mention the costly bills to support a home. It was further implied that Generosa paid my alimony while Danny was in jail, which was only a half truth.

The question of how much Mr. Ammon was worth dragged on for days, some statistics indicating over eighty-four million, others less than forty-two million. Either way it was a lot of money, which was all left to Generosa in Ted's will – a fact prosecution declared as a motive for the murder.

After spending days at court, Rachelle would mull over the facts that were presented in court. "If Generosa didn't know the will was not changed, then Daddy didn't know. How could they say Daddy was after Mr. Ammon's money if no one knew how much he had and no one knew he hadn't changed his will?" This remained a question to the end.

By the end of October Greg was subpoenaed. Carol called to let me know Greg would be taking the stand the next day. This was a disturbing difficult task for Greg to have to testify against his long-time friend. Greg may not have approved of some of Danny's antics, but he loved him none the less. We were two families that took vacations together, that celebrated Christmas's together, that watched each other's children grow from infants to teenagers. It was a terrible strain on both families.

My mother and Rachelle made it their business to be at court when Greg testified to support both Greg and Carol. They met Carol and her eldest daughter in the lobby of the fourth floor courtroom. But to their surprise they found out that my father-in-law might be taking the stand instead. They made their way to the second row seats, and sat for several anxious minutes waiting for court to begin, not knowing who would be called to testify, Danny's friend or Danny's father.

The court came to order. After the opening preliminaries, prosecution called her first witness of that day to the stand - Danny's father.

On October 21, 2004, my son Tony's fourteenth birthday, his grandfather testified for the prosecution.

It was common knowledge my father-in-law's testimony would not be in his son's favor. But it was not known how heartbreaking, volatile and detrimental it would be to Danny's case, and to my family. The two of them had not spoken to one another for well over a year, maybe more. The family was divided: those who took Danny's side and those who didn't.

The DA cut right to the quick bringing up the wedding that Danny had attended on the day of our son's eleventh birthday three years before. "Mr. Pelosi, did Danny say anything to you the night of your relatives wedding?"

"He asked me, 'if someone wanted to get rid of something so that it could never be found, what would I do?'"(New York Post, 10/22/04)

My former father-in-law explained in detail that in today's modern world with DNA and such technology that nothing could really be disposed of forever. What my father-in-law was referring to was the disappearance of the hard drive which was part of a sophisticated surveillance system with hidden cameras in the East Hampton estate. Danny, instructed by Generosa, hired an alarm company to install the intricate system. The man who installed the equipment testified that Danny was one of two people who knew where the hard drive was hidden. Prosecution was attempting to prove to the jury that it was Danny who removed the hard drive because it recorded him as the murderer.

The DA's questioning focused on the night of the wedding, what Danny's behavior was on that evening, was the subject regarding what to 'get rid of' ever brought up again and what was his relationship with his son, to which Danny's father replied, a good one. Prosecution turned the podium over to the defense.

The defense's interrogation of Danny's father went from one shattering fiery statement to another, like igniting a match to gasoline and watching the fire creep along the intentional path of destruction erupting at its final destination in an irreversible explosion.

"Could you please describe to the jury, Mr. Pelosi, what kind of relationship you had with your son Danny."

Rachelle listened to her grandfather emotionally speak about the shame and disgrace her father brought upon his family and the good name 'Pelosi'. The many times her father was in and out of jail, how her grandfather would visit him on numerous occasions, the constant disappointments and the hope that his son would one day get his electrician's license and settle down. And the passionate statement that 'I love my son. I'm not proud of the things he's done in his life, but I love him.'

Danny's lawyer broke the heart-rending moment with a startling vehement accusation on whether Danny's father had been subpoenaed to court. To which my father-in-law replied he was not.

The defending attorney hesitated just enough to allow the impact of this revealing statement to be absorbed by the jury. Then he held up a letter.

"Is this a letter you wrote to your son?" defense prodded. Determining that it was, he read excerpts of the letter out loud to the jury, the letter Danny's father wrote his son some time ago acknowledging his disappointment in Danny and how he was returning Danny's childhood possessions because he no longer wanted ownership of them.

Danny's lawyer then presented a stirring emotive letter written by Danny begging his father for forgiveness. This letter was also read aloud.

"Why did Daddy's lawyer have to read these letters to the jury? They're personal.

They're none of anybody's business." Rachelle sobbed to me late that night lying in bed next to me. "Did you know grandpa gave Daddy back his old baseball cap from when he was a little boy and his report cards and all his old things? Why did he do that?" Rachelle cried angry defensive tears for her father, not aware that it was Danny who gave his attorneys the letters.

The interrogation ensued with defense accusing Dan's dad of favoring his 'beloved' youngest son, the former police officer, and blaming Danny for that son's death.

My father-in-law fervently stated that he did not blame Danny for his younger brother's death and added emphatically, "I love Danny. I'll love him until the day I die." Then stared directly at Danny and said, "I love you Danny, whether you know it or not." (New York Post, 10/22/04)

In a harsh retaliation the defending attorney pulled the implosive trigger, "then why did you break Danny's nose?"

"You said that? That's baloney." Danny's father shook his head in a recriminating loathsome glare at his son. "You told them that! Shame on you! I broke your nose?"(New York Post, 10/22/04)

My father-in-law's testimony ended in a courtroom drama, the jury witnessing the hurtful animosity between a father and his son.

That afternoon my father-in-law came to the house to see Tony for his birthday, but he wasn't home. Dad hugged me, told me he would always love me, he said this was the hardest thing he ever had to do in his life, he hoped the kids could forgive him, and left with the two of us sad and grieving. If my father-in-law ever regretted what he did, I may never know. The day's events could never be reversed. The damage was done.

Rachelle's grandfather called her later in the evening inquiring if she was okay. He had seen her crying in the courtroom. He had hoped that Rachelle would not be in court the day he took the stand and worried how this would effect her. She respectfully told her grandfather she was confused and taken back by the shocking information she heard, she knew there had always been differences between her father and him, and that she was sad to hear about the kind of relationship they actually did have. He was crying when he hung up with her. It was the last time she spoke with her grandfather or saw him for well over a year.

Danny had given his children instructions not to speak to the man who called himself their grandfather. They were torn between the love for their father and the love for their grandfather, a man they had up to that day only fond memories. The man who gathered all his grandchildren together to bake homemade apple pies and host Easter egg hunts in his backyard. A good, loving grandfather. The happy holidays of yesterday will remain lost memories.

Greg's testimony later that same day was almost like a breath of fresh air in comparison to the heavy dramatic scene earlier in the day with my father-in-law. Although a witness for the prosecution, it was clear that Greg was Danny's buddy and not pleased with being in the hot seat. At times Greg had the jurors and the courtroom chuckling when relating the incident of the 'stun-gun-game'. When the gun Danny ordered was delivered to the New York job, Danny like a kid with a new toy, dared his workers to get zapped, offering them a hundred dollars for a zap.

The DA questioned Greg on whether he thought it abnormal for someone to intentionally zap an innocent person with a stun gun.

"No," Greg answered shrugging his shoulders, "that's just how Danny is."

Greg, not intending his honest response to cause a wave of laughter, angered the judge who pounded the gavel, ordering quiet in the courtroom. He instructed the court officers to remove anyone who showed disrespect for the law; future entry would be denied.

"That District Attorney is trying to make it sound like Daddy sneaks up behind people and jabs them with a stun gun." Rachelle complained. "His workers didn't care. It was a joke to them. She wants people to think he's mean and sadistic. Daddy couldn't even put our dog to sleep, remember how he had the vet come over everyday to give Ben an injection? He couldn't even set a mousetrap! He even made steps for the raccoons to climb out of the attic! I hate that woman!"

As the trial continued, more confusing and conflicting questions arose with the prosecution and defense competing over the disputable evidence. Each team was fully armed with their own set of high-priced specialists in their chosen field. Men who traveled the globe armed with umpteenth degrees and lifetimes of experience attesting to their professional judgement. Yet the opinions of the masters of forensic medicine differed as night to day. One expert witness for prosecution testified with a confident conclusion that the death of Mr. Ammon occurred at the time of day to incriminate Danny, between midnight and 8 a.m., based on the digestive contents found in Mr. Ammon's stomach: tuna steak, rice and asparagus along with three glasses of white wine.(CBS 2 NY News, 11/22/04) The opposing expert swore there was no way to determine the exact time of death, due to the few glasses of Chardonnay Mr. Ammon had with his dinner the night the murder occurred, which would alter the digestive process and the break down of enzymes. Defense asked the prosecution's witness if he agreed with an article published in the *American Journal of Clinical Nutrition* that said the type of foods eaten by Ammon were more likely to be digested in two to three hours rather than four to ten. To which he confidently replied, "he did not accept that information and added there are widely varying views on fixing the time of death based on a victim's stomach contents."(CBS 2 News, 11/22/04)

A second set of experts called to the stand specialized in the physical effects 'stun gun' attacks had on the human body. Here too, were contrasting testimony. Prosecution's witness testified that Ammon had puncture-type marks on his neck and back that he was unable to identify during the autopsy, but said, "the injuries were consistent with those that might have been suffered by someone who was zapped with a stun gun."(CBS 2 News, 11/22/04) It was further stated that the marks on his body could only have been caused by repeated zaps with a particular type of stun gun, the same type of stun gun Danny had purchased. But the defense witness testified there no stun gun marks found on Mr. Ammon's body. In addition the type of gun Danny had purchased would only give a slight shock like an accidental contact with a low voltage live wire.

Days were spent convincing the jury that their expert was the true expert. Neither of the opposing professionals waived their opinions. The prosecution and the defense were akin to two sleek physically fit high-endurance million-dollar race-horses running neck to neck in the famous Kentucky Derby. Occasionally one would fall back a few yards, only to catch up and gallop past.

The day the graphic autopsy photos of Mr. Ammon's na-ked, brutally beaten body was put on display, and testimony was presented as to the horrific manner in which Mr. Ammon was killed, was the day my daughter began to fall apart and the day my nightmares began. The medical examiner testified Mr. Ammon "died of blunt force of trauma, at least three dozen savage blows to his head, as well as numerous broken ribs and other injuries. The injuries were so violent they appeared to be more consistent with those suffered by a person involved in an automobile crash. The autopsy determined "that the head had the external evidence of the most severe injuries, but was unable to say the exact number of blows to Ammon's head because of 'overlapping and intersecting' wounds, but said it was at least 30-to-35."(CBS 2 News, 11/17/04)

At twenty-two years of age, I could not keep Rachelle from going to the trial, but I did convince her to go only on the days she was off from work, rather than continuing to take days off. She had been working for me part time because I didn't feel she could handle taking on more hours while the trial was go-ing on. Pounds were sliding off her already petite frame, like snow melting off a roof on a sunny afternoon. Her normally rosy healthy complexion became a pale washed-out gray. Deep circles formed under her bright beautiful dark eyes. She picked at her food with a bird-like appetite. Sleep, when it did come wasn't until the early hours of the morning and that was after hours of staring at some mindless TV movie. I'd find her curled on the couch in a drug-like sleep, hesitating to wake her. On the days she would go to court, she would be up and out without the need of a wake-up call. Ghoulish nightmares would wake her and she'd seek solace in bed with me, saying over and over again that her father could not have committed this murder, or any murder. Rachelle was positive, without an inch of doubt that her father was innocent.

"There is no way my father murdered Ted. If he can't kill an animal, how is he supposed to kill a person? He wouldn't beat anyone that way. Daddy didn't care about money, Generosa was getting twenty-five million dollars in her divorce settlement, to Daddy that's like a four-year old with twenty dollars. Generosa did this, I know it and she set Daddy up. She knew she was dying of cancer, and she didn't care. She didn't care about Ted's money, she just wanted him dead and she made it look like Daddy did it. She was a witch. An evil hateful witch. I wish they would let me go up there and testify."

There was a smoldering flame flaring in my young daughter, a blazing frustrating misdirected combustible fire with no outlet.

One evening Rachelle joined me at my mother's rather than going to the movies with her boyfriend. My mother cooked us a delicious meal, vegetable barley soup, hearty nine-grain bread and baked apples; we tried to pretend everything was normal. Rachelle gobbled her dinner down; it was the first decent meal she had eaten in days.

We did our best to avoid talking about the trial and anything related to it, but that was ridiculous. There wasn't anything on any of our minds but the trial.

Rachelle was the first to broach the subject. "Nan, you've been at the trial almost everyday, what do you think?"

"Well," Mom began looking at me for approval, glad to have the chance to let her granddaughter know what her thoughts were. "In all honesty Honey, I don't know what to say. Everyday it's more confusing than the day before, it's one mystery after another. *Every* piece of evidence is questionable. Prosecution brings on some expert that sounds very convincing, but then your father's attorney questions that witness and what sounded so plausible just a few moments before, winds up sounding doubtful. Like the stain that was found on the floor on the passenger side of Generosa's station wagon, the supposed 'get-a-way car'. The DA said it was blood. But the defense's expert said that when the car was cleaned and the carpet was shampooed, there was no way to determine if it was blood or not, that it could just as easily have been a drink one of the kids spilled. Then there's the question of a pubic hair that was supposedly found on Mr. Ammon's shoulder which defense insists was a hair from a gay lover Ammon met at a gay beach in East Hampton the night he was murdered. But the DA's expert said the hair in question was attached to Ted's shoulder. Now that hair is nowhere to be found."

"What about that drop of blood that was found near the surveillance system?" Rachelle said agreeing with my mother's notion that there was more than an air of mystery surrounding the trial.

"I know, it's been confirmed it's not your father's, but no one seems to know whose blood it is."

"How could they not know Nanny, doesn't that sound suspicious? On CSI they can identify blood that's years old."

"Yes and in one hour CSI has found the weapon, the murderer and the case is solved. Unfortunately this isn't CSI. These two attorneys are like skilled chess players, strategically maneuvering their pawn."

"Danny's lawyer did point out," Mom said momentarily directing her thoughts to me, "that the DA didn't address the undetermined source of blood found in the hidden compartment where the hard drive was set up. So that's left hanging in midair. They have a minute by minute record of Danny's cell phone activity that proves he was in Center Moriches at 1:30 in the morning, so if it's at least a forty-five minute drive to East Hampton, according to the defense experts who say that Mr.

Ammon died earlier in the evening, that would have Danny nowhere near the crime scene at the time the medical examiner says Mr. Ammon died. Then prosecution says the phone was off during the *estimated* time Mr. Ammon was murdered, implying it was off because Danny was in East Hampton committing the murder, but defense says the phone was off because Danny was sleeping."

Mom stopped for a moment - took a sip of tea - then continued with the perplexing proclamations as if we were discussing some other family's lives.

"There are these three or four inmates that were in jail with Danny who say that he confessed to them and one of them taped their conversation, but due to some legal technicality it can't be submitted as evidence. And of course there's the missing hard drive, to which the DA said no one but Danny knew where it was."

"That's a lie!" Rachelle protested. "What about the people who installed it? Or Generosa? The alarm system wasn't a secret; Daddy told everyone about it, anyone could know where the hard drive was. And *if* it was Daddy that took it, don't you think he'd be smart enough to bring a screwdriver to remove the door instead of ripping it off its hinges like that witness said?"

"I know, nothing makes any sense to me. There are too many loose ends. It's one baffling puzzle after another. Blood that can't be identified, a pubic hair that's taken a walk, a hard drive that's disappeared, confessions from convicted criminals that can't be used. Oh, and listen to this! Prosecution calls this woman to the stand; turns out she had been dating Danny. I know that's no shock, but she was going out with him around the same time that Mr. Ammon was murdered. In fact she went with Danny to his cousin's wedding. Maybe that's the reason he never made it back for Tony's birthday cake?"

"I always wondered why Generosa didn't go to the wedding with Danny." I mused.

"Maybe she was too busy planning to kill her husband." Rachelle added sarcastically.

Mom raised her eyebrows – maybe Rachelle had a point.

"I doubt if we'll ever know the answer to that one, Shelly. What we do know is this woman went to the wedding with your father and apparently they continued to date until he married Generosa. She actually believed she had a future with him until she spotted a wedding ring on his finger."

"Wait a minute, she thought *she* had a future with Danny, who wasn't even divorced from me, and was living with Generosa!"

"That's typical of Danny, isn't it?" Mom cuttingly remarked. "Anyway, she testified that Danny came to her apartment one night acting weird, paranoid is what she said, he kept looking out the windows as if he thought someone was after him. He pulled down the blinds, and whispered to her that he murdered Mr. Ammon; supposedly he gave detailed information from that night. When she asked him why he did this horrible thing, she said he pounded his chest and said 'because there is a monster inside of me.'"

"Oh my god. She said that?"

"Yes and I think her testimony is pretty damaging. Danny's attorney told the jury she had an axe to grind because she thought she and Danny had a future, but when she found out he was married, she made up this ridiculous story. According to Danny's lawyer there were several individuals who testified against Danny to get even with him, including your father-in-law. At times I'm certain the prosecution has the stronger case, but then that evidence is squashed by the defense and vice versa. There is nothing that has been said that is clear cut and of sound proof. Nothing."

The trial was coming to a close by the second week of December. The roster of witnesses had their say. For over two months experts and non-experts from every field took the stand. There were forensic experts, medical experts, stun-gun experts, pathologists and people skilled in alarm surveillance systems. Cellular records and financial accounts were investigated, bank accounts were scrutinized and gory photos of Mr. Ammon's naked body were displayed. A battery of witnesses testified to Danny's alleged confessions, and the nannies of the Ammon children attested to Generosa's temper tantrums and alcohol consumption. Various Pelosi family members took the stand, even the local merchants from the cleaners where Danny had his suits tailored, and the car mechanic that serviced Danny's vehicles and detailed the infamous station wagon. From a best friend to inmates looking for a get-out-of-jail card, to chauffeurs, business partners and girlfriends, (both Danny's and Ted's), all swore to tell the truth and nothing but the truth. Throughout the three months Danny remained confident. The papers printed that Danny would turn and look at whoever was sitting behind him and with a cocky self-assured smile, haughtily declared, "I'll be home for Christmas."

In the afternoon of Tuesday, December 7, 2004, Rachelle and my mother were sitting in the courtroom as they had been for most of the trial. Danny's attorney was at the podium finishing up with a witness when Dan turned and mouthed to Rachelle, "I'm going to testify." There was a buzz through the courtroom much like hornets fleeing after their nest is attacked. Those reporters who caught Danny's shocking whispered proclamation jumped from their seats, their heads spinning like the exorcist, 'what did Danny say?' 'Did Danny say he was going to testify?' They zipped from their seats to the lobby, and speed dialed their headquarters with the dramatic news.

Danny's attorney strolled back to his seat, presumably unaware that Danny had blabbed the astounding news to everyone who had a bird's eye view of his client.

When the court officer asked the defending attorney who his next witness was, he rose from his seat and announced, "I call Danny Pelosi to the stand."

The buzzing escalated from a hornet's hum to the drone of an entire bee colony. Outcries of utter astonishment were murmured throughout the courtroom. Prosecution, dumfounded that defense allowed his client to take the stand, exclaimed to no one in particular, "this is too good to be true," as Danny made his way to the witness stand, nervous yet composed.

In ninety seconds Danny's attorney pumped six questions at

him beginning with, 'were you in East Hampton on 10/20/2001?' and ending with 'did you murder Ted Ammon?' Danny answered each question with two simple words, "absolutely not".

The DA requested a recess until the next day to gather her massive artillery of firing weapons to be aimed directly at her target - Danny. Her statement to the press that afternoon was, "the key witness said pretty much nothing, nobody here expects to hear the murderer say, 'I did it.'" She added smugly, "Defense has evidently lost control of his client."(Court TV.com, 12/07/04)

Danny's decision to testify on his own behalf was the hottest news to come off the press, at least until the next week.

Rachelle and Little Dan were frightened at the prospect of their father taking the stand, "What if he says something stupid Mom, to tick the DA off?" Little Dan worried.

"I read in the papers that no one who takes the stand wins the case,' Rachelle cried, "Why is Daddy doing this?"

"Because he wants to tell his side of the story," Little Dan answered his sister in defense of his father.

"You just said you hope he doesn't say anything stupid."

They bickered back and forth on the pros and cons of their father testifying, understanding and not understanding their father's need to defend himself.

The two of them were at the courthouse on Wednesday morning, December 8, an hour before the doors were unlocked. My mother canceled her yoga class and met them. By the time she got to the fourth floor courtroom it was packed, as it was on the day of opening statements. The kids were on one side of the room and my mother found a seat on the opposite side, ironically among the legal community, lawyers, law students, assistant district attorneys, and her, the former mother-in-law of Danny Pelosi.

Danny was in the hot seat four hours. The District Attorney did a superb job of rapidly loading and reloading her arsenals, firing one accusation after another.

Rachelle and Little Dan both agreed that the District Attorney did her best to get Danny to lose his temper. At one point the DA sneered, "as long as Ted was alive, you couldn't have any peace with Generosa. You couldn't take it any longer," and Danny replied with, "you phrase this with such drama, it wasn't that way."

The District Attorney kept her aim on her target, hoping for a bull's eye. "You simply went out to East Hampton to knock some sense in his head, and you lost it, didn't you?"(Court TV.com, 12/09/04) She might have gotten Danny ruffled, but he never lost control. "That's absolutely not true," he answered.

The petite prosecuting attorney who could have passed for a preschool teacher continued with her battering accusations that Danny wanted Generosa's money and would go to any length to obtain it, including the apparent sadistic joy that Danny got from his supposed repeated jabbing at Mr. Ammon with the stun gun and *"bashing his brains in."*

"I think Daddy did good on the stand," my son said, "he had nothing to hide, he just wanted people to hear what really happened."

My mother on the other hand thought he sounded like a fool. "I couldn't believe what he was saying, Tami. He was talking as if he was sitting around the bar shooting the breeze with the guys, not on the witnesses stand for murder. He rambled on and on going from one thing to another. When his attorney told him to sit back and relax and asked him if he wanted some water, do you know what Danny said? He said, 'I need a drink,' and he didn't mean water! Of course that did get a few laughs. I think for a moment that everyone forgot that they were sitting in a court of law. The judge lost his patience more than once, he kept reprimanding Danny for not sticking to the questions asked. I guess giving Danny the benefit of the doubt, if I were up there I'd want to have my chance to tell my story. But I'm not sure he got his story across, whatever his story might be."

When prosecution was finished with Danny, his attorney redirected his questioning back to his client, and out of nowhere shifted the course of the case to Generosa as being the possible murderer. He questioned Danny if Generosa ever asked him to kill Mr. Ammon and naturally Danny said yes. All of a sudden the finger was pointed at Generosa and where she was the night of the murder. My mother thought it was too late in the game to start making those accusations.

"There was one thing that Danny's lawyer said that was somewhat in Danny's favor," Mom noted. "He said that 'even though Danny is a self-styled storyteller, gambler, drinker and womanizer, his vices stop short of homicide.'(Court TV.com, 12/09/04) I think most people who know Danny, especially those who've known him for years, will agree to that. Even me."

But then his lawyer said, "you've told many boastful stories in your life, haven't you?" And Danny answered proudly sitting tall in his seat as if this was some great accomplishment, "yes, I have." The attorney continued with "you could say you are a bullshitter right?" and Danny inflated even more, "absolutely."

The moment he ended his questioning, the DA jumped to her feet for one last dig, "are you *bullshitting* the jury *now*, Mr. Pelosi?" Danny said defiantly, "no, I'm not." (Court TV.com, 12/09/04)

"I think the line of questioning of Danny's lawyer missed the boat with that last comment," Mom remarked. "He throws this *bullshitting* thing in after making implications that Generosa murdered Ted. How can the jury believe Danny is a storyteller on some things and then turn around and say that what he testified to is not bullshitting?"

Mom shook her head at me, "I don't know Tami, that was one hell of a backfire as far as I'm concerned. To top it off, those were the last words the jury heard before ending for the day. And closing statements are on Friday. The judge told the jurors to pack a bag, they're going to be sequestered and will be deliberating over the weekend. This is it, Tam. Next week at this time there may be a verdict."

The burden of the trial drove a wedge deeper into my family, each of us fleeing to our own place of escape for as long as we could. My schoolwork was definitely a distraction, but a temporary one. At night I was alone with my own tormented thoughts, playing the gruesome murder scene over and over again in my mind. Rachelle and Little Dan were so certain their father was innocent. Tony was too withdrawn to know what tortured thoughts he had. And me – I didn't know anything anymore. I couldn't imagine Danny savagely beating someone to death. It wasn't possible. I knew him too well. He would not be found guilty. There wasn't even any solid proof; even the first homicide detective on the scene the day Mr. Ammon's naked battered body was found stated it was a crime of passion. If that were the case, I don't see how that would connect Danny. Danny is shrewd. *If* he intended to kill Mr. Ammon he wouldn't have left a trail leading to him. He wouldn't be so dumb to have shut the alarm system down a few minutes before committing a murder and then ripped the hard drive out that was hidden behind a wall. But *did* Generosa antagonize him to the point that he went there to knock some sense into Mr. Ammon's head like prosecution said? Was it *Generosa* with the help of someone else who beat Ted to death with repeated blows to his head? *Did* Danny come in after the fact and clean up the mess, remove the blood stained sheets and the hard drive, and promised a hefty payment in return for keeping his mouth shut? Or was I in denial like the detectives told me?

I couldn't believe I could actually possess these evil thoughts. Danny had a bad temper, it was true, he could bellow loud enough to rattle the windows; he could send the kids scurrying to their rooms with one word – NOW! But to commit a cold violent act to another human being? No. It just was not possible. But – *what if it was*?

- TWENTY-NINE -

God Works in Mysterious Ways

*"...the relation of the sexes...knows of but one great
thing; to give of one's self boundlessly, in order to
find one's self richer, deeper and better."*
—Emma Goldman, Anarchism

In spite of the daily pressure of the trial, and the haunting question of whether or not Danny committed the horrific crime, I was emotionally stronger than I had been in months. Aside from my prayer group and my faith, the only thing I can attribute my newfound strength to was Andy, a man I met just before Danny's trial began. I had prayed for God to get me through the trial and He sent me Andy. When I was with him I could forget the grief, the sadness, the shame and the fear. I could smile, relax, and be mellow. For the first time in my life I felt whole. Not used. Not a part of something or someone else.

It was interesting how I met Andy; God does work in mysterious ways. For months my friends had been pestering me to date. One of the women I worked with had been dallying in some on-line dating service and convinced me to try it. Reluctantly, I gave in. I was inundated with a variety of interested individuals who emailed me only one day after my short and to-the-point biography was listed. Friends said I should be flattered but I found it to be overwhelming. It was a lengthy process to sift

197

through their personal chronicles and weed out the ones I wasn't attracted to. The copious response did not lift my self-esteem, it only made me feel like I was shopping for a pair of shoes that I really didn't want. I finally narrowed the choices down to three, emailed each one and within a few weeks I was 'dating'.

It was weird to meet someone I didn't know at some designated place, have some superficial conversations over a meal I couldn't eat and try to get a glimpse at my watch without them noticing. They were each pleasant enough, educated, average looking businessmen. I couldn't wait for dinner to be over, brush them off with an, "I'll email you," and make a dash to my car. I'd come home from my date nauseous and swear I wouldn't do it again, but my friends continued to badger me, trying to convince me that it would get easier with each date. It didn't get easier. I took a stand and refused to subject myself to another uncomfortable evening. "If God wants me to date," I said adamantly, "then He has to bring him to my door."

Ironically at the end of June a man who was scanning the dating service saw my picture and my bio and emailed me. He wrote, "I know you're going to think this is weird, but I have a brother who is going through a divorce and I think the two of you would hit it off." After a couple of emails back and forth with the brother who was playing matchmaker, I was convinced he wasn't joking and agreed that his brother Andy could connect with me by email, which he did. We sent a few pictures and chit chatted back and forth via the Internet for a couple of weeks, then I didn't hear from him anymore. I figured he had his own problems and I certainly had mine. I was relieved of the additional pressure this email 'dating' was causing.

Surprisingly on September 13, just before Danny's trial was about to begin, I received an email from Andy wanting to know how I was. I decided it would be best to air my dirty laundry right then and there rather than popping the cork over dinner as I had done on the other dates and then watch as these men attempted to conceal their shock. Andy didn't choke or hang up on me, instead we made plans for an official date the following Saturday night. And rather than meeting at some restaurant, Andy came to pick me up – at my house – to my door. Just as I asked!

I was more nervous on this date than on the other three. First of all I didn't feel in control not having my car as a means of escape, but more than that I had that inner feeling that this would be more than a one-night date. Just to play it safe though, I made a plan that one of my friends would call me on my cell and if I needed an out I would pretend there was an emergency and have to go home.

When Saturday night arrived I had butterflies multiplying in my stomach faster than the seconds that were ticking away. When Andy's car pulled into the driveway I had to pee even though I had just gone twenty seconds ago. I ran to the bathroom, dribbled a trickle of pee, ran back through the hallway pulling up my pants, picked a few dog hairs off my sweater, grabbed the door knob, took a deep breath, then opened the door as if I'd been doing this sort of thing all my life.

Andy was drop dead gorgeous! The first thing I noticed was the twinkle in his light hazel eyes and his pleasing smile. His dark wavy hair speckled with gray was neatly combed back. He was slightly taller than average with a trim but muscular build. He was casually dressed in jeans and a blue and white striped button down long sleeve shirt. After an awkward five seconds and a quick introduction to my dogs, we headed out for our dinner date. I intentionally planned this evening when I knew each of my kids would be out. If I wasn't ready for this dating thing, I didn't expect them to be.

Andy chose a quaint restaurant with a splendid manicured lawn with grounds that were covered in a glorious array of fall foliage, topped with a captivating candlelit interior. I turned my cell phone off. I wasn't going to need any rescuing.

It was an enjoyable relaxed evening; the conversation flowed like a soft caress. I felt as if I had known him forever. I found Andy to be as comfortable as an old pair of slippers.

Andy was as different from Danny as any two individuals could be. He was stable and down to earth. He was a man who would gladly spend his hard-earned money to see his family happy without going over board and putting his family in debt. He didn't need to flash a hundred-dollar bill around in some egotistical display and then have to worry where the grocery money would come from. Andy was respectful and not one to question about my personal or public life. That wasn't necessary, all he needed to do was read the newspapers or listen to the news.

The day after Danny's father testified I came home from work to find that Andy had sent me an adorable Vermont Teddy Bear. Tucked in the bag was a thoughtful card that read, 'try not to worry so much.' This little brown bear wasn't a shut-me-up-gift or an ease-the guilty-conscious-gift, it was a gift from the heart, from someone who took the time to think of me.

Needless to say, after our first date I came home to dozens of messages on both my cell and home phone and spent the next few hours reciting the entire evening detail by detail to my mother, Rachelle and Joy.

On our way to another spectacular restaurant for our second date, I silently sent a prayer up to my *angel* asking him to send me a sign that I was doing the right thing. My sign came a few minutes later.

We were a little early for our reservation and decided to wait for our table at the bar. When I sat down at the twenty-foot long bar I couldn't help but notice *the hundreds of pennies* that were inlaid under a thick lacquered finish. My guardian angel certainly heard my prayers. I decided to share the story with Andy about the relationship I had with my brother-in-law and the *agreement* we had regarding the pennies. Amazingly he didn't think I was off my rocker and simply said, "I guess I have your angel to thank."

I relaxed and enjoyed that evening and the many other evenings that were to come. We soon began to see each other on a regular basis and spent almost every other weekend together when he didn't have his children.

Andy was exactly what the doctor ordered. A gift from God. An abeyance from the turmoil.

- THIRTY -

"It Was That Man!"

"God asks no man whether he will accept life. This is not the choice. You must take it. The only choice is how."
—Henry Ward Beecher

It was a raw windy morning on Friday, December 10, the day of the closing statements. Rachelle and Little Dan were at the courthouse early to beat the hordes of spectators, the gawkers, those individuals who have nothing else to do with their lives. The same people who must chase after ambulances and fire trucks, just so they can cluck their tongues and say how horrible it was to witness the pain.

There was a long line of freezing individuals when my mother got there, inching their way closer to the courthouse doors, eventually huddling in the wind tunnel of the entranceway like cattle in a boxcar. The press was there in droves, standing in the drafty alcove, clicking pictures of the family members. Rachelle sat next to my mother, Little Dan behind them. A nervous hum generated throughout the courtroom, attorneys shuffled their papers or filled cups of water. Occasionally a cough was heard or the crackle of a paper wrapper from a cough drop. Danny was dressed in a smart black suit, white shirt and dark tie. He was escorted to his seat by court police, as was the custom since the beginning of the trial. His usual wink was lacking confidence and for the first time his jaw was set tight. The bailiff announced the arrival of the judge, the jury entered, the court was in order.

The defending attorney was the first to present his summation. It took him three hours to remind the jury that the four principal prosecution witnesses may have had motives behind their testimonies.

"All four people have one thing in common, they come with an agenda, an axe to grind, a grudge to bear, or an advantage to gain." (Court TV.com, 12/13/04)

He recalled the attention of the jurors to the fact that Generosa had a deep hatred for her estranged husband whom she believed was hiding millions from her.

He emphatically posed the questions, "where was Generosa Ammon on that night? You haven't heard a single witness or anything about where she was that night. It was Generosa Ammon who complained, 'I can't live on $5 million dollars;' it was Generosa Ammon not Danny Pelosi who was full of hate and anger."(Court TV.com. 12/13/04)

He reiterated there was no physical evidence, no eyewitness that conclusively incriminated Danny. "What the prosecution has presented here is built on quicksand, speculation and guesswork." He contended the time of death was hours earlier based on his pathologist's analysis of the contents of Ammon's stomach, which Danny's cell phone records clearly indicate that he was no where near East Hampton. Defense closed its statements with a final reminder to the jurors that they had to reach a verdict based on evidence not emotion, probabilities or how they felt about the defendant.

"Fact is", Danny's attorney said, "Danny Pelosi is a lot of things. He's had a lot of bumps on the road in his life, but he is not a killer...this is not a referendum on whether you like Danny Pelosi, but whether there is substantial evidence."(Court TV.com, 12/13/04)

Both my mother and Rachelle called me during the lunch break in between the final summations.

"I think Daddy's lawyer did real good," Rachelle announced

hopefully. "I kept watching the jurors and I saw them nodding their heads like they were agreeing with him."

This time my mother concurred with Rachelle. "I think," my Mother said choosing her words carefully, "that Danny's attorney packaged everything together logically and sensibly, whatever doubts may have been lingering were cleared up. Even though his tactic of bringing the focus on Generosa came late in the game, I think he made substantial headway with the jurors. If nothing else, it certainly gave them something to think about. There truly is no proof at all, and every piece of circumstantial evidence is also questionable."

"How was Danny?" I asked my mother, not really wanting to know.

"He looked relieved. You can tell he puts a lot of faith in his lawyers. I think he feels pretty confident at this point. Of course let's see what the DA has to say. She doesn't miss a thing. Maybe she was a detective before becoming a lawyer. I'll call you as soon as court is over."

Whatever spark of hope defense may have lit, the prosecuting attorney quickly extinguished. Unlike Danny's attorney who referred to his notes, the DA was like an actress on the stage, her script memorized, her theatrics perfectly executed.

In a dramatizing opening statement, the DA announced "this is not a whodunit, this is not the bogey man, it's that man,"(Court TV.com, 12/13/04) and flamboyantly turned on her heel and pointed her finger at Danny. "That is the man", she continued, "the only man who entered Ted Ammon's life. That man is an alcoholic prone to fisticuffs and he's a lousy gambler."(Court TV.com, 12/13/04)

She spoke about Danny's belief that Ammon was worth $300 million and how he wanted a good chunk of that, even if he had to commit murder. The DA went on with how convenient it was for Danny to suggest that it was Generosa who committed the brutal and savage crime at this stage of the game when Generosa is not able to defend herself. She reminded the jury that Ted Ammon was a man six feet tall and Generosa a petite five foot two, and according to Danny's own testimony Generosa was drunk on the day of the murder.

"That is not a one-hundred and twenty pound Generosa Ammon who committed the vicious crime," she swung herself around again, "it was that man."(Court TV.com, 12/13/04)

This diminutive prosecuting attorney indicated the defense dug deep in the barrel to come up with that tactic after their other ploys fell by the way side, then almost sneeringly said, "the mysterious pubic hair was none other than Mr. Ammon's." She accused Danny of removing the hard drive and had a friend dispose of it. "Wasn't it the defendant's own father who testified that his son asked him on the day of the family wedding, the same day as the murder, how do you get rid of something so it's never found?"

Prosecution closed her statements saying she didn't have all the answers, but noted that the law only requires that she prove, even solely by circumstantial evidence, if necessary, that Danny Pelosi was Ted Ammon's killer.

"Do I know the exact time of death? Nope. Do any of the doctors know the exact time of death? Nope. Do I know the exact weapon? Nope. Do I have proof beyond a reasonable doubt? Nope. But take into consideration the four people who testified on oath, one being the defendant's own father. Who was the man boasting about getting Ted Ammon's money? That man! Who was already speaking about bashing Ted Ammon's brains one year before the murder? Who? It was that man!"(Court TV.com, 12/13/04)

I was already on the phone with my mother when Rachelle broke in, I told my daughter I'd call her right back, but quickly asked how she was. From the sound of her voice, I didn't think well.

"Tami, that DA pulverized Danny like an old meat grinder," Mom said, sounding defeated as if it were her battle. "Forget the optimism from Danny's lawyer. That District Attorney hammered one lethal nail after another."

"What do you mean?"

"I told you she was cunning. She went over everything; if any of those jurors had a lapse of memory in these last two months, this DA refreshed their memory - from *her* angle. It does not look good. I think you better prepare these kids for the worst."

"This is what I've been afraid of. How am I supposed to do that?" It wasn't a question I expected my mother to answer, more like a depressing quandary to myself.

"God, I don't know Tami, it's going to be hell these next few days. Who knows when they will come to a decision, they could deliberate for weeks."

"How were the kids during this?"

"Frightened."

"What about Danny?"

"Not quite so cocky. That DA is one powerful attorney. Even if she doesn't win this case, you know she has Danny squirming right now. You better call Rachelle back.

I'll see you later."

Rachelle was plainly distraught when I called her back. I told her to come right home. I didn't want her talking on her cell phone and driving at the same time, ear bud or not.

Her eyes were red and swollen by the time she got home, she must have cried all the way from Riverhead to our house.

"That DA was horrible! All she kept doing was pointing her finger at Daddy and screaming, 'that man did it, that man did it!' Like a witch."

The daunting testimonies were piled up against Danny. There wasn't enough actual evidence to prove him guilty, but there didn't appear to be sufficient evidence to prove him innocent either. I wondered how confident he was feeling. Did he have unwavering faith that his high paying lawyers could outweigh the DA's own lack of proof?

THIRTY-ONE

Guilty - With Reasonable Doubt

"The past is but the beginning of a beginning."
—H. G. Wells

My family stayed close to home that weekend; no one wanted to be too far from one another in case the verdict came in. By nine-thirty Sunday night Danny's lawyer was feeling optimistic. Over the weekend the jurors had requested the court reporter to read back several hours of testimony including asking to see the crime-scene photos and a magnifying glass. Danny's attorney seemed pleased that jurors were going over the trial data with a fine-tooth comb.

After the jurors had deliberated for twelve-and-half hours on Sunday, it didn't seem likely that a verdict would come in on Monday. I convinced Rachelle that she and I should go to work and keep our minds busy. I thought it best not to send Tony to school. I had spoken with the school administrators on Friday and they too believed he needed to be home, at least until the verdict came in. Little Dan made the wise decision not to go to work. Driving home from Nassau County, whether in jubilation of a victory or in overwhelming grief, either way could be a dangerous situation when traveling such a distance.

As soon as I woke on Monday morning I turned on the local Channel 12 News in case there was some report of a verdict. But it only mentioned that the jury was still in deliberation from Saturday and they were expected to convene by nine that morning.

Little Dan came into the kitchen to tell me about a nightmare he had. "It was weird, Mom, I dreamt I was putting food on top of Cheeney's (our pet Chinchilla) cage and then I put another cage on top of that one. When Cheeney went to get the food, the cages came tumbling down on her. I know it doesn't sound scary now, but it was in the dream. What do you think it means?"

I didn't have an answer for my son.

"I get a bad feeling from it Ma, like it's Daddy reaching for something and then everything falls on top of him."

There wasn't much I could say to that. When Rachelle and I left, Little Dan and Tony were in the living room watching the repetitive news on the local news station.

Rachelle and I drove to work in separate cars. With twenty active three-to-four- year-olds excited about Santa's close arrival, neither Rachelle nor I had the chance to think too much about what was happening at the Riverhead Criminal Court. School let out at twelve. Only five minutes after the parents picked their children up, we got a call from a friend that the verdict had come in, but it wasn't known what the verdict was. I quickly called my mother to tell her what we heard.

"Ma, put the news on, the verdict came in, we don't know what it is," I screamed in a near panic.

"Oh my god, I'm on my way back from Southampton, I'll go right to Riverhead. Where's Little Dan and Tony?"

"They're at home."

She hung up and raced to Riverhead. The parking lot was filled to capacity. She ran from the opposite end of the court building parking area, past the assemblage of TV vans to the courtroom. It was eerily quiet when she reached the fourth floor. There was no one in the lobby except the court officer who was guarding the closed doors. He would not allow her in the courtroom. She tried to peek through the crack in the door, but he warned her that when those doors opened there would be a stampede and she better stay clear. He did not know what the verdict was.

Within moments the doors banged open and as the officer had predicted a mob of reporters charged out. Mom pleaded for someone to tell her what the verdict was. She found out minutes before I did.

Rachelle, Carol and I and our other staff members, hovered around a small radio listening to 1010 WINS waiting to hear the verdict. Rachelle was sitting on the floor, her arms wrapped around her knees glaring at the radio. I felt as if I was watching a scene from an old 1940's movie, expecting to hear President Roosevelt announce the attack of Pearl Harbor.

"Oh my god," one of the girls screamed, " I think they said the verdict is guilty."

"No," Rachelle screamed back, "you must have heard it wrong."

Everyone was dashing back and forth from the computer to the radio trying to find out what was said. Someone turned the volume up and seven of us stared at the radio. Within seconds the verdict was broadcast, "the Danny Pelosi verdict is in. Danny Pelosi has been found guilty." Rachelle fell on her side, still holding her knees to her chest reeling back and forth, *"He's not guilty, he's not guilty."* She screeched a painful wailing cry of despair. Her frail body contorting as if in a seizure. Our young Program Director whom I had known since he was a child, scooped her up, rocking her in his strong bear like arms. *"Daddy!"* she sobbed.

I was momentarily frozen in my spot, incapable of taking in a breath. I found out later I screamed when the verdict came in. I shifted to automatic pilot. "The boys, I've got to call the boys." Little Dan answered the phone, but my throat was so dry I could barely get the words out.

"The verdict is guilty, the verdict is guilty." I gasped.

"What are you talking about? We didn't hear anything," Little Dan argued, unable to comprehend what I said.

"It's true Dan," I cried to my son, "they found Daddy guilty." It tore at my heart to be far away from him at that moment, and worse for being the one to break the devastating news that his father was found guilty of murder.

"No", he yelled "it can't be, we have the TV on, they haven't said anything." While I was on the phone with him he turned the volume up. I heard the verdict telecast in the background and the newscaster blare the jury's decision. Then the muffled cries.

I wanted to dash out the door and rush to my sons, but my daughter was still wrapped in the arms of the Program Director, inconsolable. When she was finally calm we headed home chauffeured by my staff who would not let either one of us drive.

My mother got to my house before I did. She told me she found Little Dan sitting on the loveseat staring at the TV with his girlfriend close next to him. He was clicking the remote from one channel to another as if he had to hear the report from all stations to be certain there were no mistakes. Tony was lying down on the couch with a blank expression on his face; tears were quietly running down the sides of his face into his ears. Mom went to each of them, but only her oldest grandson allowed her to wrap her arms around him and cry on her shoulder. Tony remained motionless on the couch; his eyes fixed on the ceiling. All my mother could do was hug his unresponsive body and tell him she knew how great his pain was.

While driving home with one of my dear friends at the wheel I had one phone call after another. Each call was interrupted by another call trying to get through. Bad news spreads like a raging wild fire, calls were coming in from one end of Long Island to the other. In between I managed to leave Andy a message.

When we pulled into my driveway, I took a deep breath. I knew my heart would break the moment I witnessed my children's agony, and worse, I knew I was powerless to take their suffering away.

Rachelle got home the same time as I did. She ran past me

into the house straight to her brother Danny. When I walked in they were in the living room, hugging and sobbing on each other, my eighteen-year old son, not quite a man, holding his older sister up. "We're *never* going to see him again, Danny. We're *never* going to see him again." They cried, intertwined as one broken heart. Mom wrapped her arms around both her grandchildren. In a little huddle, she offered them hope. "You will see your father again. It will be different, but you will see him again." I let them be and went to Tony's room. He was on his bed with his arms limp along side of him, his left foot was twitching back and forth. A steady stream of silent tortured tears rolled one after the other down his innocent face onto his pillow. He wouldn't talk to me. I ached to hold my youngest child close to me and soothe him in my arms like a baby. But he wasn't a baby, he was a fourteen-year-old 5' 7" unapproachable non-verbal adolescent. Instead I wiped his tears and stroked his face lightly with my fingers. I lay down next to him and placed my arm across him.

Everyone left us to be with our grief. The house was quiet, except for the little whimpers escaping from Rachelle's throat. She was curled on the couch with her boyfriend sitting idly next to her, helpless of what to do. Tony stayed in his room, his TV on low. Little Dan stood outside on the porch; one tear rolled down his baby hairless cheek. The memory of that Fourth of July so long ago flashed through my mind, my little son atop his father's shoulders saying 'I oh so happy, I have water coming from my eyes.' The water coming from my son's eyes this sorrowful day, was anything but happy. It was as if someone had died. And in a way it was. The death of life as we knew it. A funeral without the body. The slow and painful mourning process lay before us.

Before the day was over reporters were at my door begging for a statement. I pulled the drapes closed and the four of us huddled together in the living room. We attempted to resume some degree of normalcy the day after the crushing verdict. Little Dan went to work, but Rachelle, Tony and I stayed home.

Tony remained in his room most of the day, emerging only to get some food or use the bathroom. Rachelle spent the time crying on the phone with one friend after another. I had to delve into a forty page final paper and exam for my doctorate studies that was due that night and to which I only found out at six in the morning what my paper would be on. The professor had announced in the beginning of the course that the final paper would be a surprise, giving the students only twenty-four hours to complete and would count as half of the final grade.

Despite the fact that every newspaper had Danny's face sprawled across the front page with bold headlines, "PELOSI GUILTY IN AMMON'S SLAYING" "HE KILLED THE MILLIONAIRE" "HIS TURN TO CRY" I could not allow myself to wallow in my family's life altering event. A term paper was due; that was my focus.

In between sorting through hundreds of pages I downloaded from the Internet and trying to assemble the information needed for my paper, I answered dozens of phone calls from friends and family and spoke to at least five or six individuals who came to my door to see how we were doing. My mother came over in the afternoon with lunch then back again later with dinner ready to give me a hand with both the paper and the well meaning calls and visits. By ten that evening after sixteen hours of non-stop work, I forwarded my final paper to the professor.

Late that night even though exhausted and bleary-eyed I read some of the stories about Danny.

"Danny Pelosi swallowed hard and buried his head in his hands when a jury delivered its verdict Monday: guilty of the second-degree murder of millionaire financier Ted Ammon...."

"A jury of nine women and three men deliberated for 23 hours over three days before deciding unanimously that Pelosi was guilty beyond a reasonable doubt of beating Ammon to death in the bedroom of his expansive East Hampton beach home on October 21, 2001......"

"The Prosecuting Attorney contends that Pelosi, who crossed himself just before the jury forewoman announced the verdict, was optimistic that he was going to get away with murder....."

"Pelosi who remains jailed without bail, faces 25 years to life in prison when he is sentenced January 25......."

"Now It's His Turn To Cry," was written in bold letters across the front page of the *New York Post*.

It didn't matter how many tabloids had Danny's name and face plastered across the front page, I could not adjust to the fact that it was the man I was married to for nearly twenty years, the father of my children whom they were referring to. Who could have ever imagined that this was how our lives would end up. That night I buried my sobs in my pillow.

In the midst of the surrealistic events, my professor emailed me; I passed my final exam with a 98% and received 100% on my forty-page report. My focus on my studies was undoubtedly a therapeutic escape route.

I had to work the rest of the week and finish up before the Christmas vacation. On my way to the center I stopped for my usual 7-11 cup of coffee. From past experience I expected to see Danny's face glaring at me from the newspapers. I had warned myself not to look at them, walk past them, get my coffee and get out. But I could not ignore the latest front page, pictures of Danny and Scott Peterson, their faces side by side. Over each photo read, "Pelosi Found Guilty/Peterson Sentenced to Death." My stomach churned to see Danny's picture along side Scott Peterson's. I hadn't read much on the 'Scott Peterson case' except to hear he was accused of murdering his beautiful pregnant wife, Laci. I thought about Scott Peterson's mother, her unconditional love she must have for her son, her memories of the day he was born, his first step, his first day at school, his high school prom, his wedding day. I refused the temptation to purchase the paper. I grabbed my coffee and hurried to my car. I didn't want to read any more sadness anywhere.

- THIRTY-TWO -

Holidays and Heartbreak

"Do what you can with what you have, where you are."
—Theodore Roosevelt

I was looking forward to being with Andy on Saturday the eighteenth of December. My time with him was as comforting as a hot bath on a blustery wintry night. We originally had plans to drive into the city and do a little Christmas shopping together. When Andy called Friday night to apologize that he wouldn't be able to keep our plans since he had to work late on Saturday, I was relieved. I wasn't up to walking the streets of New York with the holiday shoppers. I wanted to stay as close to home as possible. We decided on a small local Italian restaurant to celebrate a quiet holiday dinner together. Neither of us was in the mood to be surrounded by gaiety. For the both of us it was going to be a sad holiday time. It was Andy's first year that his children would be with their mother. He was a devoted and loving father and the major change in his life was difficult for him. After dinner we went back to his apartment. While we sat on his couch enjoying a glass of wine and light conversation, he reached over and handed me a small wrapped gift that was on his coffee table, a beautiful diamond cross on a delicate white gold chain.

"I know your strong faith in God," he said as he fastened the chain around my neck.

"I've never had a person as kind as you." I answered. It was the most treasured gift I had ever received.

Andy was with his family for the holidays and I was with mine. The traditional Christmas Eve was at my house, but it sorely lacked any holiday merriment. It reminded me of the first Christmas after my grandfather's death. My family expected to see him walk into the living room as he always did on Christmas Eve, carrying his tray of home-cooked mussels and stuffed baked clams.

As the clocked ticked to midnight I had that same sense of anticipation, to see Danny make his grand entrance with an armload of presents for everyone.

My two older children made the decision the night before to visit their father in jail. Normally the inmates are allowed to sit with their family and friends at tables in a large room, but Danny was on a suicide watch. Instead, their visit consisted of them sitting on stools and peering into a small glass window of a 4 X 4-block cubicle. They were shocked to see their father not in his expensive custom tailored suit, but wearing the drab green prison uniform, his hands cuffed in front of him with a huge lock and thick chains down to his legs shackling his ankles. Their only means of communication was through a little speaker below the window. Throughout the heart-wrenching hour Danny sobbed to his children and begged for forgiveness. He was remorseful, as he should be. It was his actions alone that caused the suffering of his family. He preyed on his children's sympathies, his children who loved him unconditionally. I remember only too well how his large sad puppy eyes could melt my heart.

Like some melodramatic movie of the 1950's, the three of them touched the small glass window with their fingers. Danny pleaded with his two older children to watch over their little brother and listen to their mother. But unlike actors playing a part, they wept real tears for the end of a life as they knew it. Christmas of 2004 was not the victory Danny believed he would be celebrating, but an agonizing realistic defeat.

The New Year started off with the belief that this year everything was going to fall into place. Andy and I spent New Year's Eve together, which was a special treat for me since I had spent the last several years alone. Two weeks into January Joy came for a post holiday visit. I planned an evening where Joy and her boyfriend and my brother and his wife would have the opportunity to meet Andy for the first time. The six of us piled into my brother's big Chevy Suburban. Whenever Roger is around a good time is guaranteed, add Joy's wisecracking sarcasm and a dab of Andy's good-naturedness and you had a delightful potpourri of endless humor. The next day Roger called to tell me he had never seen me that happy. He said my eyes lit up every time I looked at Andy. He was happy for me but at the same time, concerned that Andy wasn't all he appeared to be. Perhaps my brother had a premonition.

So much for the great way the New Year began and the delightful potpourri of endless humor. Before the end of January, January 25 to be precise, I was hit with startling news. There was no warning like a radio announcement cautioning the listeners a hurricane was on the way, there was no boulder rolling in my direction. It came and left as quickly as a tsunami, leaving me to figure out what in God's name happened.

It was the day of Danny's sentencing. I had my head buried in my studies to keep from dwelling on what was happening in the courtroom. I let the message machine take my calls so I could concentrate on my work, but when I saw Andy' number come up, I took the call.

"Hi," I said happy to have such a pleasant interruption.

"Hi," he answered, not sounding so pleasant. Within two minutes Andy told me he was confused and needed some time and space.

I was stunned, to put it mildly. I mumbled something stupid to him and hung up without saying good bye or inquiring what he meant. I toyed with the idea of calling him, however that lasted only a second. I refused to ever beg another man again. But that didn't stop me from torturing myself. What did *I* do? I was convinced that *I* must have been the one responsible for him to have such a sudden change of heart.

Interesting to note, later that evening when I found out that Danny was sentenced to twenty-five years to life for second-degree murder, it wasn't nearly as devastating to me as the phone call from Andy earlier in the day.

Andy did call the next day, he said he was sorry I hung up the way I did and wanted a chance to explain his feelings, which momentarily pacified me. He told me he wasn't ready for a commitment; I answered I wasn't either. He said he couldn't give me anything more, I told him I didn't need anything more. Andy talked about the complexity of both our situations, but what I really think he meant was the complexity of *my* situation. We spoke for a few minutes more. I was relieved that he still wanted to keep our plans for the following weekend.

Whatever happened in Andy's mind from Wednesday morning to Thursday morning I may never know. But on my way to work on Thursday, two days away from seeing him, Andy called. He fumbled over his words, then spewed out life-wounding sentences, 'he was not ready for a commitment, he was terrified of one, he couldn't see me anymore, he had to put closure on his marriage,' blah, blah, blah. I nearly drove off the road listening to him ramble one hurtful statement after another. Then he added as if the next line would justify his terminating our short relationship, "You deserve more." I had to pull my car over. It was the same script but with different characters, the lines only slightly altered.

"I guess I just wasn't good enough," I said, easily falling back to the role of the victim, and why not? I played that part all my life.

Naturally he assured me his decision had nothing to do with me. For several bewildering minutes I half listened to him repeat that I did not do anything wrong, that it was him, not me.

It was remarkably easy to fall back to the ultimate martyr

role. "I can't make you like me, Andy. This is your decision and I have no choice but to accept it. I hope you find what you're looking for."

I hung up with him stymied, baffled, stumped. My emotions were tossed around like a batch of clothes agitating in the washer, with one emotion mixing with another, anger, shunned, weepy, empty, jolted, jilted.

I sat on the side of the road long enough to catch my breath and call work and tell them I wasn't coming in. I didn't say why. I drove home in a tearful blur.

I wrote Andy a letter not blaming him, but blaming my complicated life as the reason that drove him away. I thanked him for his honesty and wished him well. I packed up the few gifts he gave me and dropped them off at his apartment when I knew he wouldn't be home and tacked the letter to his door. I drove down by the water and sat in the freezing cold for hours sobbing.

For two weeks I could not function. My schoolwork, which had always been my therapy, my salvation, my escape route where I could block out everything that was going on around me and inside me, failed miserably. All my assignments were left scattered on my desk where I left them, incomplete. I could not go to work. I hid at home and told few what happened. I'd get Tony off to school and go back to bed and stay there all day. Soiled clothes piled up in the laundry room, dirty dishes piled in the sink, snotty tissues piled across my bed. I could not understand why I was taking this so hard. I had, after all, been used to heartache, being lied to was nothing new. I was unrealistic in my belief that I could dismiss Andy from my mind with a simple good bye letter.

When I finally had the courage to call Joy late that night, she was outraged.

"Why that lying no good bastard! How did he fool *me*?" Joy took Andy's behavior as a personal affront. She had taken Andy on the side on the night she met him and in her tough-girl Brooklyn dialogue threatened he better not hurt me.

"I've been around my share of bullshitting creeps, but this guy just seemed too sweet to be one. Maybe he's a goddamn detective. Don't you think it's a little suspicious Tami that he started to date you at the *beginning* of the trial and just so happened to break it off right *after* the verdict? Look at what those other detectives did to you! I'm telling you he was hired to get some dirt out of you, but when the jury came up with a guilty verdict, his mission was accomplished and you were dumped."

"You read too many trashy novels." I joked with her.

"Well then why did he dump you, huh?"

"He didn't dump me." I whined.

"Oh no, what do you call it when someone tells you out of the blue, no warning, no nothing, that they don't want to see you anymore?"

PART IV

The Healing Years

2005…

- THIRTY-THREE -

The Courage to Change the Things I Can

God grant me the serenity to accept the things
I cannot change, the courage to change the things
I can, and the wisdom to know the difference.
—Serenity prayer

Andy wasn't a detective, I am sure of that. Although Joy did have me guessing for a few seconds. It certainly would have made a good book. The truth was, I was dumped. And I'll probably never know the real reason. But I can guess that being the ex-wife of an accused murderer could have had something to do with it. Maybe Andy was pressured by his friends and family to stay away from a murderer's wife. Maybe he just couldn't handle the daily chaos of my life. Who knows? Maybe a lot of things. All I know is that I was crushed that our wonderful relationship was over.

The tears I shed and the overwhelming grief I felt when Andy chose the fork in the road that didn't include me went much deeper than the ending of a short three month relationship. His good bye was the catalyst I needed to release the emotional crap that I had to stuff in order to survive. Trapped feelings gushed forth like a broken dam. When I finally stopped crying and finally stopped feeling sorry for myself I could begin the task of chipping away the hard exterior and get down to the

223

nitty-gritty of why I stayed married to Danny. More importantly I uncovered why I clung to him after we were divorced. It was as if I took a large magnifying glass and scrutinized the flaws and blemishes of my character.

The truth of the matter is I was just a kid when I got married. A kid having kids. I was downright immature. I sort of froze in that teen mentality time zone. In my childish mind I was in competition with the other women who wanted Danny from the time we were teens. Each time Danny cheated on me and came back it was as if I won something. *I* was the one who collected the trophy. Some trophy!

In short, I was addicted to Danny. As addicted as the smoker who sucks nicotine through a hole in his throat and drags an oxygen tank around for survival. My mother tried to talk to me, but I was incapable of acknowledging Danny's lack of morals. His lack of ethics. Like those crazy mirrors at a carnival, I had a distorted view of him. Other people could see him for what he was. But I couldn't. Perhaps that would have been too painful for me.

When I thought about Andy's statement that he needed to put closure on his marriage a mega two hundred-watt light bulb went on. This huge insight suddenly popped up, like the adolescent that shoots up four inches in one season leaving last year's pants two inches over the ankles. Aha! Another mystery unfolded. I hadn't put closure on my marriage to Dan! My mother was known to say, "Tami, you may be divorced on a piece of paper, but you have not divorced yourself from Danny. You are as married to him as that fateful day you said 'I do'."

I have to give myself some credit though. It wasn't like I had time to prepare for a divorce or the emotional process of putting any sort of closure on my marriage while being bombarded by the media, harassed by detectives and investigated by LIPA. What made matters more difficult was Danny's belief that we were still married – a delusion that I went along with - he just had another wife.

As I chiseled further into my psyche, painstakingly prying

away one unyielding tier at a time, I uncovered a deep-rooted embedded untruth. I believed that when Danny left me for Generosa and when Andy terminated our friendship it was because of something I did or didn't do that was responsible for their choices. I felt abandoned and rejected because I believed these men did not love me, when in truth it was *me* who didn't love myself.

Time does heal wounds and time gave me the opportunity to step back and make unbiased observations without the emotional strings tugging at my heart. I can look back and see that I needed Andy. I needed to feel like a woman again, to experience happiness, kindness and a gentle touch. I needed to know I was capable of being loved. And I *needed* for that relationship to end so that I could take a monumental step in the direction of self-love.

Today I *know* that I did not do anything wrong. I'm not the cause of Danny's running off with Generosa – or any of his extramarital flings. I'm not the cause of Andy's decision to cut off our friendship before it had time to flourish and grow. Whatever their issues were, they were *not* mine. I was up front and candid with Andy. I entered the relationship in honesty and left it in honesty. I do not take responsibility if my life was too overwhelming for him. My life, and everything surrounding my life, was not a secret and I never attempted to keep it one. I made apologies and amends when appropriate without groveling at his feet. *And* I didn't call him and beg him to change his mind. That was definitely a change in the right direction.

I am witness to my own growth and the courage that it took to make some definitive changes. Such as controlling myself from attending Danny's trial as I so often wanted to do. It was an ongoing effort for me to keep posted in the forefront of my mind Danny's callous abusiveness or I would have slipped back into the hole that I had crawled out of. Pity would have erased from my mind the damage he caused to my children and myself. I stayed away for my own protection. That was change.

I am done beating myself up. I'm done being overcome by

shame and disgrace of being married to a man convicted of murder. I adopted that shame as if it were my own. I am not accountable for anyone else's actions. I did nothing to be ashamed of. I was a wife. I was a mother. I went to church. I went to work. I helped children. I accept that I have made choices and decisions throughout my life which were not the wisest. I accept that I cannot change or undue one fraction of a second of what occurred in my life. The past is the past. I can harbor resentments and regret that I spent my life living in a pitiful fantasy – or I can move one. I've chosen to move on. I have come to accept myself exactly the way I am, because I know that through acceptance and letting go of the past that I made room for growth and change.

Many people believe I should hate Danny, but to me hate is the flip side of love. A passion that binds you. Pastor Lydia said I needed to forgive him so I could get on with my life. To forgive Danny is a major undertaking. I don't know if I have come that far in my evolvement. But I have addressed that I needed to forgive myself. In forgiving myself I could recognize the anger I had toward myself. When I recognized this powerful negative emotion that I refused to acknowledge, I was able to force myself out of denial and encounter the jumble of emotions that I kept under lock and key. One depended on the other for healing to take place.

Am I angry with Danny? Of course I am. Anger is healthy when it is understood and dealt with in a positive manner. I am angry because of his selfish choices and decisions that caused my family to suffer. I am angry that he put me in a financial mess. I am angry that he turned my life upside down.

The detectives believed that Danny made a drunken confession to me and that I, out of fear protected him. Contrary to what the detectives assumed, I do not know what took place on that dreadful night of October 21, 2001, my son Tony's eleventh birthday and I am done obsessing over whether or not Danny committed this vicious crime. I have had to let this lingering mystery go in order to move on with my life.

- THIRTY-FOUR -

Moving On

*"When one door closes another door opens; but we
so often look so long and so regretfully upon the closed
door, that we do not see the ones which open for us."*
—Alexander Graham Bell

As I steadily dug deep within my core I came to realize that throughout my tumultuous marriage to Danny an incredible inner strength had slowly been brewing under the surface without my being aware of it. I always thought of myself as weak, too frightened to rock the boat and stand up for myself. But I did. I rocked the boat when I went to Al-Anon, even though it made Danny angry. I rocked some more when I persevered in my education, even though Danny criticized me. I rocked further when I pursued a profession, even though Danny mocked me. I had an inner strength all along. Of course I did. How else could I have come out on the other side? How else would I have found the courage to expedite major decisions, to have faith that as I closed one door a new one was waiting for me?

It is said ignorance is bliss. In my ignorance I cleared the way. I moved on. I took risks.

One of the first steps I took over the threshold of fear was making the decision to leave the center that I helped to create almost nine years before. Carol and I were more than partners;

we were close loving friends for years. We grew from two young enthusiastic women with a vision, to two mature equally enthusiastic wiser women with greater visions. We developed an organization that began with little hand puppets and evolved into a quarter-million-dollar corporation. One of the happiest days that Carol and I shared was the day we took over the nearly condemned building on sixteen beautiful acres of land. We happily swept the floors, scrubbed the toilets, raked the lawn, and decorated the center for every holiday. As a team we created unique programs to offer the community and brain stormed inventive ways to raise money. We hosted scores of fund-raisers and received dozens of awards for our undying efforts. We were an incredible team. Where I was shy and reserved and preferred to stay in the background, Carol was outgoing and extroverted. When one of us was down, the other could lift her up. We had been together so long that we could read each other's minds and finish the sentence the other one started. We melded together as a single thinking, feeling unit.

The dream I had of developing my own preschool program became a reality when Diane joined us. With her strong organizational and marketing skills and her personal financial help, the unique preschool program that I designed became a sister organization to the center and a financial success.

That dilapidated building that was granted to us and that I helped to create as a place of recognition in the community was as much a refuge and safe haven for the many distraught young people that came through its doors as it was for my children and myself. I am certain the love and support we received from everyone at the center is what saved us through the grueling days of the trial.

Yet it came time for me to move on. Change is inevitable.

Patti had already moved on years before to pursue other interests. When I made the brave decision to leave the center it wasn't entirely because the preschool had outgrown the limited space, although that was definitely true. It was because I needed to step out of my safety zone and launch a new ship.

It was a disconcerting period of time that required many meetings and many phone calls for Carol and I to understand that a separation of our business interests was not a separation of our long-term relationship. We remain close supportive friends to this day and stay a part of one another's lives.

It was a bittersweet moment on June 10, 2005, the last day of my preschool, when I tearfully said goodbye.

The second major step I took was to sell my house – the house my children grew up in – the house they did not want to leave. I swayed back and forth like a pendulum. Sell. Not sell. Sell. Not sell. I drove myself nuts trying to come up with every conceivable option of how I could remain in my home. The truth was I could not afford it. The refinancing allowed me to keep my nose above water and bought me some time. But my funds were disappearing much quicker than I had planned. Everything had looked good on paper; I had even put money aside for an emergency. But everyday there was an added expense I had not figured on. I finally bit the bullet and listed my house with a real estate agent. But when I came home on the night of January 27, right after Danny was sentenced and Andy gave me the shaft, and I saw the For Sale sign on the property, I called the realtor the next day and told her to take it off the market. I was terrified to sell and terrified to stay. I didn't know where I was going to go or how I was going to manage. The more houses I went to look at, the more depressed I became. The market was at a record high, which was beneficial for selling, but not for buying. I had already accepted that I was going to down size considerably, which was perfectly fine with me, but the homes that were in my financial bracket were practically handyman's specials. Even though I could make a sizable profit on the sale of my home, I had a lot of debt to pay out, thanks to Danny, which was going to leave me very little cash to purchase another home. I was stuck between a rock and a hard place; I couldn't afford to stay in my home, nor could I afford something to my liking. I prayed for an answer.

Jane, my real estate agent was an understanding caring lady. Once she found out who I was and who I had been married to, she treated me with kid gloves. She patiently helped me sort through my dilemma and wisely guided me through the process of selling my home. Jane was careful not to give the perspective buyers my full name to avoid any curiosity seekers. She usually introduced me simply as Tami.

The same day my house was advertised strangers were traipsing through the rooms and snooping in the closets. I felt like I was being inspected by the White-Glove Good Housekeeping Guild.

Selling a house is exhausting. Each time Jane made an appointment with a client meant I had to spiff up the house, put my little yapping ankle-biting dogs in their kennel and make sure my senile old Labrador Willy hadn't deposited an elephant-sized dump somewhere, which meant spraying the rooms with an asphyxiating dose of air freshener.

A few times I thought I had a serious buyer. One enthusiastic young family came back several times bringing different family members. They came with notepads and rulers and measured the rooms. But they never put down a deposit and soon they stopped coming. Another family did put down a fair amount of money, but their final decision was hinging on the husbands' mother who was on vacation and evidently was the financial lender. After three weeks of waiting for the matriarch to return from her travels, she turned her nose up at the deal. I was beginning to feel the house was jinxed.

So, on a cold evening in March my friend Joanne came over and we dug a hole in the hard ground and buried an eight-inch St. Joseph statue upside down on the corner of my property. I had never heard of this tradition before, but Joanne swore it helped her sell her home. I was willing to try anything anyone suggested. We said a few prayers in between giggles and wondered what the neighbors might think seeing us on our hands and knees in the semi darkness with a small gardening shovel in my hand.

It appeared to work, or almost work. A couple of months went by; finally I had a serious buyer. The gentleman put down a substantial amount of money, much more than was required. His family was hoping to be settled in time to enjoy the huge swimming pool before the summer was over.

After a somber and diligent hunt in search of a new home I found an adorable little house a few towns away that had everything I wanted and could afford and still allowed Tony to stay in the same school district. I borrowed the money I needed for my down payment from my mother and was going to repay her when I sold the house. Closing dates for the two houses were set for August.

The people I was buying my new house from wanted to be certain that I didn't need to sell my home in order to purchase another one. They were anxious to sell and didn't want to be held up in case the sale of my house fell through. I led them to believe that wouldn't be a problem. But I was nervous that something might go wrong and I would lose the little yellow house I had fallen in love with. Jane assured me things were moving smoothly and not to worry. I drove past my future home as often as I could, finally getting excited about the day I could call it mine.

In the meantime I started the overwhelming monumental task of sorting through the years of clutter that accumulated in the attic, the basement, the garage and anywhere that Danny could stash some more junk. Danny was the type of person who came home from the dumps with more trash than he brought. He also was the type of person who bought multiples of the same items. When a local store that sold an assortment of Christmas decorations closed down, Danny brought home dozens of talking Santas, life-sized lawn ornaments and enough holiday lights to decorate three houses. I told myself that by getting rid of the literal mess I'd have a good fresh start. A new home would be symbolic of the new life my family was about to embark on. That was how I felt on the good days. Other days I felt depressed. I bounced back and forth from highs to lows, excited to start anew and sad to leave behind the tender memories that are irreplaceable. I could pack the pictures and all the other treasures, but I couldn't pack those special occasions when all four of my grandparents were alive and gathered together in my living room. Nor could I take with me the traditional photo spot of the kids posing in front of the huge oak tree year after year dressed in scary Halloween costumes, or grinning nervously on the first day of school, or the angelic glow of their First Holy Communion, and the last photos of the two older kids decked out in their sophisticated grown-up prom gowns and tuxedos.

I sat on the floor in the middle of my den with boxes all around me remembering that happy Memorial Day weekend in 1989 when Danny and I settled our young and growing family in our new home. The collection of those memories are boundless and sometimes humorous, like the time Danny built Rachelle a dollhouse that turned out to be so big it had to remain in the basement where it was constructed, or when Danny set the video camera up one night in the kitchen to catch a little field mouse in action. We watched the video the next morning as the furry critter grabbed the piece of cheese and smugly sat nibbling on it while staring into the camera lens. These are the sweet fragrant memories that I can cherish and take with me wherever I go. On the other hand I was glad to say good riddance to the bitter acrid recollection of the nights I cried myself to sleep, to the LIPA investigators searching through the basement, the detectives and the media hounding me, and to the day that Danny left me and coldly walked out the door.

The sale of my home was more than the opportunity to purchase a smaller more economical home; it meant letting go of my life with Danny. Packed within the dozens of cardboard boxes was the rancid accumulation of over twenty years of the life experiences of a nuclear family gone sour, like a container of milk left out on a hot summer day.

I was on my way home from grocery shopping towards the end of July, one month from my closing dates, mentally decorating my new home when Jane called me with bad news. The buyer's young son was diagnosed with a life threatening disease. Naturally under those extreme circumstances they had to back out of the deal. I panicked. I had promised the owners of the home I was buying that I did not need to sell my home to purchase theirs. I did not want to lose the chance to buy it or lose the money I borrowed from my mother. Nor did I want to go through the aggravating process of showing my home again. I was ready to throw the towel in and give up. I began to cry.

"Listen Tami. Your house is going to sell," Jane said trying to comfort me. "It will just take a little more time, but it will sell. I know you love that little house and don't want to lose it. My husband and I have talked this over and we want to give you the money you need to buy the other house. After all that you have been through you deserve some peace and happiness. We want to do this for you."

I was speechless. It took me several minutes to absorb what Jane said. She and her husband had discussed the matter at length before she called me. Even though Jane was confident that my house would sell and she would get her money back, I was stunned that this woman would take even the slightest risk to help a perfect stranger. Jane suggested I take a couple of days to think her offer over. Once I was able to get over the shock and the embarrassment, legal papers were drawn up and within a few weeks I was given a check for $125,000!

On September 4, 2005, I literally closed the door for the last time on the home that was built on a young woman's dream. It wasn't until mid-October before Jane sold my former house and she and her husband were reimbursed for their selfless kindness.

When I got into my car from signing all the necessary papers and contracts at the closing, I saw two pennies on the front seat. Whether the pennies were there before or not, doesn't matter. As far as I was concerned my prayers were answered. The message was clear, I had made the right decision.

Moving On

Moving on from the center and moving into a new home were pieces of cake in comparison to emotionally moving on from Danny. The less that I saw or spoke with him, the easier it was. But anyone who has quit smoking knows that the psychological cravings last much longer than the physical withdrawal.

Since my children frequently spoke to their father on the phone they naturally revealed their conversations with me, which tended to make me go berserk. It was an effort for me to mentally block out of my mind what they would tell me and for me to keep my mouth shut and my lips sealed. Otherwise I would have wound up getting caught in Danny's endless drama. I had to tread carefully in this delicate matter and not bad-mouth their father and put my children in a confused defensive position.

Occasionally Danny had wanted to talk to me on the phone regarding some situation or another. I used to make my kids lie and tell him I wasn't home or I'd talk with him and then be angry with myself. Even from faraway prison he still tried to control my life. It was easier for me to find the courage to stand up to the intimidating detectives and the confidence to confront school officials on Tony's behalf than it was for me to assert myself with Danny. I needed to be extremely careful and keep my guard up at all times so that I didn't yield to the old self-destructive patterns. Once I acknowledged this ingrained characteristic within myself I was able to keep from being sucked under like a strong undertow.

I am grateful for my Al-Anon background, the incredible unconditional loving support of family and friends and my deep trust and faith in God which helped me to put one foot in front of the other and begin the journey of self-healing. It's not about how far I have to go, but how far that I have come.

I have moved on.

- THIRTY-FIVE -

"A. D." - After Dan

"I am not afraid of storms for I am learning how to sail my ship."
—Louisa May Alcott

L etting go of the past is liberating; it frees you up and allows space for new wonders to emerge. It's like weeding out a garden before planting beautiful new flowers. Virtually all aspects of my life are different today than they were. I have begun to refer to my new life as "A.D." – After Dan.

On the day before my forty-second birthday, thanks to my real estate agent Jane and her husband, I moved into the little yellow house. I didn't think that anything could top Jane's generous $125,000 loan, but she surprised me again. A huge basket wrapped in pink cellophane was waiting for me when I pulled into the driveway of my new home. Packed with the candles and the other thoughtful gifts was a small blue checkered pillow with the picture of the yellow house printed on it and *Home Sweet Home* embroidered below. A heart-warming card that brought tears to my eyes was tucked inside. Talk about the cherry on the top of the cake! I have been graced with many earth angels in this lifetime and Jane is definitely one of them.

The best birthday present I could have ever received was to wake up to a bright sunny morning in my little house. My mother and I worked like busy beavers to get my house set up and organized. Within a few days the place was decorated from top to bottom. I wanted to create a warm cozy atmosphere as quickly as possible to ease the difficult transition that my children were experiencing. Tony in particular hated everything about our new home. I thought it was perfect. I loved its quaint charm from the moment I saw it. It's adorable, like a cute dollhouse, small enough for me to manage and roomy enough for comfort. It has everything that a family needs.

I made the decision to take a year off of work, which turned out to be more like a year and a half. I had some money put aside from the sale of my home that afforded me this luxury. I felt I earned this time off. My entire family had been under tremendous stress for too long. We needed time to adjust to the major changes that were taking place. We needed some structure back in our lives. We needed to share our meals, kick our feet up on the couch and sit back, relax and enjoy.

I took advantage of my free time to concentrate on completing my doctorate studies. After years of intense study, mounds of research work and a tumultuous chaotic life filled with a frustrating endless battle of obstacles and stumbling blocks, out of sheer perseverance, I was justly rewarded for my determined efforts and finally granted the title of Doctor of Education.

It was the one area in my life that I paid heed to my mother's advice. I promised her on the day that Danny and I came to her as two foolish teenagers wanting to get married that I would continue with my education. I am grateful that I didn't give up as I often wanted to do and for my family and friends who continually encouraged me to stay with it. Am I ever relieved that it is finally behind me!

Taking time away from the work world had other added benefits as well - like raising a baby.

Seline is part of my new life. At forty-three years of age, I'm raising a baby - my half-sister - we share the same father.

My father remarried some years after my mother divorced him to a woman half his age; his new wife is only one year younger than I am. I was happy my father had picked up the pieces after his divorce and found someone to share his life with. But I was shocked, as everyone else was, including my father, when about two years into their marriage his wife became pregnant. I'm sure my father at the age of sixty-three and in very poor physical health never imagined that he could conceive another child.

There are many older men who marry younger woman and start a second family late in life. But due to unforeseen circumstances my father and his wife were not able to raise their own daughter. I don't want to get into their personal lives; let's just say that the state stepped in when Seline was less than four months old and I willingly came forward to act as her guardian. Originally it was meant to be a temporary position until Seline's parents were able to take on the responsibility of their child. As you guessed, that did not happen. Seven months later I was granted full custody of this precious little bundle of sugar and spice and all things nice.

Once again I have had to endure the snide remarks that I knew went on behind my back and the open blatant criticism of the so-called well-meaning people who asked me why I have taken on such a burden. It was not exactly a choice; it was more a necessity. Granted this wasn't in my plans for my future. With my own kids grown and independent I thought I was going to be footloose and fancy free. Obviously God had other plans for me.

I have devoted my life to helping children; how could I turn my back and allow this adorable baby, my own half-sister, who looks like I did as an infant, go into the home of strangers? That is not who I am.

I call Seline the miracle baby, not just because she survived a difficult birth, but because she seems to work miracles with everyone who comes in contact with her,beginning with my own son Tony. When Seline first came into our home Tony wanted nothing to do with her; he would barely acknowledge that she was there. Before long he was laughing at her silly antics and carrying her around in his arms. I believe it was Seline who contributed to Tony coming out of his shell and his desire to return to school. This tiny little being with a wisp of light blonde hair and big blue trusting eyes put a smile back on my son's face. Babies have a way of doing that. They can turn cloudy days bright. Seline certainly does that for me. Whenever I find myself overwhelmed or concerned about the future, one baby bear hug from my little sibling and all my problems fade away. I know I have a lifetime haul ahead of me, but I have no regrets in my decision to raise my half-sister.

I've even tried dating again. I didn't take it quite as seriously as I had before. I didn't have that obsessed need to tell my perspective date my juicy background the moment we met. Once in a while a date progressed to a few weeks before it fizzled out. I did get somewhat serious with one man, but my life was vastly different than his. He was a confirmed bachelor and I was a new mother, not exactly a match. Unlike my relationship with Andy this one ended with a mutual decision and we remain on friendly terms. The time is still not right for me in the relationship department, but that's okay. I have a full plate as it is right now. I can barely find the time to grab a cup of coffee with my girlfriends let alone go through the time consuming 'get-dolled-up' phase of dating. Besides I'm still adjusting to the 'After Danny' newness of my life.

One night when I finally found the time to have dinner with my dear friend Josephine, she said she thought of me as a neglected chair that was stuck in the back of an antique store collecting dust until the day a caring person came along and took it home. Everyday that individual worked on the old chair stripping it of its layers of blistered paints and stains it had accumulated over the years. The legs were reinforced and it was painted a glorious bright color. After the tedious painstaking chore, the abandoned piece of furniture was transformed into a magnificent chair of remarkable beauty and strength. I believe Josephine's insightful words applied to my entire family. We have each been stripped down to our core, taken apart and put back together again.

Each of my children has had a portion of their youth snatched from them that can never be replaced, special occasions spoiled by sadness and confusion. The impact of Danny's conviction will have a permanent effect on them for the rest of their lives. Each one has dealt with it and the events that led to it, according to their own coping ability and how each was affected by their father's inconsistency throughout their lives and my own often irrational behavior.

My daughter Rachelle Marie is a beautiful young woman inside and out. She has a petite slender frame and creamy smooth skin. Her warm medium brown hair is highlighted with golden hues that shimmer under the light and emphasizes her large dark eyes and long lashes that she inherited from her father. She has a quiet honest beauty that comes deep from within and resonates around her like a halo. Unlike her father she is a reserved, sensitive, kind and trustworthy giving soul. She couldn't tell a lie if you paid her. She is my best friend.

As the oldest child Rachelle was the one most exposed to the insanity of my marriage. She was the child who witnessed our brawling fistfights and wrapped her little arms around me to comfort me. As the oldest and only girl, Rachelle knew about Danny's affairs, his incarcerations, and our financial strains, a heavy weight for her young small shoulders. She was the one who sat in the courtroom nearly everyday. She is the one who firmly believes it was Generosa who set her father up. She was the one who collapsed the day her father was convicted.

It's been a stressful emotive few years for my daughter. It wasn't easy for her to drive past the county jail that her father was in while on the way to the local college where she was attempting to finish up her Associates Degree in Early Childhood Education. Several times when Rachelle was en route to campus to take an important exam Danny would call and have her in tears. By the time she made it to her class she was an emotional mess. It's no surprise that it took her a few extra years for her to complete the program or that she has decided to take some time off before furthering her education. In the meantime she's following in my footsteps and is working with children. Rachelle has moved out of the house and in with her boyfriend and his supportive loving family.

Rachelle, like all of us, has had to deal with ignorant people who make rude remarks, or is it rude people who make ignorant remarks? Either way, at one job interview the woman asked my daughter if she was related to *that Pelosi guy that's in jail for murder*. Fortunately, behind Rachelle's soft delicate exterior is a deep inner strength that has made it possible for her to begin her own healing journey.

Little Dan, as the first born son was given his father's name – Daniel Pelosi. Under other circumstances it could have been a name to be proud of. Instead the name carries with it shame and embarrassment. One day while sitting in the waiting room of the doctor's office because my son was complaining of severe chest pains, (which turned out to be due to anxiety), the nurse called his name out minutes after a radio broadcast announced that the electrician Dan Pelosi was a suspect in the Ammon murder. Patients who appeared engrossed in their books raised their eyebrows at the connection of my son's name. Scenes like that happened frequently. And my son's anxiety worsened. He was forced to leap from boyhood to manhood in one giant step, was burdened with the role of man of the house and watchdog of his younger brother. As a young man without a father figure, or more likely because of the lack of a positive father figure, my son's anxiety turned to anger. Normally quiet and reserved, he became angry with everyone and everything and lashed out with his fists on any occasion that stirred his boiling pot over. Luckily my brother stepped in and took Little Dan under his wing. He's been working with his uncle since he graduated from high school and is learning a good trade as a carpenter. The days of hassling him to get out of bed are over. He sets his own alarm and is up and out of the house before I am. I have come to depend on my son for many things, from fixing the broken doorknob to hanging the ceiling fans and keeping his brother in line.

At twenty-one he has turned out to be a fine young man whom I am very proud of. His looks resemble more mine than his father's but many of his mannerisms are so strikingly like Danny's that sometimes I think I'm looking at his father.

My oldest son is like his sister, a peaceful sensitive soul. There has been some mention of taking a few college courses down the road. With his intelligence I hope he follows through.

While Tony might have been the child born into sobriety and not subjected to his parent's fist fights and drunken scenes that his older siblings witnessed, he was also the youngest to experience the break down of the family structure. The older ones at least had their father around for more of their childhood years than Tony did, for whatever that might be worth.

Tony was only ten when Dan left for good. Prior to that there were the numerous times Danny was out of the house, either being in jail or living with Mary. For this little guy his father seemed to be gone more than he was home. It wasn't until the trial when Tony learned about his father's jail time and his sordid affairs.

The teen years are a trying time even in the best of circumstances when there are two loving supportive parents in the home. In the case of my younger son, combine a broken home and a parent's conviction with a rush of teenage hormones and a child who lacks communication and coping skills, and you're looking at a time bomb ready to go off. When Tony's teacher would call complaining he wasn't attentive or was throwing crumpled paper balls at his friends, I was elated he wasn't suicidal. I didn't care that he wasn't paying attention or had to sit in in-school suspension. I cared that he got up in the morning and made an effort to go. I could deal with some minor behavior problems in school; dealing with a depressed, emotionally unresponsive teenager was another story entirely. After a while

Tony wasn't able to meet the demands of a formal education and needed to be home tutored and even that became too much for him. I've had enough meetings with school officials, guidance counselors and child advocates that I think I know the New York State school laws inside and out.

After being out of school for more than a year, in September of 2006 Tony on his own made the decision to return. To watch my son get on the school bus, something he hadn't done in years, and participate as a functioning student is something I never thought I'd witness. I'm keeping my fingers crossed that he makes it through graduation and hopefully beyond.

Tony is almost five years younger than Little Dan. Even though he's a foot and a half taller, broader in the shoulders and a good forty pounds heavier, he respects his older brother. He's powerfully built like my deceased guardian angel brother-in-law, rather than slender like his father. My mother says he reminds her of Joaquin Phoenix.

When I asked Tony what he wanted for his sixteenth birthday, a landmark age, he asked if I would spend the day fishing with him and his brother on Little Dan's boat. I took that request as a positive sign that the horrible birthday memories of the past are beginning to fade.

My kids have come a long way from the day that Danny walked out on us, but it's been a rough road. Even after all these years the four of us continue to be judged because of the actions of one. In our small Long Island community the name Pelosi has negative connotations, eyes continue to roll, cruel remarks are heard within ear shot, father's have been known to not let their daughters go out with my sons, minor incidents with the law that other kids might get a slap on the wrist and a strong warning turn into major legal matters for both Little Danny and Tony involving costly lawyers and stiff penalties, all because of who their father is. In Al-Anon I learned that alcoholism is a family disease, to me this is the same theory. Only one family member may be behind bars, but all family members suffer.

Rachelle and Little Dan have mixed emotions; they vacillate from feeling sorry for their father to sheer anger at him. Tony has yet to acknowledge what is stirring deep beneath the surface. Periodically they take the long trek upstate New York to visit their father in prison for special occasions like Christmas or Father's Day. Although I don't feel Danny warrants any visits, my children do, so I've stepped back and let them make their own decisions. Danny tells his children that one day he will be granted an appeal that will set him free.

On April 8, 2005 after two years of anguish, and thousands of dollars on attorney fees, the LIPA charge was dismissed; justice was finally obtained. My fingerprints and mug shots have been removed from the police files as if the arrest never existed, but the trauma from this fiendish experience remains. My heart still races whenever I see a police car behind me.

It was never determined who was in my basement in April of 2002.

- THIRTY-SIX -

Recipe for Life

"There are no mistakes, no coincidences.
All events are blessings given to us to learn from"
—Elisabeth Kubler-Ross

Not long after completing my doctorate and obtaining guardianship of Seline, I was thrilled to find a position as Director of a prominent preschool center where I could use my newly achieved degree and years of working with children. I had sent my resume to dozens of facilities and although I was elated to be back to work – all were a distance away from my hometown. So instead of taking Seline for long leisurely walks that I had become accustomed to, I was taking her on a two hour ride on the snail-paced Long Island Expressway to work with me, the major perk to my job.

My experience with young children was a tremendous asset to this new challenging position that had over three hundred children in attendance, but I was unprepared to have to answer to another person. I was used to working with Carol, which was more or less like working on my own. We thought along the same line, had the same goals and allowed one another creative freedom. Working under someone else was an entirely new ball game that took some adjusting to. One night on my long ride home in the pouring rain feeling exhausted and a bit sorry for myself, I had the time to think about some of the things I accomplished in just a short time at my new position. I had organized files and important data, had the administrative offices painted, hung a bulletin board acknowledging the achievements of my staff and teachers, held weekly meetings for them to voice their grievances, and tacked up inspirational affirmations in my own office. I presented a positive attitude even when I was feeling down. I realized that the women who worked there began to find their way to my office, first for work-related problems and then for personal matters. They learned to trust me. It was as if I had a revolving door, no sooner did one person leave than another came asking advice or consolation. And it wasn't just the adults; the children flocked to me as if I was the Pied Piper himself, especially those who had been labeled with behavior problems. When word went out that I allowed one of the students who came for the after school program to sit in my office to do her homework in order to keep her out of trouble, everyone came wanting the same privilege. I realized I had become the peacemaker, the mediator, the person who actually listened to the complaints and did my best to do something about them.

When the women eventually discovered I was the ex-wife of the infamous convicted murderer, that I had once been arrested, and I, like many of them, was a single struggling parent, and that I managed to pick myself up from the bottom of the pit, they gathered around me even more. They didn't come to hear about the gossip, or the trial, or whether or not I thought Danny was guilty; they came because they wanted to know how I survived, how I could laugh and be positive after what I had experienced. They told me they wanted what I had, just as I had felt so many years before when I met Carol at my first Al-Anon meeting. I was stunned. I wasn't aware I had come that far. I thought I was still plodding along waiting for the day when things would get better.

Lulled by the steady thwack of the windshield wipers and the rain drumming on the sunroof, Pastor Lydia's words from years before came to mind; *God was going to use my experience in a way I could never imagine.* How my experience from the past had anything to do with my present position I didn't know, but I did feel that something was getting ready to surface. *But what?*

A frightening bolt of lightening sliced a huge Z across the dark sky, hitting something close by with a loud crack. I braced myself for the inevitable boom. It was as if that thunderous clap zapped a message to my brain. "I get it!" I shrieked, startling Seline who had been contentedly watching a *DORA* DVD in the backseat, oblivious to nature's fireworks. I *have* been using my experience! The impromptu short discussions I had throughout the day with the women I work with provided them with just enough confidence and self-esteem to help them make some positive changes in their own lives. The negative disgruntled atmosphere seemed to have changed overnight. They began to feel hopeful. They tacked up their own personal affirmations. They laughed.

Pondering how a few daily words of encouragement had evidently benefited this small group of women so much, I remembered what Joy had said on the day we sat around the pool in the Bahamas sipping our Pina Coladas: *When life hands you lemons, make lemonade.* That was it! I couldn't wait to get home and put my ideas on paper. The events from the past would not be in vain. I could help others because I've been there. *God was going to use my experience in a way I could never imagine.* Based on my own healing and self-discovery I found a way to guide other women who are much like myself. I turned those sour pieces of fruit - not into lemonade - but into a delicious sweet lemon meringue pie made up of the most nourishing, nurturing, replenishing, rejuvenating ingredients that have the capability of altering your life.

Recipe for Your Life

One batch of fat lemons
Begin by peeling away the layers – shame, disgrace, anger, fear
Gradually blend in self-love, self-respect, self-esteem

Add:
Two large bowls of courage

4 cups of gratitude
2 – 3 cups of responsibility
1 cup of positive thinking
5 heaping tablespoons of faith
3 tablespoons of a good sense of humor
2 ½ teaspoons each of silliness, joy, laughter
Top with a heavy coating of love
Sprinkle with an assortment of loving, supportive family and friends

Utilizing the *ingredients* I designed an eight-week program that provides women with the tools to learn from the past, to take responsibility for the present and to empower them to create a future they never dreamed of.

I have had the supreme privilege to be a part of many women's lives, to be there as each steadily makes her slow and often painful journey from despair to hope, as her deep-rooted wounds begin to heal, and as she uncovers her own hidden strengths and talents. These women have given me an incredible gift - they have helped me to see I am no longer that wretched pathetic character on some tragic daytime soap opera. I have finally given up my contract!

I know the road ahead may still be filled with obstacles and I may continue to make mistakes and have my heart broken, but with my head held high I am willing to face the daily trials of life and move ahead to the future, however uncertain it may be.

Writing this book has been a personal healing for me. I worked on it for over six years. As I healed, the book evolved. To reveal to the public my weaknesses and faults, my immaturity and naivete, and my shame and embarrassment, has had a cathartic effect. I have been purged, cleansed and renewed - I have learned to love myself.

If my story can help another woman embark on her own remarkable journey, then it will be worth exposing my private life.

It is also my wish that you will come away with an awareness, and perhaps even compassion, for the innocent individuals who have the unfortunate painful experience of living behind a crime.

Remember - whenever you see a penny, whether you believe it is from your Angel or directly sent from God; take the time to pick it up. I believe you will immediately feel better.

Newspaper Headlines

The following is a list of headlines not including the local papers such as *Suffolk Life*, *Dan's Paper*, *The Independent*, *Southampton Press*, and a few other small town papers, as well as stories written in newspapers as far away as Florida. A lengthy article was written up in *Time Magazine* in September of 2003, sensational stories were printed in *The Star* and other tabloids. National television interviews with *Paula Zahn Live* on November 14, 2003; *Primetime* on November 5, 2005; *48 Hours, Murder in The Hamptons* - Part One on February 4, 2005 and Parts Two and Three on February 6, 2005. Court TV started coverage on September 7, 2004, the last segment viewed on May 5, 2005.

This list provides a small indication of what my family lived through.

2001, Oct 24	Newsday	Exec Found Killed In Home..
2001, Oct 25	Newsday	Suffolk Investigators Widen Murder Probe
2001, Oct 30	Newsday	Mourning A Magnate-Friends Remember..
2001, Nov 6	Daily News	Slain Mogul Wife Eyed
2001, Nov 10	Daily News	Divorcing Mogul Left Will Intact
2001, Nov 15	NY Post	Cause For Alarm-Wife's Beau Knew Alarm
2002, Jan 5	NY Post	Cops Quiz Slain Mogul's Widow
2002, Jan 6	NY Post	Slay Widow's Beau Decked in Bar Brawl
2002, Jan 24	NY Post	Ammon Widow Has New Hubby
2002, Jan 26	Daily News	Lover's Spend Widow's Beau Lived Large
2002, Jan 24	NY Post	Slay-Case Tail of Woe Ammon Widow....
2002, Jan 27	NY Post	Ammon's Wife Threatened Him Over....

Newspaper Headlines

2002, Feb 6	NY Post	Ammon Told Pals: I'll Get The Kids
2002, Feb 7	NY Post	Ammon Widow's Hubby Back on L.I. for DWI
2002, Feb 7	Newsday	New Husband Of Widow In Court
2002, Feb 8	NY Post	Generosa's New Guy Is Nuts: Court Papers
2002, Feb 8	Newsday	Ammon Widow's Spouse Indicted
2002, Feb 9	NY Post	Alarm-ing Twist For Ammon-Slay Widow
2002, Feb 14	NY Post	Wife Made Hidden Videos Of Ammon
2002, Feb 15	NY Post	Generosa's Guy Grounded by DWI
2002, Feb 16	NY Post	Generosa's Hubby Put Fear In Jury
2002, Mar 1	NY Post	Ammon's Pals Offer 25G Reward
2002, Mar 5	NY Post	Ammon-Case Car Seized
2002, Mar 20	NY Post	Ammon's Mr. Fix-It Denies DWI
2002, Mar 21	NY Post	Bizarre Drug Twist In Ammon Slay Case
2002, Mar 25	NY Post	Ammon Suspected A Scam-Tol Pal...
2002, Mar 26	NY Post	Generosa's New Hubby Accused Of Extortion
2002, Mar 28	NY Post	Pelosi-Newfound Mystery Note Could Be Clue...
2002, Mar 28	Newsday	Pelosi's View On Financier's Death
2002, Apr 3	Daily News	Ammon Widow L.I. To Mourn Hubby's Kin
2002, Apr 4	NY Post	Pelosi's Cop Brother Died While Under Probe...
2002, Apr 9	NY Post	Probe Back In Gear-Slain Tycoon's Buck...
2002, Apr 19	NY Post	Pelosi: No Great In Britain
2002, May 10	NY Post	Generosa Slumming ON Long Island
2002, May 31	NY Post	Fix-It Man In A Fix: Probation Report Urges Jail...

250

2002, June 13	NY Post	Generosa Cancer Scare
2002, Sept 19	NY Post	She's Cashing Out-Generosa Sells slain Hubby's...
2002, Oct 13	Daily News	Ammon Case is Cold
2002, Oct, 13	NY Post	Ammon Kin's Year Of Pain...
2002, Oct 20	Newsday	Magnate's Murder Remains Unsolved...
2002, Oct 31	Daily News	L.I. Murder suspect May Be Jailed for DWI
2002, Oct 31	NY Post	Ammon widow's New Hubby Nixes DWI Deal
2002, Nov 1	Daily News	Seek Jail Time For Pelosi
2002, Nov 1	NY Post	Pelosi's Latest Skip And Fall
2002, Nov 16	Daily News	Pelosi's Going to Jail Drunk Driving
2002, Nov 16	Newsday	Pelosi Pleads Guilty In DWI
2002, Nov 16	NY Post	Pelosi's Surprise Guilty Plea
2003, Feb 4	NY Post	Dying Request
2003, Feb 11	NY Post	Generosa's Hubby Goes To Jail Today
2003, Feb 12	NY Post	Pelosi In Prison...
2003, Feb 12	Newsday	1 Year Sentence In DWI
2003, Feb 12	Daily News	It's The Slammer For Pelosi
2003, May 12	Daily News	Pelosi Pals Sue Suffolk Cops
2003, May 13	Daily News	Pelosi Not In The Money
2003, May 13	NY Post	Sad Tug-O-Love-In-Law Sues Generosa
2003, May 14	Newsday	Ammon Kids In Custody Battle...
2003, May 14	NY Post	Generosa Told Kids That Slain Dad OD'd
2003, May 15	NY Post	Generosa Will Move To Slay Home
2003, May 30	NY Post	Pelosi Gets Boot From Custody Suit
2003, June 11	NY Post	Ammon Probe At Last
2003, June 13	NY Post	Pelosi Free Today Under A Cloud
2003, June 14	NY Post	Zapping Pelosi

Newspaper Headlines

2003, June 16	Daily News	Ammon Wife Shrink Stink
2003, June 23	NY Post	Jury Eyes Ammon's Murder
2003, July 4	NY Post	Generosa & Hubby Now Living Apart
2003, July 6	NY Post	Ammon's Slay Fear-Told His Family...
2003, July 10	NY Post	Generosa's Living solo In Death House
2003, July 11	NY Post	Mystery DNA In Ammon Slay Mansion
2003, Aug 7	Daily News	Seek Key Laptop in Ammon Slaying
2003, Aug 7	Newsday	Linked By A Laptop/Clue to Hampton Murder...
2003, Aug 7	NY Post	Laptop May Have Ammon Slay Clues
2003, Aug 9	NY Post	Slay Whitewash
2003, Aug 25	NY Post	Ammon Widow Dies Of Cancer
2003, Aug 26	Daily News	Ashes Tug of War
2003, Aug 26	Newsday	Ammon's Will Cuts Off Her Hubby
2003, Aug 27	Daily News	Pelosi May Grab Kids
2003, Aug 27	NY Post	Pelosi Has Poppy Plan For Ashes
2003, Aug 28	Daily News	Swiped Urn Willed to Nanny Danny's...
2003, Aug 28	NY Post	Nanny Spanks Danny-Generosa Gave Her $1M...
2003, Aug 28	Newsday	Parceling Out Ammon Estate
2003, Aug 29	Daily News	Generosa Strong-Willed
2003, Aug 29	NY Post	Estate Of Chaos-Drugged Generosa Signed Will...
2003, Sept 3	NY Post	Ammon Secrets Buried-Generosa Nixed...
2003, Sept 5	Daily News	Zap Pelosi in theft Case
2003, Sept 8	NY Post	My Life with Generosa
2003, Sept 9	Daily News	Pelosi Out of Zap Trap
2003, Sept 9	NY Post	Pelosi In Electrical Rip-Off Rap

2003, Sept 10	NY Post	Generosa's Ashes In A Safe Place
2003, Sept 16	NY Post	Affairs Long Strained At Ammon House
2003, Sept 17	NY Post	Pelosi Sets Sights On Wife's Will
2003, Sept 24	Newsday	Pelosi Aims to Fight Wife's Will
2003, Sept 24	Daily News	Generosa Will Won't Do
2003, Sept 25	Daily News	Generosa Worth $35M Pelosi Fight Postnup
2003, Oct 2	Daily News	It's Pelosi, The Gigolosi
2003, Oct 22	Daily News	Lawyers Cheated Me, Pelosi Yelps
2003, Oct 22	NY Post	Pelosi Charges Ripoff
2003, Oct 29	NY Post	Juicy Murder Case Is Likely to Crumble
2003, Nov 5	NY Post	Ted's Estate Takes $10M slap At Danny
2003, Nov 6	NY Post	Pelosi: Let's Deal-He'll Talk To Ammon Jury
2003, Nov 6	Daily News	Pelosi Dares'Em Says Make My Day
2003, Nov 7	NY Post	Pelosi Docked $2.6M In Will
2003, Nov 10	NY Post	Mansion Of Blood-Chilling Glimpse Inside
2003, Nov 13	NY Post	Gay Ammon Shock-Neighbor Claims Bizarre Sex...
2003, Nov 15	Newsday	Suspect Voices Fears/Focus of Hamptons
2003, Nov 19	Daily News	Zap Pelosi as Wife Beater
2004, Mar 23	NY Post	Pelosi Charged In Ammon Slay
2004, Mar 28	Newsday	The Pelosi Trial
2004, April 21	Daily News	Pelosi's Trial Set For Sept 1
2004, April 21	NY Post	Pelosi's Trial To Begin Sept 1
2004, June 18	Newsday	East Hampton Slaying Case, Attorney Says
2004, June 23	NY Post	Jury Eyes Ammon's Murder
2004, June 28	Daily News	Pelosi Pal Stays True to DWI...

2004, July 2	Newsday	Guilty Of False Statement, Man...
2004, July 23	Daily News	Judge won't Zap Pelosi Indict...
2004, July 27	Daily News	Pelosi's Alibi Is All Relative...
2004, July 28	NY Post	Pelosi Alibi: I was At My Sisters
2004, Aug 3	Daily News	Pelosi Attorney Forced To Quit Murder
2004, Aug 3	NY Post	Car Clue In Pelosi Slay Trial
2004, Sept 5	Daily News	Pelosi Slay Trial to Begin After 3 Years
2004, Sept 5	NY Post	Pelosi: DA Case A Sham
2004, Sept 7	NY Post	Legal Haggle May Stall Pelosi Trial
2004, Sept 8	Daily News	I'm Not The Killer, Pelosi Tells Judge
2004, Sept 8	NY Post	Dangerous Dan
2004, Sept 9	NY Post	Stupid Pelosi Jury Quiz
2004, Sept 9	Daily News	Pelosi's Team Hires Durst's Jury Expert
2004, Sept 10	NY Post	Slay Suspect Pelosi Caught In Catch-22
2004, Sept 11	Newsday	Pelosi Murder Trial, Phone Message...
2004, Sept 12	Daily News	Pelosi Team Keys On Call
2004, Sept 14	Daily News	Pelosi Jury Is On Fast Track
2004, Sept 15	NY Post	Jerky Jury Disrupts Pelosi Trial
2004, Sept 15	Daily News	Juror Puts Stamp On Pelosi Pool
2004, Sept 16	Daily News	Pelosi Jurors Are Yanked
2004, Sept 21	Daily News	Possible Pelosi Juror Truly One of His Peers
2004, Sept 21	NY Post	Jail Rats Turn On Pelosi
2004, Sept 24	Daily News	Pelosi Jury Is Seated
2004, Sept 25	Newsday	Pelosi Jury Selection, His Fate In Their...
2004, Sept 25	Newsday	Picking The Jurors, The Consultants Goal...
2004, Sept 25	NY Post	Pelosi Jury Selection

2004, Sept 26	Newsday	Murder In The Hamptons
2004, Sept 27	Daily News	Pelosi confident on Eve of Slay Trial
2004, Sept 28	Daily News	Ma: Pelosi Didn't Do It
2004, Sept 29	Daily News	Boozy Pelosi Beat Wives, DA Says
2004, Sept 30	Daily News	Pelosi Confession Secret Tapes
2004, Sept 30	Newsday	Defense: In Court, It's Danny Being Danny
2004, Sept 30	NY Post	Mistrial Looms Over "Threats" To Her Kid
2004, Oct 1	Daily News	Pelosi Tattler Has Lotsa Baggage
2004, Oct 2	Daily News	Pelosi Jail Snitch Has Long Record
2004, Oct 5	Daily News	Quiz Pelosi Snitch Jail Inmate Accounts
2004, Oct 5	NY Post	I Should Of Shot Him...
2004, Oct 6	NY Post	Excerpts From Inmate Accounts
2004, Oct 6	Daily News	Add 4 Jail Snitchers to Pelosi's Trial
2004, Oct 7	Newsday	Pelosi Murder Trial, Informant Has...
2004, Oct 8	Daily News	Double Trouble for Pelosi: New Raps Rats
2004, Oct 11	NY Post	Pelosi Video Twist-Fiancé Tapes Eye
2004, Oct 13	Daily News	Witness Charge Pelosi Muscled Stoolies, Targeted
2004, Oct 13	Newsday	At Pre-Trial Hearing, Pelosi Faces New...
2004, Oct 14	NY Post	Uh, Oh Danny Boy-Pelosi
2004, Oct 14	Daily News	Ex-Girlfriend to Testify of Danny's Plan
2004, Oct 14	Newsday	Painting Two Very Different Portraits
2004, Oct 14	Newsday	Prosecution Readies Witness
2004, Oct 15	NY Post	Another Side Of The Duchess
2004, Oct 15	NY Post	Ammon Gay Bash
2004, Oct 15	Daily News	DA Slaps Pelosi Attorney

Newspaper Headlines

2004, Oct 19	Daily News	Ammon Aide's Grim Find Stumbling...
2004, Oct 20	Daily News	Pelosi Prints, Gory Pix Revealed at Slay..
2004, Oct 21	Newsday	Pelosi Murder Trial, Alarm Installer
2004, Oct 22	Daily News	Blood Will Tell, Pelosi's Dad Jolts Defense
2004, Oct 22	Newsday	Pelosi Murder Trial, Fathers Heartache
2004, Oct 22	NY Post	Son Burned in Court – Pelosi Rages At Dad
2004, Oct 26	Daily News	Ex-Buddy Details Pelosi Plot
2004, Oct 26	Newsday	Witness Testimony
2004, Oct 27	Daily News	Generosa A Lookout
2004, Oct 28	Newsday	Family Matters, Sons Unanswered Plea
2004, Oct 29	Newsday	Testimony From Wife's Attorney
2004, Oct 29	Daily News	Pelosi In Ted's Home On Slay Day
2004, Oct 31	NY Post	Sexy Tale Of Rich Gal In Ted's last Tryst
2004, Nov 1	Daily News	Pelosi's a Good Fit As L.I. Casanova
2004, Nov 2	Daily News	Bloody Pelosi Shocker Jury told Of Red...
2004, Nov 2	NY Post	Incensed Judge Warms Pelosi Is Courting
2004, Nov 2	Newsday	Pelosi Murder Trial
2004, Nov 4	Daily News	Sis: Spied For Danny
2004, Nov 5	NY Post	Danny Demon Delay-Trial Furor Over Devil
2004, Nov 5	Daily News	Devil Of A Pelosi Defense
2004, Nov 5	Newsday	Pelosi Murder Case, Trial Takes a Mystical
2004, Nov 8	Daily News	Pelosi Family, a House Divided
2004, Nov 9	Daily News	How Danny Turned $6.7M Into $308
2004, Nov 9	Newsday	Pelosi Trial Testimony

2004, Nov 10	Daily News	Say Danny Paid Family Bills Too
2004, Nov 10	NY Post	Pelosi Gave Ex Checks-Generosa Paid...
2004, Nov 11	NY Post	Nanny Nails Danny-Pelosi Trial Bombshell
2004, Nov 11	Daily News	Nanny: Pelosi Fessed Up, Said He'd Kill Me
2004, Nov 15	Newsday	Suspect Voices Fears, Focus Hamptons...
2004, Nov 16	Daily News	Phone Hangs Danny, Sez DA
2004, Nov 17	Daily News	Pelosi Tries to Hush Rats...
2004, Nov 18	Daily News	Trial Of Tears For Informer In Danny Case
2004, Nov 19	Daily News	Jailers Tipped Pelosi About Snitch, DA Sez
2004, Nov 23	Daily News	Ammon's last Meal May Skewer Pelosi
2004, Nov 24	Daily News	Pelosi Figures Be Home For Christmas
2004, Nov 24	NY Post	Stunning Testimony Against Pelosi
2004, Nov 25	Daily News	Pelosi Spews To News
2004, Dec 1	Daily News	Pelosi Defense Opening With Top Doc...
2004, Dec 2	Daily News	Pelosi's X-Rated Witness
2004, Dec 2	Newsday	Riverhead Murder Trial, Niece Adds Weight
2004, Dec 3	Daily News	State Of Ammon's Last Meal May Serve...
2004, Dec 7	Daily News	Sweating bullets, Sez Pelosi
2004, Dec 7	Daily News	Cut Pelosi Defense to 5 Days
2004, Dec 7	NY Post	Pelosi's Pass On Witness
2004, Dec 8	Daily News	See Danny As Villain Or Victim
1004, Dec 8	Newsday	Pelosi Takes The Stand
2004, Dec 11	Daily News	Danny: She Did It!
2004, Dec 12	Daily News	Pelosi Fate Up To Jury
2004, Dec 12	NY Post	Ammon witness Ignored

Newspaper Headlines

2004, Dec 13	Daily News	Jurors Have Pelosi Sweating Bullets
2004, Dec 13	NY Post	Pelosi Trial Shock-Pal Prays To Jurors
2004, Dec 13	Daily News	Pelosi's Testimony Works Against Him
2004, Dec 14	Daily News	Pelosi Guilty In Ammons Slaying, He Weeps
2004, Dec 14	Daily News	Know-It-All Danny Cooked Own Goose
2004, Dec 14	Daily News	He Confessed, but Generosa Didn't Believe
2004, Dec 14	Daily News	Generosa & Danny, Fairy Tale Gone Bad
2004, Dec 14	Newsday	How Jury Leaned To A Guilty Verdict
2004, Dec 14	Newsday	He Killed The Millionaire
2004, Dec 14	NY Post	Now It's His Turn to Cry
2004, Dec 14	NY Post	Pelosi Jurors Saw Stun gun, Ted's Cash
2004, Dec 14	Newsday	A Risk That Backfired, Daniel Pelosi
2004, Dec 16	NY Post	Heat On Pals Of Pelosi-DA Eyes Slay Raps
2004, Dec 17	Newsday	Back In Court, Pelosi, Minus The Counsel
2004, Dec 17	NY Post	Pelosi Thought Charm Would Get Him Off
2004, Dec 19	Newsday	The Pelosi Trial, Local Case National
2004, Dec, 19	NY Post	Mystery Of Mad Generosa
2005, Jan 19	Daily News	Twins To Tell Court What They Think
2005, Jan 25	Daily News	Pelosi to Hear Twins Statement
2005, Jan 26	Daily News	Tearful Ammon Children Want Pelosi To Rot
2005, Jan 26	Newsday	Danny Pelosi Gets Max 25 To Life...

ACKNOWLEDGEMENTS

Ihave been blessed with an amazing family and an awesome circle of friends, without their gentle embrace I doubt if I could have made it to where I am today. I especially thank my dearest Earth Angels who made a difficult journey easier, although "thank you" is not adequate enough to describe how much each of them means to me.

My Earth Angels –

Joy Barnett - my dear sister of choice and childhood friend - I am forever grateful for her outrageous humor and ability to make me laugh when I wanted to cry and for being my personal bodyguard. I look forward to the day when we sit on the beach as two little old ladies in our wooly sweaters!

Carol Carter- for reaching out to me nineteen years ago when I was too shy to reach out to her and the many times she held my hand and helped me see the bright side when my life was filled with darkness.

Diane Haugland - from the first day I met her I admired her clever business abilities, never realizing that one day we would be dear friends. I am deeply grateful for her generous gifts from her heart and the faith that I would one day pay her back!

Josephine Ghiringhelli– my personal psychic medium - what would Friday night dinner be like without our *long* talks that lasted way past dessert? Love ya, Kiddo.

Thanks go to Joanne Romano for attempting to coach me on business decisions, real estate, and for 'planting' St. Joseph, and especially for our daily walks that were far better than any therapy!

Patti Kelly Barker- for her never wavering faith and literally standing by me and holding me up.

My gratitude to Greg Carter for his strength and gentle kindness and for *donating* so much of his time.

I also need to thank Pam Allen for her belief in me and her devoted love for Seline – she is the best *Tip Tip* anyone could ask for!

Thank you too to Paulette Murtha, I couldn't ask for a more kind, warm-hearted and giving friend, I am grateful our paths have crossed.

A special thanks to Annie Chiuchiolo for her amazing musical talent and an incredible voice that is sure to be remembered.

The Angel Team – for their endless hours packing, gluing, stamping, organizing, hauling and 'selling the book'!

My list would not be complete without thanking the Senior Ya ya's – Lonni Campbell, my second mother and personal astrologer; Phoenix Redhawk for bringing *magic* into my life; Mary Eberhardt for making me laugh with her blatant honesty; Charyl Ozkaya for her calming touch; Helen King for understanding what it's like to be a Virgo, and Bonnie Campbell for her selfless giving of her time helping me with my schooling, and the hours she labored creating a masterpiece book design.

Nor would it be complete without acknowledging my cousins Joey and Audra Consolo, for graciously stepping in and caring for my baby sister, Seline. Without their support and love I would not have been able to finish my doctorate degree nor have a cup of coffee with a friend.

For my Father – he did the best that he knew how. He is my

Acknowledgements

father and I love him.

Very, very special thanks to my younger wiser brother, Roger Shore, for all our heart-to-heart talks and for being such a wonderful role model and terrific uncle to my boys. I am deeply, deeply grateful to him. He is my tower of strength. Words cannot measure my love.

For my mother, Susan Semerade, for standing by me and allowing me the dignity to walk my own path and for not judging me when I judged myself. I am grateful for the many, many hours she typed away, for all the rewrites, and 'no that's not how it was, it was this way,' after she thought she was finally done. This book would not have been written without her ability to capture my inner feelings and create a flowing story. Thank you, thank you, thank you. I love you.

The love I have for my three children, Shelly, Danny and Tony cannot be expressed in a few printed words. Against the odds, they blossomed into fine young adults. I am eternally grateful to each of them and proud beyond description. They are the loves of my life.

For my littlest angel, Seline, and her precious baby bear hugs. She has brought me more joy than I thought was possible.

"J" – for the pennies. I do believe in miracles.

There were many who touched my life, some briefly, but *all* in an extraordinary way. Again - my deepest thanks. If I have forgotten anyone, I apologize.

Tami

For my daughter Tami, her courage and fortitude has never ceased to amaze me. I should have known when this quiet ten-year old won Reserved Championship on top of a sixteen-hand thoroughbred mare that there was more than meets the eye. I admire her resiliency and her deep faith in God. It is my honor to be her mother. I am especially grateful for the opportunity to help her put her story into words, and continue her remarkable journey helping other women.

I am deeply grateful to my Mother, for her spunk, her spirit, our fantastic friendship and her devoted love.

Thank you Lonni Campbell, Kathleen Johnson, Joanne Phoenix, Dotty Mato, Joy Barnett, and especially Pam Allen for taking time out of their busy lives to read the manuscript, sometimes more than once, and for their constructive suggestions and all my dearest friends who continued to support and encourage me along the way.

Susan

Special thanks to Diane O'Connell's professional guidance and literary services. (http://www.docls.com)

Lastly, but certainly not least, heartfelt thanks to Mill City Press, in particular Michelle Brown. The professionalism, patience and willingness to answer numerous questions helped us transform an overwhelming project into reality.

About The Authors

Tamara Pelosi earned her Doctorate in Education in 2007, but it was the 'school of life' that was her principal teacher. *Pennies From An Angel, Innocent Lives Behind A Crime* was born out of her own experience and motivated her to come forward and reveal her personal life for the sole purpose of helping other women. She has received a number of specialty awards attesting to her charitable character and her dedication to family life. In 2005 Tamara was inducted into the Long Island Volunteers Hall of Fame; 2004 she was presented with 'The Women of the Year' award for creating a variety of programs that serviced the youth and family of the local community; in 1998 Tamara was awarded "Suffolk County Volunteer Award" for outstanding service to the youth of Suffolk County, New York. Throughout the years, Tamara has created numerous parenting workshops, developed programs specifically for teachers, and facilitates support groups that help empower women to gain their independence. Ms. Pelosi was Co-founder and Director of the Sunshine Center, a youth and family facility. She is currently working on her next book, *Recipe for Empowering Your Life.* Visit her web site at www.penniesfromanangel.com for further information. She lives on the eastern end of Long Island with her children.

264

Susan Semerade, Tamara's mother, has been in the health and healing field for over twenty years. As a seasoned yoga instructor and Certified Ayurvedic Health Consultant she writes articles on nutrition and well-being for health related magazines. Ms. Semerade says she is blessed with a unique loving relationship with her daughter and states, "a daughter's pain is your pain; a daughter's glory is your glory." Helping her daughter write her story was as healing for Susan as it was Tami.

Song of Hope
"Pennies"

Anne Chiuchiolo is another remarkable earth angel who found her way into my life more than ten years ago. She has a deep faith in God and a powerful voice that reaches deep down into your soul. Anne is a gifted songwriter with that special talent for taking simple words and turning them into heartfelt music.

One day when Anne and I were talking about the book and how pennies from my Angel would mysteriously appear when I needed comfort and encouragement, we both thought - wow, wouldn't it be great to write a song about an angel dropping pennies as a message of hope. Within an hour Anne put pen to paper and the music and lyrics of *Pennies* was born. With her musician brother Dominick Chiuchiolo, and her sister Janice Chiuchiolo adding the harmonies, *Pennies* came to fruition.

You can hear this stirring CD which was produced by Dominick, with vocals by Anne and Janice on www.pennies-fromanangel.com.

Anne, Dominick and Janice